the Modern Gentleman

the Modern Gentleman

— Second Edition —

PHINEAS MOLLOD · JASON TESAURO

TEN SPEED PRESS
Berkeley

© 2002, 2011 by Phineas Mollod and Jason Tesauro
Illustrations © 2002 by A.W. Shasteen

Published in the United States by Ten Speed Press, an imprint of the
Crown Publishing Group, a division of Random House, Inc., New York.
www.crownpublishing.com
www.tenspeed.com

Ten Speed Press and the Ten Speed Press colophon are registered
trademarks of Random House, Inc.

Permission granted to reprint material from the following publications:

D. H. Lawrence, *Lady Chatterley's Lover*. New York: Penguin, 1962.
Henry Miller, *My Life and Times*. New York: Gemini Smith/Playboy Press, 1971.
Stephen Potter, *Anti-Woo Gambits for Non-Lovers*. New York: McGraw-Hill Companies,
    1965. Excerpt reproduced with permission of the McGraw-Hill Companies.
Raymond Chandler, *The Long Goodbye*. New York: Random House, 1992.
One-Upmanship by Stephen Potter, © 1952 by Stephen Potter. Reprinted by
    permission of Henry Holt & Co., LLC.
Tom Robbins, *Fierce Invalids Home from Hot Climates*. New York: Bantam Books, 2001.
Jackie Stewart, Interview, *Playboy*, June 1972.
Amy Vanderbilt's Complete Book of Etiquette. New York: Random House, 1958.

The Library of Congress has cataloged the first edition as follows:
Mollod, Phineas.
  The modern gentleman / Phineas Mollod and Jason Tesauro.
    p. cm.
Includes bibliographical references and index.
  1. Etiquette for men. I. Tesauro, Jason. II. Title.
  BJ1855 .M65 2002
  395.1'42-dc21
2002001355

ISBN 978-1-60774-006-3

Printed in the United States of America on recycled paper (20% PCW)

Design by Colleen Cain, based on an original design
by Paul Kepple @ Headcase Design.

10 9 8 7 6 5 4 3 2 1

Second Edition

To all the books that made me think and blush, and the hidden gems of life that begged my discovery.

—P. M.

To my Pop Pop and Pop, two jazzy gents who boosted me to the upper branches of a gnarly family tree.

—J. T.

ACKNOWLEDGMENTS

A litany of fond framily thanks can be found in the first edition, yet those who contributed pointedly to the second deserve mention: an old-fashioned analog thank-you to our Facebook friends and Twitter tweeps for providing fodder for Digital Man; a hat tip to Russ, Ken, Larry and Kenan, the original MG alums, as well as new recruits Jason and Bruce, for walking the walk and tipping the flask; bravo to brother Dan for his symphonic know-how and modernist vivacity on Classical Music as well as his Farmer Brown chicken-coop smarts; a thunderous rim shot to Doc Dugan for spinning vinyl in the basement and being a primal force behind the syncopated brilliance of Jazz; fond head rub to Donny for his wisdom on all things whiskered and whiskerless; back pats to Alex for Pacific and Midwest musings on file-sharing and Life Reset; handshake to Nick for philosophizing on texting and Girl Problems; and a big shout to the epidermically prosaic Joshua for talking tattoos and lost love regained.

Grazie, Jeff Gordinier, for a chapbook's worth of poesy insight; 500 g of gratitude to Michel Emery and Petrossian for copious caviar chrestomathies; and a walk-in closet's worth of thanks to Monroe Robertson, Jake Mueser, Benton Bryan, and Philip Martin for the skinny on bespoke dress and snappy shoes. Lovin' mouthfuls of Wednesday wabbit, 1955 Sauternes, and rich Kona to intrepid gastronauts Kendra, Tim, Andrea, and Frits; a bushel of appreciation to Manakintowne Specialty Growers, Rural Virginia Market, Chelsea

Market, Sub Rosa Bread, Gearhart's Chocolates, Belmont Butchery, Chef Grandinetti, and the Union Square Greenmarket for artisanal localism, foodie knowledge, crisp Mutsu apples, and Ronnybrook's killer coconut yogurt. Gracias to Manolo for busting out the Galician orujo; thanks to Sippie for Shochu 101 and for explaining fractions to me at Stonybrook Elementary; cheers to Matthew Rowley for talking moonshine; plus caffeinated credit to Lamplighter Roasting Company, Café Grumpy, and a broad bear hug to the world below 23rd Street, the modern gentleman's modern bazaar.

Gratefulness to James River Writers for literary support in VA; dotted-line thanks to Kirk Schroder for legal muscle when we were wrasslin' for rights; and a humidor's worth of acknowledgment to John, Dina, Debbie, and Michael for turning vision into joint venture. A full decanter of thanks to David and Maria Denton, and Carol Colby for vinoventures and sommelier mentoring, with an especial PS to Bartholomew Broadbent for texted mischief and wisdom over a drained bottle of 1964 Bual. Hatfuls o' love to gents-in-training Sebastion and Brooks, and a couchful of kudos to Holli for the high-minded headshrinking. Confit and Country Style Thanks to Julia, Dean, and Jessica for Crash Pad insight; and truffle-scented appreciation for Luca, Alessandro, Chef Melissa, the Tasting Room babes, and my dear Barboursville family for friendship and franc.

A secret handshake to the dapper designer, Colleen Cain. Thanks to our sharp-eyed copyeditor, Kristi Hein; proofer, Jennifer McClain; and indexer, Ken Della Penta. Bon mots to our staunch supporters at Random House and Ten Speed Press, especially Aaron Wehner, a fellow gent, and Madame Editor Lisa Westmoreland for polishing our silver tongues. Lastly, a goodie-drawer's worth of liplocked reverence for Gillington and ALN for bringing us to our knees.

CONTENTS

INTRODUCTION

A man may possess expensive duds, slick wheels, and a tongue to match, but these are not the prerequisites of a gentleman. A gentleman is defined by how he carries himself in fairways and stormy climes. A student of the classics and a pilot of the new, he recommends sizzling reads, pays his gambling debts, mans the grill, and curbs his dog. Reserved, flamboyant, or likely somewhere in between, a gentleman's charisma is cultivated, not canned. He fosters an infectious comfort in others as they quietly marvel at his manner and know-how. Little charms performed thoughtfully ensure that inevitable faux pas are measured against a graceful reputation. He can be trusted with his word and your wife.

Nine years after *The Modern Gentleman* provided a manual for the Millennial Age, we're back for round deux. Certain fundamentals like wine smarts and guest decorum invited only limited updates, yet a brave new world of social media required a *Second Edition* addition of "The Digital Man." Also expect new sections reflecting unearthed passions for coffee, caviar, and the farmers' market, plus a renovation of the book's cultural center to spur the postliterate generation. Further, while "Jet Setting" was scrapped in the wake of TSA's increasingly unfriendly skies, we address the politics of friends and spiffed-up "Sartorial Savvy" to include Bespoke this and that. And with an ear ever cocked for word of advancement in woo and amour, we present additional commentary on "The Nooner" and "To the Power of [3]."

The Modern Gentleman, Second Edition, remains a visually stimulating, rib-tickling, thought-provoking sourcebook of manners and mischief. Enlightened and more than a little bit decadent, it's a pioneering slant on etiquette for gallery-openers and bar-closers alike. The book offers a panoramic snapshot of the gentleman: witty and poignant, traditional but spontaneous, flirtatious yet courtly. Of course, since a gentleman inevitably dabbles in the friskier areas of excess, trouble, and chance, the book's naughty nucleus, "The Potent Gentleman," explores liquid leisure, dalliance, character-defining obstacles and gaffes, and new "Sticky Situations" to navigate.

Long-forgotten cocktail recipes also pop up on these pages, reminding us of the colorful life available in fine glassware, if one is armed with an open mind and shaker. With the entire mixological oeuvre at your smartphone thumbtips, we listed ingredients without ratios. Don't kvetch, just click.

The Modern Gentleman is not a cure-all for flaccid character, though readers will absorb knowledge that vastly improves leisure. Nor is it a pickup guide for dummies, a fudge-your-way-through-life primer, or the "last word" on style or dress. We purposely avoid most topics blanketed in ordinary guy guides filled with ruler-rapping dictums about brown shoes and black belts. Also note that lover and bedmate appear more frequently here than girlfriend or lady; the Modern Gentleman knows that kindness is not gender-specific, and that a gay gentleman practices most of the same considerations as his heterosexual counterpart. For guidance in advanced matters of woo, see the MG's sexy sister volume, *The Modern Lover: A Playbook for Suitors, Spouses, & Ringless Carousers.*

The Modern Gentleman is an attainable character, not larger than life, but exactly the size of it. We all aspire to be perpetually dapper, fluent in three languages, and able to hit 300-yard drives off the blue tees, as well as quote poetry by the stanza and win a back-alley scrap. However, there is a level of gallantry more realistic than Hollywood perfection. So knot up your ascot, pour a glass of sherry, and dim the lights: your Man Cycle is peaking.

part one

The
GREGARIOUS GENTLEMAN

*Wear your learning, like your watch, in
a private pocket, and do not pull it out and strike it
merely to show you have one.
If you are asked what o'clock it is, tell it, but do not
proclaim it hourly and unasked,
like the watchman.*
—LORD CHESTERFIELD (1694–1773)

Chapter One

OUT & ABOUT

DIGITAL MAN

Those who balance avatars with their actual visage at least embody the modern half of gentleman. On the leading edge are those chaps who properly integrate technology into daily life and haven't uttered the terms "cellular telephone" or "World Wide Web" since Windows 2000 ruled the roost. There is a necessary distinction between digital and analog selves: your virtual image, like hygiene, can't be ignored, but if stripping away your snazzy updates and smartphone leaves you bland, 'tis time to unplug and recalibrate. If everyday's but an orchestrated online striptease, vid by pic by clever quip, then you've forgotten how to enjoy this thing called life.

THE BULLHORN: SOCIAL MEDIA

Social media casts a wide data stream ideal for news blasts ("Nate's taco truck spotted") and easy favors ("Need jumper cables"). It's California-wildfire fast for announcing bacchanals, get-out-the-vote rallies, or celebrity obituaries. Standard PR, crowdsourcing, and level 1–2 thanks can live here too. Intimate affairs, hushed family news, and level 3+ thank-you's (last night's bail money, borrowed summer home), however, require more pointed notice.

By now, even your parents have skin in the digital game, but establishing an account and managing it successfully are as different as do-it-yourself versus pro-grade websites. Sterling posts that hit in the late evening are lost in next day's feed, but coffee-hour weekday updates and cocktail-hour weekend posts feed the e-churn. Unlike online dating, where specificity aids in compatibility, social sites beg for discretion, particularly when prospective employers monitor the Web for unwise blurts and XXX party pix. To post something spicy without leaving a trail, consider the Ghost Post, whereby you submit a comment to an existing thread and then hit Delete; involved parties will see it, but later-comers don't get the privilege. Caginess aside, even if your avatar is a cartoon, post at least one up-to-date photo; otherwise, people presume morbid obesity or flapping linguine hair.

To keep your online rep in winning form, mind your Facebook manners when facing these common scenarios:

- **Congrats Fix**: Attaboy alerts about promotions and graduations are welcome good news, but artists, buskers, and budding virtuosos should create dedicated Fan pages to avoid turning friends into mere fanboys.

- **Sympathy Fishing**: Reportage of maladies, breakups, and sick parents eventually cross the line from human connection to irksome bathos. To commemorate the dearly departed, a post-interment mini-elegy beats live blogging the ICU flatlining.

- **Mundane Overdose**: A high percentage of posts devoted to caffeine, TGIF riffs, and the current heat wave don't pass WGAFF (Who Gives a Flying Fig) minimums.

- **AM Radio**: Hardcore partisan crossfire devolves quickly into vitriolic cable news patter.

- **TMI**: Customize certain status/alibi updates to office colleagues only ("Pig roast sounds divine, but stuck finishing a big project") or exclude second-rate chums when broadcasting private party particulars.

- **Digi-Litter**: Sending virtual daiquiris or clogging the news feed with Mafia Wars updates secures your place in the Hall of Lame.

- **Chat**: It's never impolite to ignore a Facebook chat request ("Hey, are you there?"). On the other hand, quality posts earn high marks:

- **Provocative conversation starter:** "Can I tap that?"

- **Quirky current events:** "They repealed the pasties tax . . . strip club cover charges expected to drop by 20 percent."

- **Witty innuendo:** "Jenna is finally stimulated by Bush's package."

- **Quickie Pix:** Impromptu mobile uploads, foodie porn (splendid dishes, wine labels) trump edited albums posted a month later. Proud parents should post their offspring's cuteness judiciously, though new moms are exempt from the Baby Pix Overload Doctrine.

- **You're It:** Besides friends, occasionally tag random objects for comic effect. On an empty shot glass: "Jeanine's wits last seen here," or on an overexposed tramp stamp: "The crack of Dawn."

FRIENDING

Like sex on the first date (or Arizona's border crossing law), some F'bookers have an ironclad stance regarding unsolicited new friends. Neither the No-way-José nor the All Aboard policies are ideal, so be selective without squelching serendipity. Requests sent postmidnight indicate a horny hubby pining for exes or a dissatisfied babe wanting out of the 'burbs. When making requests to relative strangers, include a memory jogger to reestablish an out-of-the-blue connection.

Managing secondary, tertiary, and quaternary social circles in real life would require endless coffee dates and happy hours, but social sites forgo face time for frequency. Over time, certain people are LinkedIn, while other obligatory friends and distant family are "hidden" from your newsfeed. In the end, your dearest friends are often the ones you encounter the least on social media sites, justifying the notion that "digital" isn't that far from "disposable" in the dictionary.

Incidentally, unless you're married, engaged, or living in sin, the relationship button is irrelevant, though gals might employ it freely to sidestep unwanted suitors. There's no need to befriend someone you're dating until you've made it through the first fight—or unless you aren't yet old enough to rent a car.

TWEETIQUETTE

Twitter, Tweethearts, & Tweeps. Like the lyrics of a country song, sometimes 140 characters are sage poetry, other times it's 129 %$#&*!@ characters too long. Think of Twitter as a mutated, post-orgy offspring, a cross between a bullhorn, a bathroom stall, a pulpit, and a haiku. The bullhorn angle means you can amplify your voice; the stall part of it renders any responsibility for profundity inapplicable; the pulpit aspect gives your passion a channel and audience, all set to a laconic haiku beat. Thus, the most successful tweets are those that boast a specific, empowered, and amped-up nugget worth lingering at a urinal for. Savvy marketers might exploit Twitter as another venue for self-promotion and celebrity spin, but others, especially Tehran protesters, see an important tool and hear tweet music in the grassroots symphony of flash mobs and hashtags. To get started, tout your one-liner chops by tweeting about a niche topic or major live event (Super Bowl, season finale) and see how many retweets and followers you earn.

Clandestine touch: Broadcast anonymously with an untraceable Twitter alias that gives you bandwidth to vent, share, or gossip (but don't tweet me on that).

OCCASION	METHOD OF COMMUNICATION					
	letter	telephone	email	text	facebook	twitter
Birth/wedding announcement	●	●	●		●	
Divorce announcement	●	●			●	
Appearance on Jeopardy	●	●	●	●	●	●
Appearance in court	●	●				●
Running with the bulls	●	●	●	●	●	●
Roommate has the runs						●
Par-tay tonight		●	●	●		
Par-tay last night rocked		●		●		
Par-tay pix posted					●	●
Blood oranges back in season					●	●
Made the dean's list	●	●	●	●		
Made the most-wanted list						●
Drinking a Belgian summer ale				●	●	●
Drinking a brewski on the job						●
Meeting canceled		●	●			
Meeting led to casual sex	●			●		●
The condom broke						●
Pregnancy test results positive (married)	●	●	●	●		
Pregnancy test results positive (married . . . to someone else)			●			
Dying of boredom						●
Dying of laughter					●	
Dying of cancer	●					
Haven't spoken in ages	●	●	●			
Haven't spoken lately		●	●	●	●	
Haven't spoken since breakfast				●	●	●

WEB SLINGING

Pages full of worthwhile reviews about books, movies, and cafés evoke a utopian view of the Web as a marketplace of ideas. Usher in the imbeciles who prove Godwin's Law: "As an online discussion grows longer, the probability of a comparison involving Nazis or Hitler approaches 1." Hiding behind a phony screen name to hurl rants or such luminary commentary as "Yeah, that sux" brands you an idle nitwit. Unless you're cruising the kind of deviants-only chat rooms that will derail a Supreme Court confirmation, use your real name or at least a repeatable pet name like a rock star's hotel check-in moniker. Tesauro, for instance, might log in to the Daily Jumble bulletin board as "Jeblum Gink," but prefers the less specific "@TheModernGent" when hashtagging "#iheartfloggers."

Not-so-nice touch: At the coffee shop, don't be the freeloader who soaks up gratis WiFi with but a small coffee on your tab and nary a crumb bun on wax paper. Bohemians and jobseekers should mete out their mochas and munchies and sit at the counter, not the primo four-top by the window.

Most everything posted online exists on a server somewhere and, if public, is trolled by search engine spiders to be saved in perpetuity. The disclosure of voluntary personal information borders on the shameful: geo-location, DNA profiles, travel itineraries, not to mention quotidian social media postings. Convenience requires responsibility. To cover your tracks and secure your data, ratchet up the privacy settings, establish multiple email accounts, and create strong passwords for your personal accounts ("iloveyou" might elude an infant, but not a hacker's simple dictionary attack). If you're still the sort to leave your home WiFi network unlocked or download sensitive docs on public computers, we know a long-lost English duke with frozen funds in Nigeria who desperately needs your Social Security number. . . .

A note on expiring gracefully: akin to a Living Will, bequeath your passwords to a confidante whose sole job is to cremate your digital corpse. Do you really want a sappy memorial residing on Facebook's servers for eternity?

DIGITAL ENTERTAINMENT

A fantasy football league or vintage Atari hooked up to a basement telly is thirty escapist minutes well spent, whereas "solving" the latest *Grand Theft Auto* takes weeks, and multiplayer fascination with the latest Madden installment can last the entire NFL season. Unless you're on the DL with a busted femur, don't let a video game fetish devolve into a proxy for internet porn addiction. Ideally, explore the panoramic wonders of gaming by the hour at a pal's pad, leaving you curious, rather than numb after an entire night of hunting down the Islamist insurgency in Kandahar. For house party diversions, however, don't scoff if *Rock Band 3* trumps Celebrity when it comes to parlor games amongst the iPad generation. As for virtual universe denizens, before spending real money on imaginary land, invest first in your IRA, then colored pixels.

TELEPHONY

Quickie mobile calls on the run confirming "What stop again?" or "I've got the baguettes and the Banyuls, there in five" are fine, but spare fellow depositors on the bank line the minutiae of your day. Recognize the humanity of the counterperson by muting the phone, finishing the transaction, and then resuming the call. If you glean nothing else from this book, let this new tenet rule the land: to avoid the "Khaaaaaan!"-inducing frustration of two phones dialing one another unsuccessfully after a dropped call, if disconnected, whosoever initiated the call shall call back.

Not-so-nice touch: For hassle-free loitering and avoiding unwanted neighbor interactions, practice the phony phone diversion. Pretend to punch buttons, check voice mail, and bring the unit to your ear to mimic actually being occupado.

Phones are best kept on low or vibrate, since most ringtones are a near-universal annoyance worse than a tweezered nose hair, particularly when officemates are forced to hear six rounds of Ludacris's "Sex Room" while you're at the copier. Plain vanilla rings suffice for the vast majority of calls, but for novelty's sake, reserve customized ding-a-lings for randy pals or love interests.

"While You Were Out" pads were replaced by answering machines, which were superannuated by voice mail, which has been rendered quaint by email, which has been marginalized by texting, but you will occasionally encounter last century's message-saving telephone technology. However, unless you've heard the answering-machine squawk or confirmed the existence of a rolling minicassette, a gentleman needn't prate, "Are you there Grandma . . . pick up . . . are you there?"

TEXTING

This generation's telegram, the text message has become physiological: the mere ping of an alert releases a dopamine surge akin to catching a wisp of breast when a buxom lass in a low-cut blouse bends to buckle her shoe. Has any other modern convenience proved a more significant discovery in the advancement of woo? The handwritten love note shan't ever lose its appeal, but when the over/under for length of most romances has been reduced by the speed of life to 2.375 weekends, snail mail might arrive long after the notion has expired. Despite static relations, most prospects remain in SIM card limbo, and a casual love interest who failed to answer three prior texts can often be repropositioned with a light tap: "Tribeca penthouse soiree tonight? Wanna join?"

Texting is the great social leveler, allowing the formerly inarticulate to thrive in the formerly face-to-face dating world. In addition to eliminating the frightening immediacy of the cold call ask out, texting permits mobile fishing expeditions and booty messages masquerading as genteel hellos that seek to lure recipients into a "What r u up to?" exchange that hopefully culminates in "c u in 10." Plus, for multitasking rapscallions, texting offers the two-places-at-once ability to break bread with one honey whilst buttering up another for later. But beware the wimpiness of hiding behind technology's protective cloak; early rapport requires personalized contact. Also remember that the method of e-woo varies with the age and seriousness of the prospective mate, as the banker and the scatterbrained coed use technology quite differently.

Incidentally, work emails can be sent anytime, but business texting runs on the "-1, +2 restriction": from one hour before the workday to two hours after. Text beyond those parameters and you're either a certified brownnosing overachiever or a no-lifer underling in need of a warm body.

LENS WITH BENEFITS . . .

Essential mobile acumen includes surreptitious photograph taking. Learn the vectors of your lens so you can occasionally mimic phone usage while actually playing spy.

- Keep any romance simmering with "Good morning" images that offer a sexy morning jolt.

- Even if giddily deleted in the afterglow, snapping in-the-act pics adds paparazzi glam to a steamy moment.

· At a formal affair, blush-worthy transmissions beamed from the powder room are digital footsies.

Necessary touch: Sexting lovers are wise to establish a code to foretell incoming filthiness so that a phone in plain sight on the conference table doesn't light up with a snatch of your honeybunch's. . . .

DIGITALITIS

With the average chap's attention span having dipped below the cycle of a traffic light, nothing says "I find you rather insipid" than futzing with your phone alongside an acquaintance, never mind challenging your Breakout high score. Those whose perspectives are forever filtered through ear buds might occasionally soak in the chirping birds or snippets of humanity, if only to forestall hearing loss for another few years.

Incidentally, a transcontinental game of Scrabble via mobiles brings to mind Philip Marlowe's chess games by mail, but harness technology beyond mere frippery: tune your guitar, practice a foreign tongue on a long queue, or e-locate a café beside a railroad depot and order refreshments while on board, to be picked up platform-side three stops hence.

A note on P2P: After at least four format changes that culminated in the record companies blithely asking listeners to purchase *Pet Sounds* one more time—this time as a $17.99 compact disc—the digital MP3 revolt was on. Music file-sharing is theft, but there are less egregious examples (such as obtaining an album owned in another format; filling in your back catalog of a band's lesser works; sampling songs of a well-known act with a six-figure Pepsi sponsorship; or poaching from a deceased band, such that you deny Yoko another dollar from the sale of *Revolver*). However, before gorging on the BitTorrent buffet, have a pang of conscience and explore legal sites and support favored bands by attending live shows and being so gauche as to occasionally buy their music.

ANALOG ESSENTIALS

A mini empire can be run in flip-flops with nothing but a credit card, a smartphone, a laptop, and a squishy stress ball. But stark digital efficiency isn't everything. Certain hallmarks of the past should remain in the gentlemanly canon.

- **Vinyl:** An entire music collection can amazingly reside on a teeny MP3 player, but the LP remains a gorgeous fixture. Let audiophiles and rabid collectors argue over the science of sound fidelity, but vinyl delivers the beautiful listening ritual, including the double gatefold album artwork, the sight of a spinning disc, and the initial crackle of needle on wax. Listen to old soul or jazz from an anonymous online stream and you'll miss the 180-gram love.

- **Newspapers:** The daily paper is a dreamer's privilege that slows down a hectic a.m. or evening commute with just a few flips of newsprint. Stellar stories that never seem to stand out online wait to be discovered.

- **Puzzles:** Can the rainy-day beach house enjoyment of a group poring over a thousand-piece jigsaw puzzle really be replicated by the solitary dragging of digital pieces by a computer mouse?

- **Journals:** A personal journal can be a dazzling palimpsest of emotion, with all the margin doodling, smudged ink, and heavy script of a noteworthy life.

- **Photo albums:** While over 98 percent of photos should reside as 1s and 0s, there's still the simple joy of an organized album of primo vacation pics and predigital-life snapshots. Don't just say thanks for coming to the party . . . mail a card with enclosed photos to warm-blooded friends.

ARTFUL CONVERSATION

Eavesdropping would be a juicier sport if dialogue were more exciting than a litany of tired phrases:

"S'up?"

"Nuthin'."

"What's goin' on with you?"

"Not much."

"Job's okay? Sciatica acting up again?"

"Same old, same old."

Every gentleman should banish this conversational game of chicken—waiting for the other to share. Scores of intelligent and discerning minds get stuck in small talk when mixing with strangers. Limber the wit with trifling matters and internet memes before steering talk to greater issues. Mine too soon, and conversation sputters due to a premature leap into personal space. Yet good chat begins when one person pushes talk forward with personal news or wild ideas. Counterbalance the usual Q&A with pointed questions about alternate career yens, spirituality, current affairs, and after-hours pursuits. Be a beacon. Make it your responsibility to wade through a crowd of shallow souls, looking for the deep end.

Clichés and hackneyed language are pollutants that litter bad poetry, not daily discourse. Pet jargon spices diction, yet the hallmark of a good keynoter is freshness. To avoid being annoying ("and stuff"), root out overused exclamations and superlatives ("Whoa dude"), yet in the right moment, savor the occasional animated outburst that turns heads.

Engage, don't disparage. Verbal interplay is not a strike of braggadocio upon those down on their luck or a haughty high-hat pounce on introverts. Better to break ice with hobbies than with how unemployment is going. The unthinking tighten the circle around lofty topics of singular specialty. Perhaps Argentinean fiscal policy isn't another's forte; sports and the holidays might be more accessible starters. Don't shy away from the perpetually shy, but refrain from needling with a smug and smarmy, "Having a good time?"

Hot topics are less a list of things to discuss and more a mandate to probe further. Delving into lesser-explored areas of interest leads to surprising discoveries and deepened connections. Clever conversation includes the following, used in light rotation:

· **Witty Devices**: puns, hyperbole, double entendre, homophones.

· **Recitations**: literary quotations, movie lines, song lyrics, poetry.

· **Interjections**: trenchant asides, sound effects, exclamations.

· **Rehearsed Material**: jokes (very limited), stories, tall tales.

· **Interrogatives**: questions that get heads scratching.

· **Bullhorns**: large-group addresses (know when to pass the mic).

· **Proofreading**: corrections of fact, tactfully offered, that spur continued discussion.

· **Carnal Byways**: gentle nudges toward sexuality, choice proclivities, and lost loves.

The gentleman is as comfortable trading esoteric talk with bow-tied theatre-goers as he is regaling toweled locker-room buddies with the one about the pope and the seven dwarves. Deft talk is not about grandiloquence, rather raising the comfort level of those around by sharing knowledge and wit befitting the moment. Adapt and employ conversational dexterity like a Swiss Army knife of the tongue: for most occasions, the three-inch blade will suffice; however, certain company may warrant the saw (cut through the thick of it), spoon (speak in small doses), toothpick (get into hard-to-reach places), or tweezers (be pointed and delicate). But cool the jaw—too much is overwhelming. A constant entertainer who is always "on" is like tiresome telethon shtick. Some nights, be the group's emcee; on others, turn off the spotlight and enjoy friendly chat traded over a pint.

BUTTING IN

Bouts of spirited wordplay in storytelling circles are soulful music, not henhouse cacophony. Sharp interjections pitch a story to greater heights, extracting juicy details and creating operatic tension. But beware the verbal blue jay: this predator lacks the originality to start meaningful conversation, but not the temerity to barge into your nest during the hot pants climax. Bland asides and chirping interruptions sully a hot retelling. Bleats of "Ooh," "Ahh," and "No foolin'!" are oxygen. Too often, the unthinking listener needlessly footnotes or fact-checks ("Well actually, Montpelier is the capital of Vermont"), or worse, prematurely follows up and murders the punch line ("The same thing happened to a friend of mine"). Only a world-class schmendrick drains the conversational momentum with worthless tangents or untimely transitions.

Despite your full quiver of anecdotes and accomplishments, curtail showboating and needless rodomontade. Ask questions and gain insight into others' character instead of trumpeting your own. Share reason and realizations, not résumés.

Some talking pointers:

- When others are basking in a moment of grandeur, do not engage in one-upmanship simply to tout vast experience.
- Stir energy into flailing circles. Instigate easy chat by finding a touchstone ("Dugan, haven't you just returned from Walla Walla?").
- The cloak of new acquaintanceship allows for daring inquiries. In relaxed environs, mature people will answer almost any probing question.

- Keep an eye out for these feckless perpetrators and discomfiting yakkers of nervous interlocution whose tics make them matchmaking risks: shifty-eyed ceiling starers, closed-eyed pensives, obsessive nose scratchers, mouth watchers, snorting snits, slithering blatherers, tongue wetters, cheek clickers, ear cockers, gum smackers, hair twirlers, brow wrinklers, lobe pullers, lane shifters, mobile checkers, beard strokers, surprising crescendoers, and dorky guffawers—not to mention the warblers, mumblers, spittlers, ummers, and whistlers.

PROFANITY & VULGARITY

I believe in having a good heart, a chirpy penis, a lively intelligence, and the courage to say "shit" in front of a lady.
—D. H. LAWRENCE, *Lady Chatterley's Lover*

A well-rounded gentleman possesses a mature vocabulary, including deviation from the Queen's English. The proper timing and judicious use of profanity separate the nimble jawsmith from the colloquial fool. Keep it for friends, foes, and excited utterances. When making first impressions, even if your behavior is cavalier, your conversation oughtn't be. Tread lightly when meeting a lady, professional colleague, or parent. Used poorly, profanity is a steamroll of useless acrimony, the stamp of a bumptious fool. The quickest route to a bureaucratic clusterfuck is the raging-lunatic motif—swear at the clerk between you and a stand-by flight or student loan deferment and you'll be denied. Act differently. Don't lean over the counter, elbows akimbo, and demand. Hold it in and get results. Reserve your speed-bag flurry of vituperative slurry for irksome telemarketers who've somehow bypassed the federal Do Not Call list. To convey profanity over a distance, build a database of vulgar gestures. Unfurl

The Finger in both its clenched East Coast grip and the languid West Coast, up-yours flip.

Vulgar behavior such as groin thrusts is the lowest common denominator. Behind the polished veneer and stiff ascot, a man's basic settings are rooted in the hunt and the hot blood of libido. The balanced gentleman knows when to peel back layers of correctness. The sharpest vulgarities are unexpected slips revealing fundamental traits: anger, lust, hunger, and fear. Examples include lewd tongue-and-mouth gestures, the ol' in-and-out index-finger poke, beating fists, and flashed nudity. Don't be a prude; those who can handle sophistication, but not its antithesis, are missing the grotesque beauty of vulgarity. Master the art of diffusing a lover's tiff or punctuating a friendly squabble with a big smile, choice expletive, or exaggerated crotch grab.

PROVOCATEUR

Amid vibrant chatter, deft charmers might sprinkle harmless hints encoded with secondary meaning. The listener hears either an ordinary query or a fantastical invitation, somewhere between asking a lady to see your etchings and wondering whether her mind also wanders every afternoon at 3 p.m. Establish your own personal boundaries that are open enough to welcome flirty exchanges yet firm enough to avoid seductive come-ons. The attached gent might induce a veiled blush through a rich compliment, but only a drunken lout paws a close friend or new acquaintance in close quarters and blames it on the booze. It's like a firefighter starting a controlled fire not to save the mansions on the cul-de-sac but to contain a larger blaze of intrigue. This subtle exchange becomes fodder for the mind and another layer of complexity onto a mature relationship, and if both parties find themselves liberated in the future, then a simple lunch reignites the once forbidden flame.

JUKEBOXING

As Lou Gramm of Foreigner once crooned, be a jukebox hero. A jukebox affords a public opportunity to select moodful tunes and display an eclectic musical canon. In the right hands, greatest hits are tabled so that B-sides may shine.

Your $1-2 buys a well-considered three-act passion play, not a heedless afterthought. Do not feel constrained by random shuffle play—put a set together. Range the emotions and forage deep. Do a "double shot" and your genius will be noticed. Avoid the pitfalls of the vapid and eschew standards of heavy rotation. Avoid making the patrons' ears bleed with "Brown-Eyed Girl" or "Margaritaville." Be underground radio, not retrograde with a 1990s hit parade medley of Stone Pearl Temple Jam Pilots. When rushed to return for your pool shot, toss in a guaranteed crowd-pleaser. In the event of sudden dead air, make a quick choice from the current screen, though the "no Justin Bieber" lamp is always lit.

Percolating CD and vinyl-stocked Wurlitzers have been mostly replaced by TouchTunes models that put virtually the entire digital catalog of popular music at your debit card's disposal. There's little excuse for selecting a dud. While the pay-to-bump option springs your selections to the front of the queue, it had better be a bona fide toe-tapper, lest the dude whose ditty you usurped decides that Built to Spill isn't just an indie band. Also, exercise restraint before fulfilling some inner-alcoholic, inexplicable need for a tired AOR staple from Thin Lizzy. All these guidelines are suspended, however, when "impairment" becomes an understatement, the waitress has joined your party, or you are a regular patron.

TABLETOP DINER MODELS

Famished in a Jersey diner late one evening, you encounter a diminutive, tabletop, twenty-five-cent mono jukebox nestled behind the sugar caddy. Soak in the playlist: ne'er heard Billy Joel singles sit beside Elton John's "I'm Still Standing," just above Bobby Darin's "Mack the Knife," to the left of "That's Amore!" If you're at least a booth's length from the nearest revelers, punch up the volume from LO to HI.

CREAMED KORN

After an especially horrible experience of poor service, repeated short pours, or unsavory clientele, it's clearly time to leave the bar. Even if you harbor enough resentment to piss in the corner pocket, stop and instead use your underdeveloped superego to produce a gift for everyone. Pure fury is much sweeter when spread out over the course of $5. This is the time for creaming them with Korn; stuff the jukebox with nu-metal and leave the room gobsmacked with Godsmack. For pubby venues with more cougars than kittens, look for "Let's Get Physical" or put that dusty Irish Drinking Songs disc on repeat. Perhaps you might go for the darker side—select the old school juke downer trio—"The End," "Heroin," and "When the Music's Over" . . . scenes from inside the goldmine, indeed. If *you* get creamed with Korn, simply yank the plug, ask the barkeep to reboot the machine, or else admit defeat and hit the pavement.

FLASKMANSHIP

[cap]

[monogram]

The flask provides a gentleman with a dash of home-style comfort, a liquid élan, and portable panache in less than nine ounces. It is essential clandestine equipment, favored during live shows, train trips, and motoring (for passengers).

While the gentleman's daily chapeau remains out of current favor, a flask is classic and need not connote whiskey-induced dipsomania . . . unless you carry one in the breast pocket of your three-buttoned, notched-lapel jacket and swig during Tuesday's board meeting.

Purchase wisely and steer clear of downtown discount tobacco shops or delis that also peddle Graffix bongs and pipes under the glass counter to local teens. Select tastefully: no corporate swag models, molded from lightweight synthetics,* or stamped from flimsy alloys by the Franklin Mint. Select silver, pewter, leather-bound glass, or fine stainless steel styles, with that ergonomic curve for easy portability. A small funnel aids in liquor transfer.

Carry a flask in a breast or coat pocket; if this is not possible, you are underdressed for flasking. The only exception to this rule is the ripped back pocket of your redheaded girlfriend's faded dungarees. A monogrammed flask makes an exceptional gift, especially for the clever lady.

* Though you *should* employ a flimsy flask when tailgating or otherwise facing impending seizure or loss (customs, principal's office, skydiving).

Better: Relish these shining moments to display your guarded suavity, and to season an evening or solitary moment with a delicate sip.

Better Not: Do not unduly flaunt your flask. Certain instances do not warrant open consumption, lest you be perceived unfairly.

BETTER	BETTER NOT
Between acts at the theatre or when cinema houselights dim.	At school plays (though perfect for the Pinewood Derby winner's circle).
Before any special-teams play at a football game.	A flask is for intermittent sips, not collegiate gulps.
Anywhere you can see your breath, especially on a blustery platform awaiting a homebound commuter train.	Any place where there is already available liquor.
A fall day at the beach or a wetting of the lips for taxi cab trips.	Pints of rotgut from a clerk behind bulletproof glass.
At the track as your horse rounds the home stretch.	Inexcusable during a job interview (a callback interview for an Internet start-up, maybe).
In the guest bathroom after meeting your lover's puritanical parents.	During Lamaze class (but okay after "It's a girl!" is shouted to the rafters).

ELEVATOR ETIQUETTE

Ah, the elevator: tarnished brass walls, clanking exhaust fan, and the ever-tempting red STOP button. Savvy urbanites quickly learn that an empty, uninterrupted elevator ride is a rare treat, the crème brûlée of your day. Thus, do not feel like a misanthrope as you "appear to" fumble with the DOOR OPEN button while shrill cries of "Hold the door" echo down the lobby. Yet if you are courteously "saved" by a Samaritan who kindly reopens the door, reciprocate accordingly within five business days.

Joy of solitude aside, certain conventions must be followed for a seamless trip. While it is not improper to stand impassively in the lift among disgruntled employees mesmerized by the whirr whirr of their Blackberry thumb wheel, a friendly solicitation, climate comment, or witticism may enrich the lives of work-obsessed riders. There is only a small window in which to proffer elevatorial banter—like the rodeo and that ne'er seen Luke Perry movie—about eight seconds. After this period, the pall of awkwardness has indelibly clouded the car.

If the carriage is crowded, do not wantonly snake an arm for the controls. Rather, politely inquire of the lovely lady near the buttons: "Could you mash five, please?" As when riding in a subway car, don't hold up transit with chivalry; promptly step in and out.

Reserve the elevator for trips over three floors, except when toting parcels or hobbling to podiatrist appointments with a nasty hammer toe. If lucky enough to ride a manual elevator, have a smile and salutation ready for the attendant. Moreover, allow at least a fourteen-floor buffer for the retelling of a long, filthy joke. Similarly, must you press and repress the lit call button in the lobby, demonstrating egotistical mistrust of another's push?

Note: When the elevator car stops or the DMV line stalls, ready the climatic small talk. Don't fret over Tropical Depression Liza off the Lesser Antilles or the location of the prevailing jet stream; but at a minimum, shouldn't a man be heard to offer, "Feels like rain today"?

AT TABLE

Lesser men are ogres at the kitchen table and little better when dining out. Politeness is a gentleman's constant, and he plays by the rules with fork and knife, especially on the road. If etiquette feels constricting, take latitude in the attitude, not the manners. Preserve outward decorum but maintain your inner maverick. Dessert conversation might make the maitre d' blush, but two tables over, they're marveling at your manners and wishing they could eavesdrop.

Here are a few tips for the well-mannered man at the bistro:

- Whistling, snapping, or signaling unduly for a waiter's attention is unnecessary; good servers are trained to spot needy eye contact.

- When an escort rises from the table, exhibit a fingerbowlful of punctilio and stand, if only into an acceptable three-quarter crouch where gravity hasn't yet tugged the napkin from your lap to the floor.

- Ordering meat well done is implicit permission for the chef to give you a less choice cut.

- Refrain from crude sawing, poking, or bowing a knife through the fork tines. Skip the precut woodpiles of meat and slice one tender forkful at a time. Cutting linguini into tatters insults all of Italy; twirl long noodles with a fork and pasta spoon.

- Enjoy the pampering: abstain from piling plates, self-crumbing your place mat, or bussing your own table.

- The liquid lunch is a *Mad Men* relic, yet there's still room for a sole drink, especially when conducting business with Europeans. Nothing evinces self-control and cultural savvy like the wherewithal to manage a single glass of sauvignon blanc beside a plate of scallops and nail the product pitch. Instead of "Bottoms up!" show practiced restraint by leaving behind a last sip.

Incidentally, master chopsticks. A fork is an affront to the beauty of sushi and *kaiseki*. To hone dexterity, take two days of home-cooked meals exclusively with chopsticks, even slippery noodles.

TEXTING AT TABLE

For weekday lunches and freelance confabs, phones can remain untouched on the table to view the numbers and texts you're ignoring. If expecting a ring, alert guests in advance and either take it quickly at table ("Hello. Buy low, sell high. Bye.") or escape to the lobby. Social media jezebels should announce that they're broadcasting a host's vino and vittles and not merely scrolling.

TIPPING

Step up to the charge-card plate—former waiters and gray-haired regulars shouldn't be the only decent tippers. Fifteen percent is reasonable and appreciated. If the food is well prepared, and timely and professionally served, tip 20 percent. If special requests were honored without gripe or if service greatly enhanced your enjoyment, consider more. Leave extra when the difference between a good tip and a great tip is minimal; for delivery orders, tip handsomely for hot food transported in gelid conditions. Yet don't be goaded into a gratuity unless extra consideration has been proffered. A to-go cup of java poured from a coffee shop carafe is not service. However, be kind to teenage girls who toil at beachside ice cream/snack bar shops for near-slave wages.

Nice touch: When out to eat amidst tight-wadded friends, drop the Supplement: upon departure, surreptitiously slip a few extra dollars to compensate for a host's parsimony.

DINER BEHAVIOR

Despite any postmidnight impairment at the all-night diner, draw the first line in the sand: breakfast foods (eggiwegs or French toast?) or not (bison burger deluxe, moussaka), but never seafood, even if the bluefish blue-plate special comes with a nice rice pilaf. Never mind inquiring about toast types—order the rye for its optimal crunch and butter-soaking qualities, but skip the packets of colored corn syrup masquerading as grape jelly. In keeping with the group's mildly raucous boothsmanship, it's the optimal time for off-the-wall digestive wagering. Bet your comrade a ten-spot to eat his entire plate of silver-dollar pancakes in one bite; twenty for anything involving A-1 sauce. When pats of butter and onion halves are gobbled, everybody wins.

CATSUP

Easy with the Heinz. Give it a light rattle before tilting. If the viscosity or level does not allow for quick pouring, force a light rap on the bottle's sternum—the upper bulge where the neck meets the torso. As a last resort, use a fresh knife to coax the sauce forth. It is not ungentlemanly to offer catsup to a friend first; politeness notwithstanding, there is the wily avoidance of that first watery discharge out of a fallow bottle.

BUFFETIQUETTE

Reconnoiter the smorgasbord before ever ladling a dollop of country-style anything onto your dish. Course it out: minimalism is the secret to maximizing a buffet. Several small trips are more elegant, satisfying, and dollar-stretching than a single, bloated, Thanksgiving-style plate. Lesser souls litter a plate with breads and filler foods before noticing the carving station and raw bar. Return serving utensils to a utility plate or hang them unsoiled upon the handles. Close a steaming chafer if an inconsiderate guest has allowed the trout almandine to cool or the biscuit gravy to skin over.

Nice touches: Offer fresh plates to your escort and the person immediately following. At the dessert station, swirl raspberry and chocolate sauces around brioche and flapjacks and make geometric shapes on plate rims for personal presentation.

SKINNY-DIPPING

What better end to an evening of group revelry, romantic frolic, or solitary mischief than a refreshing rinse and spin? Breaststroke sans a slap in the face, the skinny-dip is the most laudable of swims. Like the ways of a woman's heart, a skinny-dip can't be forced when the dynamic isn't light and naughty. But once a small band has shared a bare splash, all bonds are reinforced. Besides, you've always wanted to see your pal's girlfriend naked anyway.

Even without drawers, the after-hours puddle plash is no time for a gentleman to lose his shirt.

Here are a few recommended scenarios:

- **Oceanfront Foray**: A moonlight jaunt is a must for any beach stay.

- **Disco Dip**: After bouts of the Hustle, sweaty friends assuage the heat by dodging into a local hotel water hole.

- **Lakeside Isolation**: Nobody's around, so it's a day or night treat (watch for snapping turtles).

- **Polar Drench**: Have a warm robe and a hot toddy waiting.

- **Postlove Lave:** Beyond the bath . . . lagoons aren't just for Brooke Shields and seven stranded castaways.

- **Chlorine Nightcap:** Why don't we all go back to my place for a float?

- **Solo Soak:** Spiritual "me time" in quiet waters.

Before diving in, enlist a confederate from the opposite sex so that at least one member from the Pink team joins—ask the wild one you've known the longest, or the party gal who's logged more than one Mardi Gras. Then, be the first one in with a Rebel Yell cannon-ball into the deep end.

Even when the only thing between him and her is H2O, casting off clothing doesn't signal the loss of manners. Despite primal urges to take to the bleacher seats with binoculars and peanuts, glance but furtively upon disrobing others. A callipygian lady should be allowed to slip languidly into the water without probing eyeballs keeping her in the crosshairs like a turkey shoot. Likewise, while assessment of fellow men's equipment is generally more open here than at the local YMCA (where a glance and a toe tap might land you a phone number or a black eye), refrain from applause-o-meter-like responses. Like savvy investors, some chaps retain hidden assets.

While a quorum is necessary to begin, sometimes not all parties are eager participants. In this case, excuses like "It's too cold" or "There might be jellyfish" should be left unchallenged, even if deeper issues are clearly at stake. A skinny-dip is no time to purge someone's genuine fears of murky water, incarceration, or physical insecurity. Do not reprimand a swimmer who retains skivvies—all levels of daring are encouraged. On the other hand, a small mob of friends may overtake a noisy flapdoodler or oafish bore and toss him gleefully into the drink.

Skinny-dipping already carries a badge of rascality, but the experienced rabble-rouser does not rule out private pools. The exhilaration of backstrokes in the buff is nearly matched by the thrill of scaling a neighbor's fence or tiptoeing into the hotel whirlpool. A dripping posse of scampering nudes is more likely to elicit giggles and envy than an actual summons. When necessary, keep it quiet, fun, and light on the libido; chicken fights are more efficient without the hydrodynamic drag of an uninvited erection.

Nice touch: It worked for securing that hot bistro table on a Saturday night, so slip an understanding security guard a twenty to look the other way as the gang has a midnight swim.

Skinny-dipping etiquette translates to hot tubs, where the cloak of rising steam shouldn't cloud conduct. Normal rules of personal space are suspended when abutting another's nakedness. However, don't commit the posttub flub of projected hot-water fantasies until a continued connection is proven on land.

COMINGS & GOINGS

Fanfare can announce a gentleman's arrival, but not every entrance will be punctuated with tickertape and or an electronic check-in. The keys to a proper entrance are rooted in the assessment of conditions, ranging from hushed to raucous. When knocking, step back, enjoy the porch daisies, and afford the host space when the door opens. Yet, burst into the "Welcome Home" celebration with fire; slink past the boss's door at 9:35 a.m. Avoid even the slightest disgrace of under- or overstaying a welcome. Just as lingering past the host's yawns is pitiable, jumping ship prematurely is insulting to the host's group dynamic, especially when it's you who dashes the faerie dust of abandon and causes the party's high to collapse in a cavalcade of "I should really go . . ."

Here's a matching exercise to relate tactics and timing.

ENTRANCES

The sneak-in, when you'd rather be invisible or avoid the cover charge. Low profile, best executed alone or in small groups. De rigueur for gate-crashing and ideal for excessive lateness. *Pairs best with French Leave or Slip-Out.*	STEALTH
Pomp, grandeur, maybe a cape. Hoopla is the name of the game. Reserved for guests of honor, dress-up affairs, and Halloween. *Pairs best with Jim Brown.*	THE PREMIERE
Peeking in long enough to realize that you don't want to be there. You're a double scoop and they're lactose intolerant. A short visit triggers a gut-instinct abort. The club is too crowded or the party has pooped. *Pairs best with The Ditch.*	FLY-BY
Despite other engagements, the brief appearance, as promised. Obligatory visit with one-drink minimum and two-yawn maximum. Only there long enough for an extended hostess hug and a brief conversation with a spry stranger. *Pairs best with The Godfather or Jim Brown.*	POP-IN
"You didn't see me. I was never here." Hatching a conspiratorial lie in the face of trouble and cell phone cameras—rarely successful. Used for feigned office illnesses and infidelities. *Pairs best with the Slip-Out.*	PERJURED
Arriving arm-in-arm or with ruckus in tow. A cheerful pair or bunch incites fresh life. Unlike poker, wild pairs beat a subdued three of a kind. *Return with a Curtain Call.*	PAIR/GROUP
Lying about whereabouts: "Whatd'ya mean? I was there for an hour!" *Since you were never there, no accompanying exit.*	GHOST
With one hand still on the doorjamb, a quick reconnoiter: "Is this the right place?" *Plot your next move based on the guest list and vibe.*	THE LEAN-IN

EXITS

FRENCH LEAVE	No one knows you've left until thirty minutes have passed. Best reserved for after-hours living room hangouts and among never-to-be-seen-again acquaintances. Great for anonymous opting out of 'round the clock benders and avoiding The Godfather (see below). Exit smoothly before the fun ends and group dynamic peters out.
SLIP-OUT	When a formal goodbye is undesirable, tell a few key players and forgo the burdensome receiving line. A sober end to a bad night or the most dignified exit after a colossal gaffe. The group is having more fun than you: get out before your sluggish mood befouls festivities.
IN-OUTS	Revolving door of "Hi" or "Bye," repeated multiple times. Coming and going, with or without hand stamp; the staple of party-hopping. Usually, out to the parking lot for indiscretions or the hallway to arrange plans discreetly.
THE GODFATHER	An offer to stay that you can't refuse. The tractor beam of peer pressure, new arrivals, and the optimistic promise of potential merriment. "Every time I try to get out, they pull me back in." Employ the French Leave.
CURTAIN CALL	"I'm back!" Unexpected encore presentation, often to retrieve forgotten items. A fallback when secondary plans falter. Use rarely, since it spoils the tidiness of a well-orchestrated goodbye. To mitigate, return bearing alms: six-pack, candy.
JIM BROWN	Retiring in your prime, with admirers wanting more. Going four-for-four, with three numbers and one kiss landed, and two assists to your credit . . . then pulling yourself from the game.
"BE RIGHT BACK" DITCH	Says it all.

SERENDIPITOUS STUMBLE-IN

It is impolite to intrude upon an affair (especially a White House gala) where you are explicitly not welcome. Yet under darkness and quiet of night, sound travels far and an alluring beat cocks your ear. You had no idea there was a party. Invariably, you are on the way home and suddenly have to decide whether to sniff out the source or continue on. Besides listening for the volume trail, look for a mass of parked cars, bodies in the window frame, or the hard-to-spot, fenced-in backyard bash. Now strategize. Do you make a move on the house perimeter and engage outdoor guests in conversation, or head for the front door, drafting behind others before the buzz-in expires? It's a crapshoot; likely, though, the Modern Gentleman is a good candidate for a late invitation.

Upon entry, look for clues as to the event's nature. A baby shower, bon voyage, or anniversary indicates a closed group, where your presence is unwanted. If you spot a steady stream of traffic or "party this way" signage, this is likely a more public affair. Note the theme. How are people dressed? Are they sipping martinis or quaffing keg beer from party cups? Stick to the high-traffic areas, as this is no time to peek into side rooms or interrupt corner tête-à-têtes. Get yourself a drink and acquaint yourself with a larger circle—start from the punch bowl area and work around the room in concentric circles. Wandering preserves your anonymity longer; if you remain in constant motion, no one can get a fix on the mystery guest.

TARDINESS

How long does one wait? For loose engagements, a grace period of thirty minutes is standard and given gratis. Beyond this, evaluate on a case-by-case basis. For close friends, call or text; for acquaintances with tardy tendencies, have another drink or exercise jukebox etiquette. For the late date or untested acquaintance, you get one phone call, like an incarcerated perp. A second call or text is saved for updated information or aborting the mission. Tardy parties should courteously transmit their amended ETA in real time (plus or minus two traffic lights).

Nice touch: Running late for vittles or vino on the town? Turn tardiness into gallantry by alerting the restaurant. "Rendezvousing with a redhead and two chaps. I'm a few minutes behind. Won't you put your best appetizer and a round of Prosecco on the table, please?" Instead of being greeted by perturbed glares, you'll arrive the hero as friends wash down calamari with bubbles. This also works when her moony eyes and smooth thighs have bumped up against pretheatre dinner reservations. Phone ahead and request that they start stirring the risotto so you won't miss the curtain going up.

FAMILY REUNIONS

Once emancipated, drop the yellowed photograph and step away from the drama. Make the most of it when the whole gang descends on you to sling career advice and offer criticism of the homemade cranberry tofu sauce. Keep your ears open for dramatic one-liners or family secrets (especially if spoken in the ancestral tongue). These can be retold for years to come. When it's all over, consider who's flourishing and who's floundering. Next year, seek out wisdom from the former and off-color jokes from the latter.

Family gatherings are a karmic yardstick: like measuring a growing boy's height on the wall in pencil, note your social progress. Answering probing inquiries with an indifferent "not much" or other rote nonsense marks a stunted growth. Once matriculated from the "kids' table," speak up like Flipper, stir the pot, and ask the ever-affable Uncle Arnie about his love of the ponies and your aunt's Jordache jeans.

Bemuse those who remember only your churlish days in braces. If you are lucky enough to have living grandparents, cultivate such relations. Sip a bourbon and branch with Pop; take a Rob Roy with Nana. They are living history and should be mined for golden lore and life lessons. If you think you're a smarty-pants at thirty, triple that and imagine what Grandpa knows. As for Great Aunt Georgia— the wily one with tissues up her sleeve and a $20 bill tucked in her bosom—ask her for a dance at the next wedding.

Climb your family tree or at least carve your initials into it. Learn whether any branches have been pruned or disowned in the past. Run down the family checklist: immigration and surname history; how parents and grandparents met; embarrassing adolescent anecdotes; names of men who sought Mother's hand before Dad. Leave creepy Cousin Morton snoozing in the La-Z-Boy, and repair to the back porch with Uncle Thelonius. Discover why Mom's side is so neurotic— it can't be all genetics (you hope). Sift through topics not highlighted in the reunion getaway brochure. Find out which kin ran counter to the law, who's on a first-name basis with the pharmacist, and which ne'er-do-well eloped to Vegas for the loose slots. Steer the conversation with rack-and-pinion precision and chuckle at the candor.

Reunions, like kidney stones, are typically uncomfortable, but bearable with medication. For the more challenging affairs, especially outdoor galas, carry the bottomless day-drink. Your wine glass is perpetually half-full from 1 to 6 p.m. When conversation yawns or devolves into an incessant medical ailment show-and-tell, spice things with a dash of hot topics ("Goodness gracious, they're closing down the Nude Emporium!").

Incest-dentally, it is not discourteous to express lingering affections for single, peripheral kinfolk, as begetting a child with your wife's sister is no longer a misdemeanor in Tennessee. Nonetheless, it's inadvisable to upgrade fantasy into actual nookie; it would make next year's Thanksgiving extra awkward.

AMEN CORNER

Whether secular as a dead church mouse or more orthodox than the Lord's personal CPA, a gentleman is occasionally invited to exalt the heavens. Sometimes shoes are left outside, other times hands are washed, and occasionally a *sheygats* is scrutinized for any trace of facial features that might suggest a distant Semitic heritage. While a fire ceremony at dawn in a Japanese Shinto temple is hard to beat, below are two ceremonies best attended with an informed air.

THE LAST SIPPER

With family gathered 'round the table, a Passover seder is a bittersweet celebration of the emancipation of the Israelites from slavery in ancient Egypt as told in the Book of Exodus. This story of the pre-Heston Moses and the Pharaoh, the ten plagues, and the Israelites includes a harrowing escape through a parted Red Sea and across the Sinai Desert into the Promised Land. During their flight to freedom, there was no time to wait for the bread to rise—hence the ban on all *chametz*, or leavened products, and the munching of unleavened matzo. In fact, truly observant Jews presciently remove all traces of carb-heavy *chametz* from their homes during the entire

Passover holiday, a practice that predates the South Beach Diet by at least two thousand years.

For guests with an interest in ancient theology and myth, a Passover seder is a nice invite; besides, anyone who has slurped matzo ball soup before is already an honorary Landsman. Dress smartly, play follow the leader, soak in the culture, skim the English translation of the service in your Haggadah (Passover service book) to see if it was the plague of frogs or the killing of the firstborn that finally convinced the Pharaoh to free the Jews. The length of the evening depends on the orthodoxy and guilt factor of the host family, but at least everyone is at dinner, as opposed to stuck in pews.

While a traditional seder has more breaks for hand washing than an OCD group therapy session, it is a boon for boozers. Four glasses of wine are raised, symbolizing the four promises God made to Moses. Thirsty dogs who don't mind facing the wrath of the Lord—not to mention the hostess—might filch Elijah's vino (an extra chair and glass of wine is traditionally reserved for the celebrated prophet). During the seder, the wine is customarily sipped while leaning symbolically to the left toward freedom; conveniently, the alcoholic buzz itself might leave you lurching a bit to the port side anyway. After enduring the endless litany of prayers on an empty stomach with the smell of delicious brisket in the air, must the Jews (and their guests) continue to suffer?

Kosher wines need not be subpar or—oy!—teeth-rottingly sweet. There are fine domestic producers of party-tested, rabbi-approved kosher wines. Try Napa's Hagafen Cellars, Central Coast's Baron Herzog, and a boutique kosher Cab called Covenant. With super-observant hosts, look for wines labeled *mevushal*, which denotes wines that have been flash-pasteurized for handling by gentiles (and red-headed *shikshas*) without compromising kosher status.

Incidentally, at the close of dinner, you may gleefully aid the kids hunting the *afikoman*, a hidden sheet of matzo—though, as many a disappointed suitor has discovered, it's invariably behind the couch cushions, not under the skirt of the eldest daughter.

HYMNS & MYRRHS

What's a gent to do when faced with trespassers, debtors, and Sunday kneelers when mentions of Virgin Mary make you wonder who forgot the vodka and celery at brunch? Whether you're seeking solace, redemption, revelation, or just a members' discount for the rummage sale, you'll hopefully find peace and joy and not just a dour hour of demagoguery.

Upon the offering plate, pay your fare according to how far your soul needs to go. Akin to curbside trombonists, organists and pastors are buskers in the pulpit, and congregations pass the basket for ducats to support the mission. A fiver for walk-ins is fine, but big holidays beg an upcharge. If modest, use a diminutive envelope so that your tithe is more elegant than two crumpled Washingtons and less garish than a fat wad. As with the pizzeria tip jar, even if no one sees you put the Jackson in, never attempt to retrieve a bill, lest the usher accuse you of degreasing the palm of God.

When offered the bread or wafer, either open your maw for direct feeding or present cupped hands. You may then sip from the communal chalice (no mentions of backwash in the Gospels) or dip your bread/wafer/planchet into the wine. If skipping Holy Communion, remain in the pew and use the time for your preferred method of quiet reflection. Blogging and texts ("OMG, I'm totally into this unionized, I mean organized religion thing!") are out, but 140 postblessing characters ("Got my Amen on @StPauls. Caught acolytes toking frankincense after mass. Hottie makes me wanna break Commandments 7 & 10. #ilovesinnersdogma") are acceptable outside of the Lenten season.

Chapter Two

ENTERTAINING

GROUP DYNAMICS

No need for a whistle or head coach's clipboard to keep a score of scallywags on task. A gentleman understands the delicate interplay between friends and acquaintances whether during playtime in the park or nights on the town. Cultivate the subtle skills of making introductions, setting a charismatic table, and coaxing the most out of groups. A host invites according to the nature of the evening. A good roster matches temperament and charisma to environment and expression. For example, certain pals are better for a lecture and others for a Frisbee picnic. Likewise, intimate evenings are closed affairs for the inner circle; don't set out plates for casual work chums.

SIZING

Groups come in small, medium, and unwieldy sizes. The small bunch ranges from two to five and comes with a low degree of management difficulty, as there is quick response time, easy transport, and nearly limitless possibility. Medium collectives range from six to nine and carry a small degree of complexity regarding tables or beach spots at crowded venues, forcing tougher transportation and more involved decision making. The unwieldy horde starts at ten, feels like twenty, moves with the speed of fifty, and makes decisions like a bureaucracy of one hundred. Its half-life is usually one event; membership falls off as soon as there's a change of place.

BRINGING IT IN BEFORE TAKING IT OUT

When conjoining couples and individuals for a shared event, "bring it in" by gluing the group together first. A preactivity beverage or quick tourney of Ping-Pong in someone's basement turns a collection of factions into a cohesive group. There's no substitute for the shared experience of a meal and sober conversation to forge common ground before "taking it out" on the town. If you don't have a home base, roll into a quiet spot prior to tossing the group into a noisy locale with tight quarters. Bringing it in is the huddle before a sandlot football game, when you figure out who's on your side before telling everybody to go deep.

INTRODUCTIONS

If I could remember the names of all these particles,
I'd be a botanist.

—ENRICO FERMI, Nobel Prize—winning physicist

Nameless faces equals weak dynamic. It is imperative to stress introductions early in the evening, especially with appellations like Thalia and Kerensa. Do not waste breath on fruitless, large-scale introductions that invariably lead to a slew of missed names. Rather, introduce guests to key players and let them make at-large acquaintances on their own. Treat each introduction as a personal connection and offer a short résumé or commonality. For example, "Maeve, may I introduce Sandor, a crazy cat who drove from New Delhi to Bangalore on an old Enfield motorcycle."

To reinforce new familiarity, repeat each guest's name first aloud and then silently to yourself. Stick the landing on tricky ethnic names. If the name is especially syllabic, the person is likely patient with new friends and will gladly explain the phonics and derivation. Acting as liaison and bolstering name recall thwart proliferation of the impersonal monikers "Hey" and "Dude." Be proactive and alleviate the awkwardness of someone having forgotten your name. Upon subsequent contact and until name recall is apparent, reintroduce yourself ("Hello Ms. Zevitas. Phineas Mollod. A treat to see you again.").

Incidentally, streetside run-ins require less formality. Spare your escort the meaningless exchange of names with an assembly of acquaintances who will never be crossed again. Introductions are pointless when they would last longer than the ensuing polite chatter, unless the lady would be offended at the lack of introduction, taking it to mean she's temporary arm candy rather than a more permanent fixture worthy of public pronouncement to all comers.

INERTIA & FRICTION

Objects at rest tend to stay at rest; objects in motion tend to remain in motion. For small groups, starting and stopping takes little more than a nimble spank. Hordes, on the other hand, take time to accelerate and, once going, rarely stop or alter course. Friction refers to the forces of motion within the group that can mar a dynamic if they are not socially lubricated. In small groups, persons of differing ilk can easily slip and twist without complaint after their ideas are considered and compromises reached ("Wait. We'll get a large pie with half anchovy and half black olive."). In hordes, it is inevitable that not everyone's needs will be congruous with the group's mission. With so many bodies, expect the squeaky wheels of limitations, preferences, and issues to require more grease. For decreased inertia, eschew early-evening dope on the veranda, and when the hour strikes, spur a hasty departure.

THE CORE

Within every horde is a nucleus. A gentleman always allies himself with this small band committed to making the most fun, even if it requires late-night secession from the rest of the group. As the dynamic winds down, expect to jettison those flagging and pining for bed. The remaining core group will invariably catch a secondary wind and end up with highlights begging to be told over brunch. The core is made up of two or more of these usual players.

- **The Locomotive:** Never runs out of energy or fun; keeps it going.

- **The Local Expert:** Knows the best sushi, nightclub, and picnic spot.

- **The Wanderer:** Goes missing, but always returns with a hot story.

- **The Aloof Couple:** Moody twosome who keep to themselves.

- **The Token:** Beloved lone rep for an ethnicity, alt-lifestyle, or political fringe outside your group's median.

- **The Catalyst:** Buys the first round or starts the dancing.

- **The Pumpkin:** Cashes in the chips early . . . for an early morning meeting or not.

- **The Liaison:** Mixes with other groups and the bartenders; has vice on speed-dial.

- **The Quiet Champ:** Seemingly vanilla persona who proves wildly insightful.

- **The Publicist:** Hypes the party, tags everyone in photos, and geolocates the group's movements.

- **The Heavy:** Show of muscle or six-foot-plus height that quells unrest.

- **The Whiner:** No matter what the group does, it sucks.

DINING EN MASSE

Birthdays and celebrations promise a bustling crowd that fills the back room at the bistro. Passing dishes, ordering family style, or otherwise tearing at the same *injera* at the Ethiopian café forges intimacy among acquaintances. Absent an obvious host, the gentleman quells any hunger-induced unrest by taking control and ordering popular starters for the table. Unless there are other knowledgeable winos, slyly palm the wine list so it doesn't fall into the wrong California cabernet-centric hands. To avoid the label of vinous tyrant, drape an arm across the adjacent diner and "include" him or her in the decision making. As table leader, you are the point man for the waiter and will be consulted before any new bottles are ordered; you may even get one line-item veto when shared vittles are ordered. Though implicitly, as table leader, you're responsible for tallying the totals and collecting funds to pay the check. There is the danger of being short-changed when the stack of cash is light and you're forced to add an extra sawbuck to make it square because of the sipping freeloader who just "stopped by for dessert." Per-person splitting is standard, never mind that Little Michael's pasta was under $20 or that lithesome Katy ordered the "gold-plated" margarita. Yet when your consumption was especially baronial, throw in a little extra without being asked.

Incidentally, group dining requires everyone to shelve persnickety dietary needs. For the sake of celebration, just pick out the onions and focus on the fellowship. You'd almost rather quietly stick yourself with an EpiPen in the bathroom than ruin a grand feast with protestations about your bothersome mustard allergy.

SPLINTERING

Splintering is the sinister foe to a group dynamic. To counter the dynamic dysfunction of multiple venue changes, keep large numbers together by finding a single place with a multiplicity of activities. Try a pub that has pool and darts or a part of town with a cluster of clubs within walking distance. In this fashion, even if the mass splinters into grouplets, they're still reachable by white courtesy cell phone. To prevent splintering, it might be necessary to rehuddle, which may be followed by a vote of no confidence and a hostile coup against the current group leadership.

The friendly flake-out is a minor form of splintering, when last-minute surprises spur otherwise reliable people to disappear without warning. Should one or two crewmembers join a winsome blonde in a separate pedicab, stick with the remaining gang and move on. Don't have a hissy fit or an episode of separation anxiety, unless stuck waiting for the cavalry alone. If this is a weekly phenomenon, reevaluate friendships.

Ultimately, when the mood has palled, jump-start the dynamic by acknowledging the lull before the group collapses: "Does anyone else find this band sonically dreadful?" A gentleman plays a cameo role in the revival of a flailing host's fading dynamic by usurping the iPod, dimming the lights, or texting some fresh provocateurs. Though, don't be the rosy kindergarten teacher forcing a game of kickball on a rainy day—if a night's spunk is irretrievable, allow it to splinter or expire with grace.

HOSTING

Entertaining is the most revealing form of home expression, a gentleman's time to impart his charms, fetishes, and qualities of life to friends and lovers. Lesser hosts allow an affair to unravel into a diluted and polluted free-for-all, with half the party stuffed in the kitchen and the other half within the glower of the idiot box. Not so the modern man in his own home, who exudes full-frontal personality with structure and style.

It's HQ and you are the majordomo with supreme control over ambiance. Ideal atmosphere includes thoughtful consideration of the event, attendees, time, and season. Are the lights soft and cozy or bright and revealing? Adjust your dimmer switches and thermostats according to your joie de vivre, and download an app to magically control iTunes. Is it a quiet living-room-floor bout of gaming or a hot Saturday eve shakedown with ceiling fans on high speed? It is the host's responsibility to bestow ample comforts upon guests and fix the first drink.

Duties do not end when the party begins. Make a point to spend time with most everyone throughout an affair, including wayward sheep otherwise abandoned on couch corners. Around the room, circles should be made of newly acquainted company and not homogenized groups that arrived together. Like an experienced referee, interpose yourself on couples or familiar friends who have slumped into a clinch like tired heavyweights. Foster new connections— say those odd names a few more times and make across-the-room introductions with flair ("Roey, may I present Ishmael, lately of Wedgewood. Izzy and I did time back in Sing Sing for running that spam-bot operation back in the early oughts."

PETIQUETTE

Good hosting involves the proper training of household pets. A guest should not have to guard his designer luggage or family jewels from an overzealous Labradoodle. If you lack the time to clean or the resources to hire a chambermaid, avoid fur-shedding animals that foist shaggy clumps onto a hapless guest's threads after only a brief sit on the living-room sofa. Rabbit-cage linings and ferret mulch provide an olfactory assault akin to an overstocked mall pet shop. Keep such creatures at least one floor away from the common space.

Side note: If you can't handle the trials of a newborn puppy or milk-feed a baby goat, try a hearty ficus or cactus, which require only air and an occasional, accidental misting. Be smart: if you cannot provide proper love and environs, don't shove a Siberian husky into your four-hundred-square-foot studio. Cat owners must invest the extra bucks for scoopable litter that minimizes odors.

Incidentally, small mammals like guinea pigs, hamsters, and rabbits aren't the best investments. Like the new car that depreciates 50 percent upon leaving the lot, the novelty of rodentia fades quickly. After the honeymoon, you are left with a pea-brained, pellet-producing varmint.

For the ova-forward eco set, the new "it" pet is the chicken. For short money, you can preorder a set of days-old, pre-sexed chicks to be delivered via overnight mail in the spring, often in batches of eight. A good catalogue like the one from McMurray Hatchery will tell you which breeds are the best layers—or you can simply pick varieties that look the most appealing but are less "productive." Watch your babies grow under a heat lamp for two months, transfer them to your backyard coop (which offers nesting boxes and protection from the elements and marauding species), wait three more months, and it's brunch time. How many eggs? About one every thirty-six hours per mature chicken. Like any twenty-first century lesbian couple who wants children, chickens don't actually need any "cocks" around to produce eggs, so if possible, avoid buying any roosters (hence the need for pre-sexed chicks), which will only cause a ruckus, eat your feed, and result in the occasional unsavory fertilized egg. Chickens are nature's composters and will eat most table scraps, and they require little daily management beyond egg-collecting, water changing, and the occasional foul coop cleaning.

PRE- OR POSTCOCKTAILS

Host a cocktail hour when you're not prepared to supply 100 percent of the fun. Provide the opening or closing ceremonies for an evening out, with or without torch lighting and dove release. Home serves as a central gathering place to wet whistles, make introductions, and divvy up the crowd into cars/taxis. This is not the time for knife-and-fork food, rather a bowl of olives and chitchat on your collective feet until the tardy arrive. Keep one eye on the clock and the other on the ice bucket; once the empty glasses denote a decent median buzz, shoo the party onward.

Nice touch: Get your dairy on with a cocktail hour cheese plate. Drop the aerosol cheese and step away from the pre-cubed cheddar. Hit a gourmet shop and play proper fromager by mixing up textures (soft, crumbly, firm), styles (runny, stinky, nutty), countries, and milks (sheep, cow, goat, wet nurse). Apportion one-quarter to one-third pound per person, total, and remove cheese from the fridge in time for it to rise to room temperature. Slice, chunk, or crumble accordingly to spur shy munchers, and serve with delectable accoutrements: local honey, berry preserves, quince paste, nuts, crackers, and sliced fruits.

For end-of-the-night gatherings, shoes are kicked off and lighter drinks, digestifs, or beer allow the group to wind down. Rules are relaxed at this hour as smoking patrons huddle on the balcony and the record collection is rummaged through for forgotten gems. The morning remnants of a successful postparty gathering are a teetering stack of unsheathed LPs, a batch of spent glassware, and a full recycling bin.

CAVIAR

These aren't the marble-sized, orange pellets you used as bait to catch pickerel in Lake Rickabear. The finest caviar is the roe of three prized varieties of female sturgeon—beluga, sevruga, and osetra. In an age of depleted wild Caspian sturgeon and oceanic irresponsibility, callously satisfying a craving is akin to picnicking on Spotted Owl croquettes, yet caviar is a storied delicacy worth preserving. People reluctant to buy underground caviar during U.S. import bans can support 100 percent sustainable American farm-raised sturgeon or wild-caught paddlefish, hackleback sturgeon, or *tobiko* (the flying fish roe associated with sushi).

To host a tasting, apportion ten to thirty grams per person; anything less and you may incur a row over roe. Chop some ice in a blender to create a cold bed for the jars/tins to rest upon, or scoop natural snow into pretty bowls. Snuggled in the coldest part of the fridge, caviar shelf life is two months from the packing date (like croissants or love notes, though, caviar ought to be enjoyed at the next leisurely moment). Taste it atop warm toast points or blinis, or straight from the spoon. Standard flatware reacts undesirably with caviar and imparts a metallic flavor; hence traditional caviar spoons are made of nonreactive mother-of-pearl, and their sea-formed iridescence adds to the aesthetic ritual. As for elegant pairings, go classic: cold vodka or very dry champagne cleanses the palate and amplifies the sensory experience.

A flight of caviar ought to be served in order of softest/mildest to boldest/most fishy, cool to taste. Like white wine or artisanal cheeses, when caviar's served too cold, nuanced flavors of mineral, earthiness, and nuttiness are lost. Whilst exercising your caviar tongue, practice some proper nomenclature and connoisseurship. Refer to the eggs as "beads," "berries," or "grains." Note their size, color (from golden hues to obsidian), rich or coarse texture, soft or firm pop, and briny or buttery taste.

Nice touch: When the night begs for eggs, place caviar in the tender spot on your hand where tequila salt traditionally goes, or else spoon it onto a lover's upturned wrist and feast from warm, alabaster skin.

SOIRÉE

A soirée is an after-eight planned affair for thirty (give or take), with a selective guest list. With or without written invitations, goers dress per a theme—martini attire for the swank, tiki for summer rum shindigs, or pyjamas for a winter lingerie party. After the bossa nova, booze, and boiled shrimp, stage a parlor game. The evening is not structured, but a commemorative toast or announcement of exciting news fuels the frolic. Ask musicians to bring guitars, poets to share verse, and contortionists to climb into the étagère. Before widespread cosmopolitan illiteracy, soirées meant a memorable evening around the piano and a good story. Revive this salon environment and guests will remember the night for more than munchie-slaking pizza rolls and your Wii bowling acumen.

BACCHANAL

The big bash should have a clever thrust, capturing the naughtiness of Halloween and the frivolity of New Year's Eve, but needn't devolve into property damage; if the squad cars aren't on their way, don't consider your little callithump a flop. Find a theme among the calendar's alternative holidays: Arbor Day, an equinox, or a lunar eclipse. String lights, hang streamers, and add food coloring to the liquor. Decorations are an essential expression of festivity, not a twenty-minutes-prior, tacked-up afterthought. If you want a full house, send an e-vite or post to your Local Favorites Facebook list. Lastly, name the affair—why call it a party when you could host a St. Patrick's Day shivaree or Groundhog Day après-ski? Once a century, host a toga party and channel your inner Caligula.

Provide a motley experience, including electronica playlists for dancing, corners for window carousing, and lounge areas for new lovers and discreet activities. Buy twice as many cups and bags of ice as you think you'll need and tap the keg in an uncarpeted, low-traffic corner, like the porch or guest shower. If you expect a mob, there's no shame in politely asking guests to bring a favorite poison. This may be a loose affair, but don't forget your chores. Deputize close friends to help work the door, mind the trash, and attend the bar. You are the floater, the ringmaster, so wear something unmistakable and introduce yourself to choice strangers and find the sixth degree of separation that sourced their invitation.

Nice touch: For outdoor bashes, an ice-block booze delivery system is a chilly novelty for encouraging even the timid to drink middling tequila. Google "party ice" and buy a forty-pound-plus, body-sized shot block. Use hot water and a chisel to carve a Y-shaped luge; two channels feed from the top into a well-excavated central waterway. Finish by chipping out a chin rest at the bottom. Elevate the top end of the ice block to facilitate speedy flow. Invite guests to lay an open mouth at one end as the tender pours a clear spirit down one lane, a mixer down the other, meeting at the maw.

INTIMATE GATHERINGS

An intimate gathering offers dinner as dénouement, a lavish affair for a hand-picked few who appreciate tempered tableside affections, long glances, and the sumptuousness of seared delights, linen napkins, chilled salad forks, and warmed dinner plates. A smaller group facilitates more deliberate eye contact, subtler undertones, and a greater premium on individual needs (vegetarians, discriminating Virgos). So that the artichoke and arugula insalata isn't better dressed than the guests, encourage gentlemen and their escorts to don eveningwear.

Think sensuous: candles trump fluorescent lighting, flowers over potpourri, cool jazz over radio pop. Swap the extra hours of hanging decorations for added attention to epicurean presentation and a scripted menu with wine pairings. Languid pacing is key; woo a waitstaffer or two away from the restaurant to help with service and cleanup in exchange for a couple of Franklins, a few bottles, and leftovers. Conduct a tactile symphony in which biorhythms are synchronized in a dance of shared secrets and open affections across the table's four corners. Red-wine whispers are perfume upon the nape of the evening. Guests are under your subtle control, and conversation is steeped in the positive, personal, and pleasurable; daily triflings and what you did at work that day should be left for family dinner.

Nice touch: Create a blissful state of escapism by moving the table to an irregular eating spot. City dwellers might serve dinner with a view on the roof; others might eat alfresco in the yard, surrounded by torches and the velvet protection of the Mosquito Magnet.

THE ACTIVE TABLE

In classic tomes such as *Emily Post's Etiquette* and *Vogue's Book of Etiquette and Good Manners*, the order of seating around the table is a "rigid and unbreakable" representation of social rank. The Modern Gentleman offers a contemporary alternative. Instead of arranging place cards according to caste and importance, manage the personalities to mix the boisterous with the shy and catalyze curious conversation. Done well, no one will suspect they were part of some mad gentleman scientist's social bingo experiment.

Food and drink are but the excuse for gathering. Fostering new bonds and introducing new friends to the old circle is not haphazard; it requires a deft hosting strategy. Instead of playing musical chairs when the dinner bell sounds, plot ahead according to gender, familiarity, and personality for an active evening around the roasted turducken.

Nice touch: Reclaim the lost art of carving. Invest in a whetstone and hone your knife skills on small chickens and whole fish so that you can dress a Dover sole and deftly cut a saddle of rabbit without splashing gravy on tablemates. Snip by snip: spread the legs, separate them from the breast, and cut legs away from the thighs. Next, slice along the breastbone down to the wishbone and remove the breast meat. Repeat on the other side. Keep the wishbone facing front and flip the bird to push out the two oyster-sized nuggets of tenderloin that are the carver's compensation for services rendered.

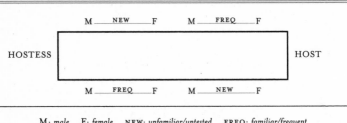

M: *male*   F: *female*   NEW: *unfamiliar/untested*   FREQ: *familiar/frequent*
_____ : *denotes couples*

Consider the table arrangement above for a typical dinner party of ten. General rules of ratio and alternating gender are followed, with Host and Hostess at the table ends. Two couples (M FREQ F) are old friends or frequent guests, the kind that help in the kitchen without asking. Each of these two couples sits adjacent to an unfamiliar couple (M NEW F) who've just learned where the bathroom is located. New couples include first-time dinner guests, new bedmates, or hoped-to-be compatible strangers, and sit near the comforting ballast of a Host or Hostess. Note that the two pairs of frequent couples aren't packed tightly into an insular clique at one end of the table. Also, even if the compatible strangers aren't so compatible with one another, there's always help from the charismatic frequent guest seated nearby.

Next, within these parameters, mix up the seating chart according to personality.

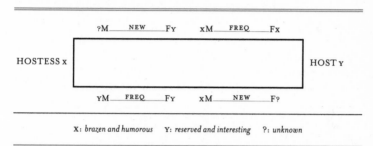

X: *brazen and humorous*   Y: *reserved and interesting*   ?: *unknown*

This is the same table, but arranged to account for charisma (X is a lively jokester and conversation starter; Y is fascinating yet low-key; ? is an untested wild card, such as a friend's new flame or a host-appointed escort). Here, the Host/Hostess and a FREQ couple flank an unfamiliar ?, whose zest is in question. The Host's and Hostess's own personalities balance the ends of the table. Foment cross fire, taking care that no one is left out to dry. In the table below, the X Hostess enlivens the unknown (M?) and the Y couple (MY FREQ FY). The Y Host engages unknown (F?) and feeds off the vivacious X couple (MX FREQ FX).

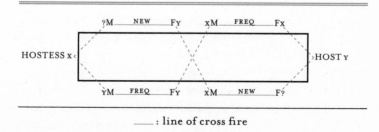

⎯⎯ : line of cross fire

Notice the additional lines of crossfire in the third diagram. Make sure there are opposites and like minds available across, adjacent, or diagonal. As the Host and Hostess handle the table ends, crossfire intermingles the middle of the table, lest these poor souls be caught with nothing between them but the centerpiece.

HOUSEGUESTS

"My roof is too low for you."
**—JEAN SIBELIUS, on welcoming the great contralto,
Marion Anderson, to his home**

Guests aren't complete strangers, so personalize the arrangements for their stay. Make room in the crisper for the vegetarian, buy local microbrews for the discriminating lager-head, and stock up on organic almond milk when a new-age, lactose-intolerant pal hits town. Indulge guests by upgrading to the butcher's choicest cuts, sniffing out imported cheeses, dialing up four-star meals, jump-starting the kitchen mixer, or dusting off a decorative platter for a festive antipasto. Special snacks, cereals, and rented films always garner praise.

Polite guests often feel chary of hospitality. Anticipate needs and offer extras up front; before the first shiver, spare the timid the awkward request for an extra degree of warmth on the thermostat. Excessive coddling can be overbearing, so don't mother guests to death with comfort checks: "Are the five bed pillows fluffy enough?"; "My pet tarantula isn't bothering you, is he?" To quell feelings of imposition is to demonstrate your comfort with a guest's presence. Saying, "Make yourself at home" is passive hosting and is almost a coded warning not to touch anything. Rather, a good host creates an inviting space where comfort is as easy to find as the phosphorescent bedroom light switch.

Nice touch: When "guestitute" pals arrive in town bearing a scuffed duffel bag and staggering credit card debt, open your heart and wallet and cover the first and last experiences to bookend their visit with generosity.

GUEST QUARTERS

When buying a futon or convertible couch, upgrade the mattress and insert a foam pad so guests don't wake up on a flimsy pallet with a gnarled spine. Stock the guest room with an abundance of towels, pillows, blankets, and linens. Mind the helplessly chilled or perpetually warm; keep an extra fan in the summertime. In any season, only a skimping host issues one meager, paper-thin, phyllo-dough coverlet. A down comforter is rarely amiss, and an afghan, space heater, or warm-bodied trollop is welcome for wintry visits. With easy cell phone alarms, guests are responsible for their own reveille at 0500 to catch the discount 6:30 a.m. flight. Otherwise, pad lightly around the common space. After nine hours of REM, however, conduct business as usual; grind coffee with impunity, split cordwood in the yard, and rouse that slugabed.

Type up instructions for deciphering your home's more curious peccadilloes: the entertainment center's army of remotes, pesky doors, forbidden cabinets, broken stairs, and tricky switches. Guest-proof for large groups, children, and first-time guests by stashing away sensitive documents and extra-special breakables. Take a quick look in the guest bathroom and remove provocative prescription drugs and embarrassing ointments.

CRASH PAD

Blankets on the floor are a last resort when there's no room at the inn. For guest comfort, purchase any of the following: sleeping bag, collapsible cot, inflatable mattress, or convertible futon. When a lover finally moves in, the extra mattress you'll acquire is usually the beginning of guest accommodations. Special guests or married couples passing through a bachelor pad warrant the gentlemanly offer of his bed for the night (with full conjugal privileges, less laundress costs). Sometimes the best choice for a leftover party intoxicate is the sofa. Remove the back cushions, wrap the seats in a fitted sheet, and dress the couch up like a four-poster. No need to furnish all the trappings—your gifts of shelter and a shower are adequate.

Incidentally, visiting pals may be temporarily blacklisted if they've abused universal rules of decency, such as returning a borrowed auto on empty and covered in mud and pollen dust, or gouging your lustrous Corian countertop while slicing lime wedges without a cutting board.

CHARCOAL BRIQUETIQUETTE

Every gentleman is fully conversant in the ceremonial Olympic lighting of the charcoal grill, from its light-it-yourself briquette ancestors to today's infrared, push-button propane styles. BBQ means blue skies, piles of potato salad, dry rubs, secret marinades, and carefree, shoeless demeanors. Fingers come first.

Isn't it time to branch out past the dynamic duo of hamburgers and hot dogs? Exhibit creativity short of epicurean haughtiness by flaming on such fantastic trimmings as vegetable kabobs, corn on the cob, and varied burgers (pork and lamb). Mold reasonably-sized hamburgers to avoid ovoid flying saucers; to prevent a bulging middle, press a dimple in the center before grilling. Italian apple sausages and bratwurst are always welcome, as are, for the meat-averse, fish fillets, shrimp, and killer vinegared coleslaw. To prevent fish from sticking to the grill, oil both sides of the fillet, then wipe the cleaned grill grates with oil using a balled-up paper towel held by long tongs. Place skin side down, and after several minutes, flip using two spatulas to avoid breakage. For a seasoned waft, sprinkle mesquite chips into the grill. Hot dogs are a beloved staple (especially with fresh or bagged, not canned, sauerkraut), but even if an heir to the late Frank Purdue, no chicken franks.

BBQ tools should be sturdy. Look for the all-in-one flipper (a combo spatula/bottle opener) for easy grilling and hosting. Before tending the dogs, a gentleman masters the delicate art of the tongs and long-handled fork (though never needlessly puncturing juicy steaks). On the road, defer to a proficient host and never commandeer the spatula. If you come upon an unattended grill, quell any emergencies, move cooked sausage to the edges, and flip darkening patties . . . then slowly slink away. But don't tarry—otherwise, you'll get wedged behind the grill, barked at by hungry throngs like a short-order cook. For a lazy merrymaker who wants to appear helpful, arrive at the grill right around "cheese time" and assist in top-shelf bun toasting or mustard squirting.

Nice touch: Picnics range from brown-bag lunches under a shady tree to gourmet treats spread on table linens set with candelabra and silverware. Don't limit picnics to daytime hours or the warmest climes. Set a well-dressed table for moonlit noshes in the sand or a candlelit interlude on the porch.

Relish intimate tête-à-têtes around the grill; the warm coals and air redolent of charred meat foster camaraderie. Note quickly which side is upwind and shift accordingly. Like the soothing patter of rain, there's something about the sizzling of meats that brings out humor and confidences.

Final thoughts for the casual outdoor affair:

- If hosting a BBQ, deputize a trusted acquaintance for grilling duties to allow freer socializing with guests. Mix a batch of homemade lemonade or boozy punch for all-day sipping.

- Eschew the no-frills-brand, black lung charcoal reminiscent of antediluvian carbon and kerosene. For easy lighting without mephitic lighter fluid, use a handy chimney starter that facilitates hot coals with nothing but yesterday's sports page. Also, skip stuffing the burgers with chopped anything (meatloaf night is Wednesday) and no frozen, prepattied 50 percent befatted chuck, rivaling Gaines Burgers (with cheese). Spend the extra few dollars or visit the butcher.

- Don't panic over a "burgercide" (unfinished patty falling through the grill slots). If tongs can't orchestrate a rescue, look up, genuflect, and close the grill cover to hide your incompetence, allowing the sacrificed meat to become indecipherable ash.

- Hit a pizzeria for some dough. Flatten it out, rub with oil, salt, and rosemary, and in four minutes, voilà! Grilled flatbread.

- Fire up dessert on the coals too: filet pineapples, peaches, and watermelons for juicy treats right off the hot grill.

- Bring booze to an occupied grill man sweating over hot coals. At night, strategically placed citronella candles fend off tsetse swarms.

DAY AT THE BEACH

At beach gambols and clambakes, sand pervades everything, limiting your entertainment options to the most primitive electronics. Poseidon's polyphony of meditative wave and crash is far more melodic than anything on the airwaves, though quiet play-by-play on a transistor radio is perfect for the baseball enthusiast. Also, museful guitar strumming is an ideal low-tech fit for sing-alongs and sea chanteys. Bocce and ladder ball are two crowd favorites that even the athletically disinclined can master in an afternoon.

Bring a GFO (gentleman's flying object); box, Hargrave, or tetrahedral kites are the most playful. For the casual kiter, beware the 300 percent markup on styles sold in lazy beach-community shops. Don't be the old sourpuss who fails to share the spool; a gentleman plays well with others. As for boomerangs, find a vast open space, mostly devoid of people or property. Try Western Australia.

Nice touch: Leave the beach better than you found it. Tote one small piece of foreign trash from your immediate sandy area.

BACHELOR PARTY

[reels]

[MPAA rating]

[blue movie]

More hype than substance, the bachelor party has long since lost its Roman-orgy mystique. Invite the groom's closest compadres, the male future in-laws, and a few seasoned married gentlemen—not for chaperoning but for insightful rounding. Many bachelors now prefer to spend their final fling over a moderately sane long weekend of skiing, golfing, or gambling with close friends. Pack your rec gear, humidor, and top-shelf spirits—whatever the climate dictates. For atmospheric elegance, quietly pack two issues of low-grade pornography for the coffee table. On these last hurrahs, spend less time on shots and more around the clam bake, steeling the groom to the responsibilities of marriage. Invoke ceremony to celebrate the rite of passage, such as by burning the bridegroom's black book in effigy.

On the other hand, when the crowd cries for blood and the bachelor himself wishes a grand finale, a corrupt and sinful outing is on the mark. The best man must shadow the groom to ensure a seamless, trouble-free twenty-four hours of debauchery. Evaluate the core group to determine the groom's agenda. The troika of vice (alcohol, sex, and gambling) may seem trite, but it's a solid foundation for a decadent evening. Instead of squandering precious resources on Vegas accommodations, reinvest locally in a nearby bustling metropolis that can accommodate the gang without the joyless ritual of Sunday afternoon hungover air travel.

- **Entertainment:** Favorite convivial restaurant; cocktail lounges/bars; live music; establishments with dress-code requirements; lively acquaintances for the guest list; only the fondest, softest farm animals.

- **Sport:** Billiards/parlor games; golf outing; kayaking or other active venture; ballgame; boating/fishing; Russian steam baths; late-night air hockey; playing in traffic.

- **Gambling:** Casino; never-ending poker game with chips and cigars as entrée; inexpensive, all-you-can-eat sushi.

- **Fleshy Vice**: Gentleman's club; hired help performance in hotel room; Mardi Gras gala; PG-13 video rental (new release for a special evening).

Nice touch: Make it a surprise Saturday to remember and lead the groom through a day-night of unknown agenda, with staggered arrivals for attendees to add to the mystery.

In any case, shoot for abundance of camaraderie, cheer, mockery, humor, and excess. Start your engines with a revving round of toasts and conversation, building the dynamic before taking it out on the town. Compel the bachelor to wear something distinctive—nothing too outlandish, merely a spirited cravat or smoking jacket. Arise the next afternoon feeling satisfied, woozy, and slightly offended.

Some prefer the cityscape tour. To accommodate the entire group, arrange a central mode of transportation to cement the dynamic and prevent group splintering. Several town cars can be useful; however, the ideal arrangement is a limousine or party bus— perhaps a converted yellow school bus with long benches and a large cooler in the back.

Should professional help be desired, plan ahead. Peruse the back pages of a free weekly for services; phone several listings to compare rates, activities, and policies. Do not offer your credit card digits until informed of the itinerary, level of involvement, and the inclusion of props. Hard-earned dollars should purchase at least some novelty and shock. The higher the tips, the better the service.

Final note: Though bachelor parties are mostly harmless mafficking, appearances of impropriety may prompt a next-day interrogation. Keep mum. If the bridal party remains insistent after a censored recap, unresolved trust issues remain—nothing a few years of marriage or a private investigator won't iron out.

BEST MANNING

As weddings differ in formality and micromanagement, the head groomsman is faced with either a thimbleful or a heaping armful of duties. In general, the best man is the driving force behind the bachelor party, as well as the point man for formalwear snags and eleventh-hour minutiae. Moreover, he's the ceremony's centerfielder, mingling among guests, lending an ear to quell service personnel flare-ups. The best man dutifully handles the groom's wallet for gratuities and checks in with the bartender to keep the ice and the bridegroom well supplied.

On the day itself, the best man keeps the groom loose, like a rubdown before a prizefight. The nonchalant toss of a ball after the morning shave calms nerves. Share a final hit on the flask or a glass of rosé before boutonnières are pinned on, and take a moment alone with the groom to bid farewell to his bachelorhood.

PREWEDDING

An attentive best man is a minority shareholder in the marriage and establishes his own rapport with the bride. Early on, the best man is a confidant and sounding board for a groom overwhelmed with logistics. Late-night phone calls assuage concerns of love, lost innocence, and the transition to wedded stability. A best man doesn't wait for the cry for help the week before, but regularly takes the groom's pulse to preserve a cool head. The best man is a warm soak when caterers and catfighting have driven a groom to cold feet.

THE TOAST

Toast preparation starts two months before the ceremony. It's surprising how many funnies are recalled when you're not pressured on the eve of the knot tying. Childhood pals can dredge up ancient playtime relics, the raw materials for a singular speech. Suitable for the flower girls and in-laws, a clever toast still has imbedded code to make insiders chuckle. If anyone can recycle your toast by merely changing the name in the opening, you have disgraced the bubbly and the groom.

Classic etiquette sanctions four libations for a proper toast: champagne, wine, whiskey, or beer. If you are quaffing a screwdriver or inexplicably sipping a white-wine spritzer, upgrade before proceeding.

Surround the speech's body with a sharp opening and winsome conclusion. A potent lead-off seizes attention—relate a classic joke, apocryphal pronouncement, or captivating quotation. If especially creative, try beginning with a gimmick such as a top ten list or uproarious roasting (details follow), followed by warm words. No matter your toasting style, final remarks should be succinct and sober best wishes for a rosy future. To amp up the import, integrate the bride's foreign culture and the groom's beloved quirkiness, winding up the toast with something symbolic and honest.

Unless possessed of stentorian voice, regale briefly and effectively. Instead of fumbling about lack of preparation or public speaking experience, grasp the moment. Despite a fiendish, boyish charm, don't shower guests with explicit stories, instances of substance abuse, or anything that happened last night. Shirk rambling collegiate mischief tales that cause nonalums to roll their eyes. A few minutes of heartfelt gravity make for great copy and a fine setup for a raucous finish. Leave the crowd guffawing and wanting more. Trite recollections ("I knew right away they were meant to be") make for limp toasts and reflexive gagging. Do better.

Incidentally, once the guests are rapt, don't forget to introduce yourself before proceeding with the toast.

ROASTING

A roast is an exquisite form of comedic address in which love and reverence are cloaked in seemingly mean-spirited and wry hilarity. Only those experienced with public speaking or possessing an impeccable sense of timing should attempt this style. Careful where you tread; when in doubt, tell a funny story instead. Bush-league roasting is worse than the cut-rate schmaltz from the annals of Hallmark. Despite the vituperative opening and body, a roast's final act is all warm sentiment, a bearlike hug that smoothes the sting and confirms affection. Perform a reading for a mutual friend for eleventh-hour edits.

CAVEATS

Despite the humorous or crowd-pleasing value, certain topics are rightfully taboo. Dodge the hisses by refusing to spin tales about the groom's prior lovers, brushes with the law, hoary secrets, the couple's rocky relationship history, divorce, deaths in the family, genitalia, and, most important, anything disparaging (even in jest) about the bride or her parents.

WOOING

FLIRTATION

Flirtation is a distinct act of charisma, a give-and-take less like chess and more akin to backgammon. Indeed, skill is involved, but the thrill of chance is always at play. Gentlemen recognize the differences between deeds of charm, manners of flirtation, and tactics of seduction.

Flirtation kicks in like a thermostat when mood and attraction are right. If you fumble for the perfect retort or regularly curse inaction ("I shoulda said something to that cute Amish girl in the black hat at the checkout line"), recall the first rule of standardized tests: trust first instincts and don't allow fear to occlude your social awareness. It is overkill to flirt everywhere with everyone, but do celebrate a heightened groove of self-assurance or a great hair day. At such times, flirting will find you.

The best techniques can't be listed because they are employed impromptu as a natural extension of demeanor and charm. Solid eye contact, the occasional wink, and first-name recall are always welcome ("Looking lovely, Carolyn"). In the freshly squeezed realm of genuine flirtation, uninvited bad techniques are sickly sweet canned orange drink. Shelve these lesser tactics:

- **The Jeweler:** A sudden reach for a lady's necklace too near the bustline.

- **The Excessive Endearer:** Sugary overdose of presumptuous pet names like "baby," "sweetie," "darling," and that boardwalk prize-wheel favorite, "hon."

- **The Restaurant Voyeur:** Flirting with a server, then leaving only 14 percent; asking the bartender when she "gets off."

- **The Cunning Linguist:** Overpunning with sexual terms.

- **The Surprise Toucher:** The "Guess Who?" hands over the eyes game or the unsolicited, two-handed neck massage.

- **The Persistent Hello/Goodbye Hugger:** Clinging with extra-expressive squeezes, pats, and circular back rubbing.

- **The Sarcastic Flirt-Beggar:** "Wait . . . you're leaving, and you haven't said goodbye?"

SEDUCTION VS. FLIRTATION

Flirtation is the exchange of peripheral sexual energy for mutual glee and confidence boosting. Seduction is flirtation with a specific thrust to further action. Thus seduction is successful only when consummated, whereas the gaiety of flirtation is itself the reward.

PICK-ME-UP
· Cognac · Dubonnet blanc · Dash of anisette · One egg white · Lemon twist ·

Flirtation is light and fleeting, even if continuous. Ideally, it is spontaneous, without thought to long-term effect. It need not be reciprocated, though hopefully it will be returned with at least a smirk or smile. The most intense flirtation involves dancing close to the line—as close as another implicitly allows. With seduction, you are luring the intended to cross the line and anticipating the ideal moment to cross it yourself.

DOUBLE STANDARD

If a woman flirts, respond in kind and check the vibe before presuming ulterior motives. Men are expected to flirt, but when women are playful, lesser picaroons with pulsing ids assume the mating ritual has begun. This type of behavior causes ladies to reserve their winsome chitchat; women are entitled to flirt harmlessly without being asked for their cell numbers and gmail addresses.

DANCING

The well-expressed dancing gentleman is a magnet who draws in like-minded spirits. Even if little is exchanged on the floor besides strong moves, gimlet eyes, and deep sighs, consider an intimate dance a clothed intercourse that's as breathless as the naked variety. Still, dancing is not an unmitigated tit-smash insinuating foreplay. A well-disciplined monogamous man relishes the metaphor of dance as a medium to channel sexuality without the vow-crushing infringements of exchanged digits and kisses.

In the nightclub, don't fear a circle, where the empty space is an exhibitionist's chance for inspired monologues. Hop atop a speaker when feeling brazen. Slug more water than gin and dress for twirling. Never mind your witty tongue; speak in the primal words of hips, dips, and writhes. When the room is synchronized in a deejay's vortex of bass and shake, let out a scream and wave your arms. As for foxtrot, cha cha, merengue, and the like, lead confidently—no one likes a limp wrist. And you don't have to know the steps to feeeel the tango or execute a daring knee slide that punctuates a brilliant dance even as it threatens your good slacks.

Incidentally, know when to bow out. A single splendid whirl is not reason to affix yourself to a partner like a ballroom barnacle. Say thank you and step into the washroom for a splash break, then take another's hand or resume solo action. A reprise with an early-night partner is like comin' home.

FLIRTING AND MONOGAMY

The married or involved gent can share a gleaming smile and innocuous flirt without temptation. Still, biologically speaking, flirtation demonstrates health and virility as a mate. Ensure that you aren't falsely flashing your feathers, leading someone to believe that you are available. Double-check the temperature before misplaced lust unwisely invites someone for a dip into your venerable gene pool. Make it a motiveless venture. Good flirtation affirms vitality but does not leave you holding a motel key.

RELATIONSHIP FLIRTATION

Don't reserve all enticements for alluring strangers. Renew your passions at home lest they expire. Billing and cooing are essential to relationship nurturing, whether through passing whispers or tantalizing glances at your short-shorts-wearing honey.

ILL-TIMED FLIRTING

Don't be a sugary sycophant, trumpeting loaded compliments indiscriminately. One does not turn on the charm at a funeral or woo the bride at her own wedding; similarly, flirtation is ineffectual when the recipient is harried with other tasks. Flirting with a married woman can be a tasteful affirmation of her attractiveness. However, overamorousness is unseemly in the presence of a spouse.

Incidentally, when someone stands between you and a simple goal, charisma can grease the wheels. An extra smile at the deli counter might get you a free sample or a bigger piece.

DATES

Dating is an audition. You are both reading lines cold, looking for the spark of chemistry that leads to a continuing role. Put aside the posturing and the scoring pad; dates are meant to be fun encounters on the town. No more preparation is necessary than the personal-growth homework you've already put into making yourself attractive and interesting. Isn't that how you got the date anyway?

Thoughts for the dating gentleman:

· Squelch indecision. During the logistics stage, present a menu of firm, lively options. It doesn't have to be dinner or an after-dusk date. How about a brunch picnic, hike, or planetarium visit?

· Dress appropriately: neither Sunday best nor funkiest eclectic. Slick shoes are an imperative; smart slacks trump khakis.

· Be interested, not just interesting. Humor is essential, but the date is not a slapstick sketch or an *Airplane!* outtake.

· Praise a date's features without invading personal space. A well-placed comment about earrings is welcome and evinces a keen eye. Overly personal compliments give the willies ("I love that mole on your right thigh").

· A run of first dates in the same place is unimaginative. Multi-task your romantic calendar by exploring the many metropolitan curiosities. At worst, a string of bad dates leads to a pocketful of restaurant reviews.

· Too many wooing bells and whistles create a false impression. Select venues within your fiscal element. Overspending is betting $500 bottles of wine against your blandness. Overdoting with chivalry is less expensive but just as gaudy.

- When the topic swings to sex or drugs, follow the leader. Less is more, and scant hints of a tawdry résumé are better than locker-room roll calls of your vast experience.

- During gorilla August, carry a handkerchief or napkin to pat your brow and neck before first contact, so as not to appear a complete drip.

Thoughts for the dating lout:

- Show up late, slouch in your seat, don't offer to share a morsel of monkfish, and steamroll your date with extroversion.

- Be the Smothering Solicitor: "Are you comfortable? Do you want another drink? Are you having fun? Do you wanna go somewhere else?" To make her smile vanish, off-handedly comment, "Do you feel all right? You look tired."

- Mistreat the service staff, giving your date a preview of what she can expect on a future Sunday morning.

- Select a venue so loud that pantomime and mouth-cupped yelling are the only methods of communication. Exception: a vibrant tapas joint enriches, as does the third carafe of sangria.

BODY LANGUAGE

Collate character clues early on. Note her entrance. Were you hugged? How does she hold her glass? Is she leaning into the conversation or searchlighting the room as if waiting for her "real" date?

A date is neither pedigree check nor portfolio review. No need to expose all desires and profiles like one of Picasso's Dora Maar portraits. Heat the pot and then prime the stew with the best ingredients and raciest conversation. Shared professions are a bridge, but bungee-jump into deeper interests like foodie philosophy, outlandish dreams, and the arts. It's a great date when conversation hums long after the foam has caked in your empty pint glass.

You may mash each other's toes or knock knees. Don't be afraid of awkward moments or brief silences, but shoulder the responsibility to moderate and stimulate. If necessary, call a time-out and consider an avenue change.

A great date leaves a mystery that won't be solved until the second episode, like a juicy cliffhanger. What was that coy smirk at the end of the night? When did she live in England? Did Tony Soprano get whacked in the diner or not?

ST. VALENTINE'S DAY

A dubious holiday, famous for the Chicago massacre and unfulfilled, chalky candy hearts. Can't remember the last time you bestowed flowers? Don't start now. And no eleventh-hour runs to CVS for a heart-shaped box and no-frills tray of Russell Stover chocolates (the only brand that says, "Not only don't I love you, I don't particularly care for you in any lasting manner"). Surprise her instead with a whisk to a favorite bistro or a boffo homemade repast. The holiday might be recognized on the fourteenth, but not always celebrated then. Despite the lack of crayon-adorned desk pouches, send your friends and associates cartoonish Valentine cards like you did in elementary school.

For proper chocolate affections, exotic spices like star anise, pink peppercorn, Earl Grey, or cardamom create a flavor experience, and cacao activates cannabinoid receptors, inducing a chocoholic euphoria. Instead of grinding their own beans, chocolatiers buy a base chocolate called the "couverture." Rejoice if it's Valrhona, Pralus, Cluizel, Amedei, or Domori—and cue the sad trombone if it's Nestlé or ADM. Strong chocolate is a catalyst of arousal, so occasionally descend to the pillows and place it on strategic body parts (chocolate breaks down at 80–90 degrees). As an edible lubricant, though, it burns skin after too long, so let it melt in your mouth, not in your glands.

DRINKING

A woman drove me to drink and I didn't even have
the decency to thank her.
—W. C. FIELDS

Cocktail management is a practical extension of personality. Do not arrive with a head start. If you are early or your date is late, order one drink to pass the time. Should plans disintegrate, kill the pain of rejection with rueful abandon.

Pace yourself. Not all rambunctious dates are Olympic tosspots. It is bad manners to drink ahead and lap a slow-sipping companion who's lumbering around the oval like a sputtering Indy car. Avoid a deplorable evening that finds you rummied up on Captain Morgan as your date shrugs with a Chardonnay. For ungoverned elbow-benders, beach booze in pitchers and bottles of wine mask consumption rates, permitting drinking at natural speeds without reproach.

Unexplained teetotaling causes as much alarm as a besotted date who calls for whiskey by the bottle like an extra in a spaghetti Western. The latter may be seeking a codependent, not a lover, and the former suggests an AA alum or an uptight rookie who lacks the social grace for even a champagne toast.

THE CLOSE

A first kiss shouldn't be first affection. A vibrant date warrants a stroke of the hair or a nibble on the fingers. Before the evening ends and the ride home begins, take a reading on the love meter to determine a date's conclusion. You should know by now whether the future holds a kiss, a nightcap, or a handshake before reaching the awkward confines of the apartment-building vestibule.

A FEW DATES LATER

Certain barriers have dropped with familiarity. Reach across the table with an offered hand without even breaking eye contact. Enjoy same-side seating or corner-booth canoodling. Close proximity affords entrée sharing and furtive nestling.

Single-fingered swinging or interlaced fingers forge an unassuming bond. Offer friction in moderation, as the continuous caress numbs the receiver to the unpredictable pleasures of casual touch. For the arm-in-arm escort, offer neither a limp spaghetti forearm nor a dominant elbow—it's a lady's supple arm, not a pigskin that mustn't be fumbled.

Learn from Hitchcock's *Rope*: sometimes the ideal arrangement is in the span of two rooms. Declare the home-field advantage and rearrange the furniture for comfort. For rented black-and-white classics, schedule intermissions to take air on the balcony, fluff pillows, and steal a smooch.

Incidentally, an aquarium is a winsome venue. For advanced wooers, immerse yourself in this oceanic theme date as if it were a Jacques Cousteau bathysphere and break for sushi or a bowl of clam chowder.

SO, YOUR FIRST DATE IS
GOING INTO THE TANK

Scenario: As dinner progresses, you realize your date is not nearly as attractive as she seemed last Saturday, nor as witty as her emails; and frankly, the anecdote about formative years spent in a Jovian cult was creepy. Each passing moment is disenchanting. To avoid this quagmire, schedule a preliminary cocktail summit before committing to the blind potluck of dinner. Enter the first full date with a backlog of rapport to drive communication and prevent uneasiness.

Bad dates vary in degree from innocuous to intolerable. If you find yourself starring in the classic first-date debacle, use the following graded list to help gauge hopelessness. For ease of discussion, these examples presume you are the innocent victim of incompatibility. (Though, any poor-date scenario can find you in the seat of culpability—off your game, clumsy, underattractive—with a squirming mate itching to flee.)

- **C:** *A Flat Affair.* After too many long pauses, intermittent sparks fail to keep the pilot light lit. Frequent interruptions to text pals and fruitless conversation of missed innuendo: the brows never fully unfurrow. Both parties have previewed peccadilloes and committed a few mood-neutralizing conversational gaffes (off-color jokes, nail biting, excessive use of pet phrase).

- **D:** *A Chilly Affair.* All of the above AND striking polarity, a mine-field of schisms (Marlboro Man vs. fitness instructor, Mac vs. PC), morose temperament, or poor table manners. Hot chem-istry has iced over into a job interview. Feels like jury duty was more blythe.

- **F:** *A Fiasco.* All of the above AND an outstanding annoying habit such as a hyena's shrill laugh, irksome germophobia, coked-out teeth grinding, or revealed tragic flaw. Feels like a peer counseling session. There's been plenty of sharing, but too much, too soon.

Incidentally, a flat date can become a good date once both parties acknowledge the dynamic. In the best cases, a next-day follow-up text directly addressing a Grade C+ bad date can foster a shared laugh and desire for a do-over or merely furnish kind closure.

LOVE COCKTAIL

• • • • Sloe gin • One egg white • 2 dashes lemon juice • Fresh raspberries • • • •

≡ WEEKEND GETAWAY ≡

Upping the ante, this three-day crash course in cohabitation previews relationship potential. By the ride home, you'll both have a keener sense of compatibility and toothpaste brands. The long drive to the inn fosters deeper exploration without time constraints or the usual date insecurities. The beach or mountain getaway is ideal for filling in the blanks of personal history and outing odd music tastes on the rental-car stereo. Pack sundries for romance and mood: candles, bubbles, toys, Duraflame logs, stimulants. They may not make it out of the duffel bag, but one should prepare for budding coupling. A cozy weekend getaway acknowledges mutual desires and acceptance of the invitation usually implies sex. Though, examining uncovered idiosyncrasies so closely might cool attraction and cause one party to reconsider. Despite passions bubbling over in the bedroom, tread lightly and respect the remaining boundaries of personal space, especially with closed bathroom doors and zipped duffel bags.

PERSEVERANCE

See a poor date through to a speedy finish: decline dessert, skip the next round, and politely call it an early night. Better yet, treat the date as an anthropological survey. Revel in hearing another's life story, even if it lacks plot and intrigue. Conversing candidly with strangers develops skills as a social animal. When all else stalls, be brazen and introduce off-the-wall queries ("You mentioned you're in PETA. What's your stance on furry handcuffs?").

Don't be tempted to end the affair with a concocted excuse—the conversational equivalent of a bad toupee. Feigned medical emergencies and phantom phone calls are laughable. Consider a salvage operation if a spark remains and chalk up discomfort to the uninspired music, long wait, or low blood sugar. A simple "Can we start over someplace else?" and an open-air stroll might remind both of you why you wanted a date in the first place.

THE OPEN TRIANGLE

I think it's quite possible for a man to take care of more than one woman—
on condition that the parties concerned realize fully what they're in for.... .
A friend of mine thinks that a man should take care of as many women as he
can keep happy. But then there are economic problems, no?
—**HENRY MILLER**, *My Life and Times*

The terms "bachelor," "divorced," and "living in sin" once carried a stigma. But society's marital mandate, obliterated by the Summer of Love and Studio 54 sexcapades, and then revived by the HIV scare, has again been splintered by the rise of career-minded women, secularism, contraceptive advances, sperm banks, easy digital wooing, and the mainstreaming of sport sex and porn, as well as hetero acceptance of the responsible homosexual's hedonist model of success. The result: little reason to rush, fewer tangible perks, and a generation of yoga-trim, moisturized, age-defying forty-plus-year-old men dating younger. Multiball dating, formerly done on the sly, is now done on consent and often sanctioned under the Friends with Benefits HMO (Horniness Maintenance Organization) Plan.

Courtship isn't always a prelude to nuptials, and healthy couplings can exist without monogamy. Back-to-back three-year relationships can eat up some clock during the prime-time marryin' decade (twenty-five to thirty-five), pushing back any eventual knot tying. Rarely, a gentleman finds himself immersed in a successful network of affairs where thirsts are sated from a host of cups, a veritable two-fer of relationship experience points. Multiball play typically occurs when a man emerges from a dry spell. Fast-forward a few weeks to when two semifinalists have surged ahead in the polls. Before choosing exclusivity, consider the open triangle.

Ideal scenario: MG is wooing lovers X and Y. X is also seeing gent A as Y sees gent B. All parties are physically intimate and nonexclusive. Outside of each twosome, none of the lovers are acquainted.

Before sexual relations are fully consummated, it's time for unambiguous disclosure. Open consent from both lovers is mandatory. Discussion might cover condom use and other logistics, but do not dwell on intimate details ("She's into leather and Mallomars"). Relationships of similar intensity should depart in style and content. Maintain confidence that your particular gift is unique and desirable, despite a lover's overnighter with someone else. For instance, MG and X go for heli-skiing and salsa clubs, while MG and Y hit the coffeehouses and galleries. X isn't shortchanged, because MG's foibles are A's abundant strengths. Likewise, as long as what Y brings to the table is different from what X brings, MG needn't fret over whom to like best. Still, triangulating varietists observe the No Unannounced Visits rule, and for propriety's sake, look out for loose barrettes and stray undies and consider locking their phones.

No mere serial flings for logging notches on the bedpost, these relationships are grounded and bordering on serious. Triangles demand more than the sustenance of casual sex and routine telephone check-ins. They work best with lovers who are mature, sane, and a little bit wild. At the crossroads? Not quite ready for the supreme soul mate? Explore multiplicity and see how two flames yield such wildly varying results in heart and bed. Should one relationship crumble, the broken triangle lists to one side, leaving the MG to lean heavily on Y for what he used to get from X. When entropy sets in, the affair either goes bust or booms into a committed relationship now that amorous attention is undivided. Try the triangle on for size, but if all girlfriends are plotted in this arrangement, reexamine your fear of monogamy.

DO-IT-YOURSELF

As table-manners expert Marjabelle Young Stewart's credo states: stroke the meat, don't saw it. The authors will not provide a guiding hand regarding the "solitary rumba" or "han solo." We assume a gentleman has honed this skill through years of trial and little error. We will not chair a panel concerning the alleged myopic effects from running a "testicular time trial" or its use as a prenap sleep aid. Rather, the following concerns the ins and outs of "fisting one's mister" during a grounded relationship, when sexual relations and intimacy are touchstones.

Certain instances require an immediate "hand shandy." No matter how stupendous a sex life, the occasional, undeniable fantasy ought to be slaked. "Giving Yul Brynner a high five" is a mild affirmation of autonomy that's as right as rain. Should slavish devotion to "backstroke roulette" lead to elbow pain and corrective Tommy John surgery, however, "drive the skin bus" only half as much. This pocket polo shouldn't take more than $7^1/_2$ minutes anyhow—the length of a regulation chukker. For cheap thrills, Internet porn has sadly replaced lunchtime ogling and binocular-aided voyeurism. Laptop denizens should never become so inured to e-smut that analog fantasies fail to arouse and expectations emerge that every goodtime gal relishes coarse sexual antics.

No main squeeze, however wonderful, can oblige all needs, all the time. When in love, "hitchhiking under the big top" appears somehow fresh. Though, after a few years in a committed relationship and away from varied live action, formerly sizzling memories of past affairs and bungled opportunities fade from regular rotation and a poor, goatish gent is left with only a few can't-miss gems on the highlight reel. At this point, it is important to engage your imagination, meet new people, and harness simple flirtation into new scenarios, even if it means producing your own indie short starring that buxom neighbor with the undrawn curtains. So "pump gas at the self-service island" and "pan for white gold" (and afterward make sure to Clear Recent History or offline equivalent), because cheating with yourself is not cheating.

LONG-DISTANCE RUNAROUND

The transcontinental affair has become spicier since email and video technology replaced protracted post and telegraph. Mutual attraction struck at last week's actuarial convention in Reno. What to do? Consider the following points before you embark.

BROAD ATTRACTION

Seafaring yeomen may revel in casual flings with many a girl of port, but the energy to maintain a landlubbing long-distance romance requires mutual, multitiered passion. Creativity must compensate for geographical constraints that consign mates to second-hand contact. The majority of interaction will be cerebral and full of fanciful yearning, so make certain neurons are fluttering as strongly as your loins are aching.

PARAMETERS

Once ensconced, establish the possibility of a conjoined future in the same area code. Ask the foundation questions: Is one party seeking a career or venue change? Are intangibles such as professional licenses, property ownership, or family proximity a factor? Glean answers early on with frank issue exchange, especially as intimacy grows lush like plush moss on a rotten log.

Establish parameters early: Is it exclusive or not? Given the failure rate, don't foreclose an active roving eye in ascetic observance of an untested, distant love stationed in Antarctica. Near-monogamy can be maintained through dedication and subliminal audiotape seminars without precluding harmless "catch and release" dalliances on the town. A constant interrogation of whereabouts or lately answered texts is smothering. If you're the jealous type, pop a Quaalude or lower your carbon footprint by dating local.

FREQUENT ATTENTION

Distance must be offset with frequent correspondence. In this manner, uncover naughty thoughts and preferences for everything from the cinema to bondage strategies. In lieu of face time, unexpected flowers, gushing letters, and weekend jaunts are the tools of woo. Skype-ing is important, yet daily video communion can be tedious, resulting in laptop battery drain. Tired of the reciprocal visit routine every three to four weeks? Instead of the usual home-and-away schedule, plan a rendezvous on neutral ground in an equidistant city.

CAVEATS

Inequality of effort and affection is fatal. The relationship is inherently flawed, as each party observes libidinal discipline without tasting the daily fruits of hand-holding and nocturnal waltzing. During visits, intimacy is focused but limited. Departure dates and luggage in the corner loom over time together. Long evenings on the porch swing are far different from the hustle-bustle of time-conscious nights on the town. Discern whether rapture is fueled by love or the artificial excitement of intermittent trysts. Permanent transplants may unearth the specter of incompatibility. Before moving vans are rented, scrutinize your pairing.

A failed long-distance relationship or two is a poignant lesson in anticipation. Distanced relations should be fortuitous, unplanned acts, not fallback solutions for twice-bitten souls. A series of affairs from afar signals more than a nomadic lifestyle: namely, a fiery strain of independence or an unwillingness to tackle complex, local relationships. It's easy to participate when interaction and meaningful pillow talk are rarities. Be certain that proximate relationships are still within your capabilities.

ESTABLISHED RELATIONS

Sometimes engaged couples are temporally separated by an out-of-state job assignment. With the perspective of space and candid conversation, see an established lover from a new perch. Ponder what aspects of your relationship need fine-tuning. Upon reunion, plot any course corrections discussed via hotel phone.

Incidentally, don't worry—all those plane tickets aren't a complete waste. You'll tally enough frequent flier miles for an island trip, where you can wallow in self-pity after the relationship crumbles.

EXES & OHS

While deep emotional ties with every ex suggest lingering issues, a gentleman invariably remains in contact with most old flames, if only through the effortless tentacle of social media. Postrelationship interaction is a sign of maturity, and maintenance should be cultivated, if cautiously. Whether the underlying motivation for remaining friends is continued attraction or mere friendship, don't delude yourself and romanticize a rocky past; all the hang-ups are still there. Never forget why the relationship ended, even as you exchange fond hellos from afar.

Some postscripts resolve into deep platonic affections; others gel into light friendships or infrequent email curiosities. At most, be able to write an outline of her current life, but leave any extended essay questions blank. Don't be presumptuous: requests for cocktails can be rain-checked and voice mails left dormant for a spell.

Incidentally, throaty telephone calls after 10 p.m. are booty calls, not innocent chitchat. Avoid texting an ex while drunk or horny (especially drunk and horny).

THE INVOLVED EX

Don't be a barnacle on the side of a spoken-for lady and make her answer to a jealous husband. Call her at the office or stick to email. Repeat calls without leaving a message indicate misguided pining.

Even worse, the hovering vulture—the loathsome creature who lunges at the first sign of heartache before staging the canned "concerned" lean-in ("Oh really, trouble at home?"). Successful long-awaited sequels are rare and fleeting, as needs change over time. Don't carry an Olympic torch for a long-past ex. Keep those old crushes pint-sized, especially if it was your fault the relationship soured. In short, if your phone voice decidedly dips when your current squeeze comes within earshot during your call to an ex, beware a possible breach. Lines of flirtation blur when you've already danced on the other side. To avoid trust issues, disclose your status with an ex to a present love.

EX SEX

In a perfect world, two people break up graciously, respect differences, and soon after sleep together for no reason other than hedonism. On Earth, sex with exes is fraught with renewed jealousies, clingy bad habits, and unwise reprises. Take a closer look at casual sex with an ex. Often there is inequality, as just one party longs for reconciliation. Eventually, one screws while the other makes love, setting up a dramatic take-two of the crack-up when someone inevitably cries, "I can't do this anymore!" As a gentleman matures, easy sex with exes is weighed against the selfish exploitation of vulnerabilities.

TAKING A BREAK

In the context of dating, taking a break is a natural consequence of growing pains. Many long-term mates can cite an early break that later either crystallized true desires or spurred years of ennui to an overdue finale. Mere mention of a break initiates candid talk of "Where is this going?" that itself may resolve the impasse. And just as being laid off isn't the same as getting fired, taking a break is not a breakup . . . although it may lead to one.

There are three essential motives for taking a break:

- **The Breather:** Life and love have gotten too hectic or intense, requiring a step-back. During time apart, are you broken-hearted or relieved? Separation reveals hidden depths of affection, or a lack thereof.

- **Dastardly Diversion:** When a potential soul mate in short-shorts enters the picture and exclusivity feels like a straitjacket, the break is a semi-legal loophole for the rascal who's test-driving a new hot rod before defaulting on the current leased sedan.

- **Aftermath:** After an affair or act of treachery is discovered, a time-out offers space to decide the future.

BIG BREAK

If you're initiating a break, your partner deserves a reasonable explanation of why you want one in the first place. Gauge the response:
(1) *Acceptance:* "Yes, we need some time apart"; (2) *Dismay:* "You bas-
tard! I expected a ring"; or (3) *Resignation:* "You want a break? We're
broken up. Happy?" The first response leads to an amicable time-
out, the second ushers in a serious tête-à-tête, the third triggers an
emotional brawl. Afterward, set a deadline and plan to call a vote or
adjourn for another fortnight; though a break lasting longer than
six weeks starts to smell like Splitsville.

THE SEXUAL FINE PRINT

Whether beneficial or not, partners on break are not bound by
monogamy, yet neither are they granted amnesty for a Spring Break
feast of unprotected promiscuity. Also, even if the topic wasn't discussed beforehand, do not assume the other hasn't buzzed an alluring ex or unofficial friend/suitor-in-waiting for a frivolous romp.
Often, horniness and habit lead back to sex with one another, but
this rarely ends the break or solves the problem. After a break ends,
all flings and misadventures are sealed, so assume the worst, respect
your mate, and move on. Despite this policy, sins will undoubtedly
be bitched until gray days: "I know we said it was okay . . . but you
still shouldn't have shacked up with what's-her-name!" The following sample contract may help clarify matters.

TAKING A BREAK CONTRACT

WITNESSETH:

THAT, WHEREAS, the lovers had a successful run of dinner dates and make-out sessions, and thereafter the parties began a monogamous relationship, but now wandering eyes, boredom, and seven-month itches have rendered it undesirable to continue dating exclusively, by reason whereof they have decided to take a Break and are hereby temporarily separated as of __last Tuesday__ ; and

WHEREAS, there were no children born out of wedlock during the relationship; and

WHEREAS, they desire to confirm this Break and to make arrangements in connection therewith, including the temporary suspension of monogamous obligations, nightly check-ins, and dog-walking favors; and

WHEREAS, having had the opportunity to seek legal counsel and the advice of a married confidant, each lover considers this Contract to be fair and reasonable, until such time as jealousy or revived passion prompts a reunion, or both lovers have found suitable replacement mates or devices and wish to terminate this relationship; and

NOW, THEREFORE, in consideration of the mutual promises and undertakings herein contained, on this __3rd__ day of __our second year living in sin__ , by and between __Dell__ , lover of the first part ("Boyfriend"), and __Leah__ , lover of the second part ("Girlfriend"), the parties do hereby stipulate, agree, and covenant as follows:

1. **Time Period.** The Break shall run for a period of three weeks from the signing of this Contract. At that point, the parties shall meet to discuss the relationship's status. Each party may ask for one two-week adjournment, but after a total of nine weeks from the date of the signing of this Contract, time is of the essence and a Final Decision (reconciliation or breakup) must be made within forty-eight hours.

2. **Interference.** Boyfriend and Girlfriend each shall be free from interference, restraint, authority, and control by the other, as fully as if he or she were single and unmarried. Neither party hereto shall hereafter disturb, annoy, molest, harass, or in any way interfere with the other's daily whereabouts or nightly entertainment. Calls and texts made from 10 a.m. to 7 p.m. (the "Safe Period") will be courteously answered, but communications outside the Safe Period will be answered at the other's discretion.

3. **Sexual Relations.** Unless otherwise agreed to as a Non-Riding Rider (an extra "all flings prohibited" clause) to this Contract, safe sexual relations with Eligible Partners are limited to one (1) new encounter per Break. Eligible Partners shall not include young hussies/studs, mutual friends, coworkers, or any smarmy personal trainers

who fomented jealousy during the relationship. Relations between the parties ("Mid-Break Sex") are permitted and shall be considered "For Pleasure Only" and do not in any way affect the rights, timing, or obligations under this Contract, nor terminate this Contract even if the intercourse is deemed "otherworldly." Before any Mid-Break Sex, the hosting party must render his/her living space in broom-clean condition, erasing any evidence of a previous Eligible Partner or general slovenliness.

4. **Amendments.** Neither this Contract nor any provision hereof may be changed, amended, waived, discharged, or terminated orally or while in the blissful afterglow following Mid-Break Sex, but only by an instrument in writing, signed by both parties.

5. **Publicity.** Prior to and during the Break, the Parties shall consult with each other prior to posting any social media announcements or changing electronic relationship status or otherwise making public statements with respect to the Break except to close friends and Eligible Partners on a need-to-know basis.

6. **Disputes.** This Contract shall be governed by the laws of the State of Good Taste, and any disputes arising from this Break shall be heard only in the Court of Love, wherein friendly public opinion, nosy sisters' judgments, and guys'-night wisdom are admissible as evidence.

7. **Termination.** Within forty-eight hours of any positive reconciliation, the party who moved for a Break ("Movant") is obligated to furnish a romantic evening of woo ("Reconciliation Repast"), with all the trappings to which the other was accustomed during the first month of courtship. The Movant is solely responsible for costs and fees associated with the Reconciliation Repast, including bistro tabs, concert tickets, and hotel rates (nightly or hourly). If a breakup is negotiated, both parties shall attempt civility.

8. **Entire Understanding.** Each party hereby stipulates that they have read the entire Contract and sign the Contract with complete and full understanding of its contents and meaning. The parties further acknowledge and agree that this is the entire understanding of the parties with regard to the subject matter hereof and that there are no other agreements related thereto, including any oversized oral promises made during romantic getaways or admissions made to the other's best friend under the cursed influence of alcohol.

Dell Lastname Signed _____ *Leah Othername* _____ Signed

THE CRACK-UP

First Suspicion of Crack, 8.0:
With absolute ease . . . both agree to differ on liking football . . . or completely
modern chairs . . . and both agree not to talk much more about these subjects.
Fissure, 23.0:
He has long wondered, now he is sure. He would rather not be present
when she is with her best female friend.
Crevasse, 64.0:
When you start in private practicing things you are going to say to her,
just as you did when you were falling in love with her.
Now with a heavy difference.
—STEPHEN POTTER, *Anti-Woo Gambits for Non-Lovers*

A breakup is defined as the end point of a sexual relationship that has lasted for any period over a fortnight, or the termination of a physically intimate, nonconjugal relation of at least one calendar month. The brush-off of a brief interaction with an extra base hit requires no stratagem and is the only exception to the "never by email" rule.

The denouement is rarely clean and swift; most relationships end with bitterness and regret, and in some cases a distinct promise never to speak again. Outside of Act-of-God breakups, most are doomed by a gross inequality of desire and motive. Ultimately, a teeny number of breakups are handled with utter maturity. The rest are ham-handed, half-bungled affairs that require at least three long post-breakup convos, two tear-filled rolls in the hay, and one silly, ill-fated reconciliation before a Pax Romana, or an uneasy peace, sets in.

Indeed, it's not easy to let go. The gentleman does his best to remain whole when crushed by circumstance. Temper the pall of a broken heart or the call to revenge. Evade Medea's fate: after hearing that her lover Jason had fallen for King Creon's daughter, she killed Jason's lover and the two sons of Medea and Jason, then fled to Athens for more high adventure.

Even if you aren't grinning like Bruce Jenner (before *E!*) on a Wheaties box, avoid the common pitfalls following a fallout. How many of the following Despondent Decathlon events did you gold-medal in during a previous breakup?

The 100m Denial: First hints of doom are ignored and precious time for real communication is squandered.

The Furious Discus Throw: Initial aftermath of restrained anger, characterized by seething and a few temperamental outbursts.

THE FIZZLE

You've bribed the planning board and gotten all the permits, but no construction has actually begun. A few dates and vibrant email exchanges suggest a promising beginning. Still, loose plans fall through, poor timing intrudes, a vague text message goes unanswered, and the whole thing goes dormant. The fizzle is a flame of interest allowed to smolder out without the bellows of continued contact. Is there a spark to salvage? Will a candid email revive a static connection? Either invigorate relations with a second chance ("We keep missing one another, and if I don't see you soon, I'm going to forget why I like you"), or shelve it for a later reprise. All it takes is one serendipitous encounter or perfectly worded message to rekindle the chemistry: "Care to try this again?"

The Shot Put of Fury: Late-night phone calls that begin with drunken colloquy and end with . . . more drunken colloquy.

The 400m Lobby: Cherry-picking accentuation of your remaining positive traits; pleading to friends for diplomatic intervention.

The Long Jump of Lamentation: Guess who's been standing on her stoop the entire evening with a bottle of Old Grand Dad in one hand and a shaky cigarette in the other?

The Mutual Javelin Throw: The true war of negativity, when patience and niceties burst and torrents ensue.

The 110m Emotional Hurdle: The pit of despair, in which crying and pleading haven't patched things up; idle threats of "I can't live without you" are bandied about.

The Heights of the Pole Vault: The false hope in the eye of the crack-up hurricane, when nurturing sentiments of "I miss you" and "I care about you" are misconstrued as signs of reconciliation.

The High Jump to the Bar: The trite, week-long swims in whiskey at the Irish pub, with head in hand.

The 1500m Plead: "I was wrong and you were right to leave me. I'll change, I'll do anything. I'll even stop seeing Ellie on the side."

WEEP NO MORE

· · · · · · · · · Brandy · Dubonnet · ¹/₃ lime · Dash maraschino · · · · · · · · ·

FOUR TYPES OF CRACK-UPS

Mutual: When budding romance backtracks into indifference: a relationship's growth, connectedness, and practicality have reached a natural stopping point. Nothing has really gone awry, but sexual chemistry and date frequency have sharply abated. Long-range scanners indicate potential obstacles and little future along the current course. Rather than forcing an unfeasible togetherness, both parties agree to part ways. Following an amicable split, the opportunity remains to cultivate warm acquaintanceship. The least destructive breakup, the Mutual augurs the best chance of romantic revisitation.

Symptoms of mutual breakup:

- After a night together, one fails to call, the other doesn't care.

- Four or five days of unknown whereabouts go unquestioned.

- Both parties have left items at the other's apartment, but are unconcerned (his Bulova watch can sit a spell; so can her pearls).

- Neither references the other (or the relationship) in mixed company.

Inequality: The corrosion of balanced affection, when one party earns a poor return on his or her emotional investment; compassion and kindness are monopolized; thoughtful notions and gifts are unheeded; one side is forthcoming, the other withholding, in communication and in bed. The relationship is consumed by unilateral whims, and the teeter-totter of affection is leaving one person in the air. The same person who picks up the check is also left holding the bag.

Unlike a Mutual split, the Inequality breakup has an insidious undercurrent, since no single episode caused the rift. It's a slow cancer, steadily eroding a relationship until the crevasse is wide. One person is left to question his or her attractiveness, second-guess efforts made, and rethink an open heart. Ironically, the more this person gave, the less he or she received in return.

A rebuffed gentleman needs time to recover from a war in which no shots were fired. After replaying relationship game film, highlight bad decisions and poor execution. Rebound relationships are improbable during introspective healing.

A selfish gentleman whose decreased affections hastened the corrosion must reevaluate his relationship manners. Instead of orchestrating a courageous fix or definitive exit, the sheepish lad allowed the souring relationship to curdle. Next time, go for the clean cut instead of a protracted withdrawal.

Act of God: The Fates intervene: a better job is offered in a far-away city, a saucy new soul mate inexplicably falls like manna from heaven, the lottery hits, or a false pregnancy reveals hidden cracks. There is little red tape here; one priority trumps another. Acts of God can be permanent splits or mere sabbaticals. Parting shots range from handshakes to tender swan songs of lovemaking.

Bitter: Transgressions and fiery passions explode: keys dragged across simonized surfaces, hate mail slid under the door, photos shredded, anonymous rants concerning sexual inadequacy posted online, and rabbits boiled on the Amana range. Straddled between acts of war, anticipate caustic telephone calls, hang-ups, and a cesspool of pejoratives spat in the name of vengeance. In this drama, the victim thirsts for the wrongdoer's matched suffering. To avoid a Greek tragedy, a gentleman does not succumb to the black bile of retribution. Constrain jilted emotions to short retorts, as bitter maledictions gradually subside.

In the Bitter breakup, the gentleman typically assumes one of two classic roles:

Protagonist: Living well is the gentleman's best revenge. Instead of firing salvos that stall healing, listen to the blues, dust off your collar, and reenter the scene. Schedule a singular evening of buddy-sponsored debauchery to pave over old hurt. During the postmortem, lean upon your inner circle for support, but beware an easy rebound to the very shoulder you cried upon most. Flip many (or infinite) calendar pages before entertaining thoughts of recontact with your ex.

Antagonist: A gentleman deserves his former love's malice when despicable lies are uncovered, abhorrent truths are revealed, dastardly deeds are detected, and the rapier of abuse has fatally slashed the relationship to tatters. The most respectable way to behave in the aftermath is to bear witness to the victim's pain, express remorse, and deal compassionately on her terms. Reflect upon your ruinous ways and lay off the serious dating scene until you've served penance.

FINAL DOS AND DON'TS

- Never end it by phone, text, third-party agent, or grapevine.

- If a breakup of live-in lovers forces one party to move out, the gentleman still offers his burly shoulders. For bitter breakups, victims may slyly reserve all local U-Hauls on moving day.

- Do not follow a hot night or sexual romp with, "We should talk." Either forgo the encounter or postpone the decision.

- Don't incinerate old photos, letters, or gifts until your rational mind deems it a sober decision.

- Before sending jilted love letters or posting mawkish 3 a.m. Facebook posts, sleep on it. After waking, tear up the envelope or instead inform your friends about your organic tomato garden.

part two

The

INNER
GENTLEMAN

*The sun, with all those planets revolving around it
and dependent on it, can still ripen a bunch of grapes
as if it had nothing else in the universe to do.*
—GALILEO GALILEI (1564–1642)

Chapter Four

GENTLEMANLY KNOWLEDGE

LITERATURE

Reading is a personal pleasure, a splash into authors, genres, and eras. Skip the CliffsNotes cram for tomorrow's *Wuthering Heights* discussion and write your own curriculum.

Skim newspapers or free weeklies for book reviews or ask like-minded friends for recommendations. Return to a few pet authors for a familiar voice. Be a few books behind; your reading inbox should be piled medium-high with waiting volumes. But don't be afraid to occasionally cut the line for an urgent must-read that fits a current mood. During winter sabbatical, pick up a tome; on the rocks from a failed relationship, get lost in a therapeutic epic. If you're adrift between Auster and Zola, take a look at our All-Season Reading List that follows.

Keep a mental list of others' literary track records. After a string of hits, a reliable source shouldn't be dropped for promoting one dud. Though if an acquaintance's first selection is a dull wordfest or a shiny airport novelette, decline like a coy schoolgirl ("Thank you for offering, but I just broke off a long engagement with Kerouac, and I'm involved with another novel right now").

Don't be the persistent book pusher. The cry-wolf refrain of "You gotta read this" wears thin; not everyone cares to read every book on your nightstand. Maintain quality control: a gentleman's recommendation batting average should be 1.000, with only limited at-bats.

An offline book club is an effortless way to find good reads and meet an eclectic mix of fellow readers. Before diving in, find out how each month's selections are chosen: is it a democratic process, the host's choice, or some shady, local zoning board–like scheme? Book clubs are fun and should boast more wine than cheese: equal parts book discussion and carousing. Skipping a month for an overactive social life is acceptable.

Rather than frequenting megastores with trendy upstairs cafés, linger in independent bookshops that favor overstuffed shelves and a lazy cat asnooze in the biographies. Hunt down vintage hardbacks on the Web for half price and wonder over an ancient dedication or long-forgotten bookmark.

Allow the creamy goodness of a sublime read to soak in. Appreciate the gentle mind as it tosses around characters and memorable plot twists for days after a book has been shelved. The characters and themes in a gentleman's book du jour should peek into conversations. Talking about the book preserves its effect. Similarly, the shared experience of a book in common forges an immediate bond and breathless respect. The more books you read, the greater the chance of forging connections (and developing myopia).

Carve out time for brown study. Turn lengthy train commutes into quiet book time; turn off the phone for extended stints or burn the lamp until 3 a.m. for late-night page-turning sessions. Underline favorite passages, look up unknown words, or jot crib notes in the margin; your scribbles, or their digital equivalent, will demark hot chapters and chart personal growth.

It's acceptable to string out a read over time, savoring every bite like a marbleized Kobe steak. Tougher tomes are like frozen lasagna and take a hundred pages or so to thaw. Keep at it, but don't be afraid to pull your bookmark out of a discount-bin snoozer.

OH HENRY!
• • • • • • • • • • • • Bénédictine • Whiskey • Ginger ale • • • • • • • • • • • •

Mimic the best heavyweights: after a long, fifteen-round intellectual challenge, schedule a glass-jawed softie for your next read to maintain stamina; perhaps a smart thriller or fun mystery. You're on your own if you move from *Infinite Jest* to *Gravity's Rainbow*.

Are you a serial reader who tackles several books simultaneously or a dedicated one-book-at-a-timer? Serial readers are an odd bunch: should they be applauded for their thirst or treated for attention deficit disorder? Some books require undivided attention and must be your main squeeze. Other times, your coffee table can be a five-subject notebook, piled with studies. Ebooks have made simultaneous sampling effortless. As for the nostalgic re-re-rereader, who consistently turns to the same volume, they just can't let go.

A bookshelf, like a music collection, is a mirror, revealing interests and personal history. Short of the Dewey Decimal System, organize it to eliminate extraneous piles. View the spines and ruminate over a treasured volume. When did you read it? Who was your lover?

BOOKMARKS

A bookmark holds your place while life continues outside the hardback. Bookmarks hawked at bookshop counters should be avoided like a thatch of poison sumac. Haphazard scraps of paper are better than laminated strips of cutesy bookworms spouting inane exclamations like "Look Where I Left Off!" Instead, use a heartifact or unorthodox bookmark to revisit a fond moment. Slip in a train pass from a recent excursion or a blue-movie ticket stub from a red-letter viewing.

Incidentally, some first editions are priceless and call for display, but books are not curios to be left out for intellectual machismo ("How did *Ulysses* end up on the coffee table?").

Nice touch: Take fifteen minutes a night to read aloud a rousing bedtime tale to a pillowmate. Might we suggest poetry, Dr. Seuss, or vibrant classics such as *1001 Arabian Nights* or the Lord of the Rings trilogy?

THE MODERN GENTLEMAN'S
ALL-SEASON READING LIST

The following is a wide-ranging fiction survey for a gentleman venturing beyond the best-seller list.

- **Donald Antrim**: His sardonic books twist sharply in the end, like a leg fracture. Try *Elect Mr. Robinson for a Better World* or *The Verificationist*; for family travails, *The Afterlife: A Memoir.*

- **Paul Auster**: Thoughtful tale-spinner. Pick up *The New York Trilogy* and the brilliant *The Book of Illusions.*

- **Mikhail Bulgakov**: A Russian virtuoso. *The Master and Margarita* is an amazing journey through deception, selfishness, and love. Where else can you find a six-foot tomcat, Jesus Christ, and Satan in one novel?

- **Tom Drury**: Simple prose about fictional Grouse County. Intelligent, probing, and full of dry wit. First novel, *The End of Vandalism*, and the singular *The Driftless Area.*

- **Steve Erickson**: Magical realism that joyously goes hog wild. For film buffs, *Zeroville* is mandatory; for dreamers, *Days Between Stations* will take you way out there.

- **Frederick Exley:** *A Fan's Notes* begins a humorous, engrossing trilogy. *Last Notes from Home* is poignant and sidesplitting.

- **Kinky Friedman:** Pure joy. Marry any woman who elicits this same feeling. Begin with *Elvis, Jesus & Coca-Cola* and keep flipping.

- **William Gaddis:** The writer's writer, with a singular style of telling a story through dialogue. Begin with *Carpenter's Gothic* or *JR*.

- **Graham Greene:** Well known but still underread. For anyone who has ever dwelled on loves lost (i.e., everyone), *The End of the Affair* is the last word. For darker political fare, *The Comedians*, and for a fast-paced jaunt in WWII Britain, *Ministry of Fear*.

- **Katherine Mansfield:** Short stories that stay with you. "Je Ne Pas Parle Français," "A Dill Pickle," "A Garden Party" . . . a modern storyteller ahead of her time.

- **Carson McCullers:** Her *The Heart Is a Lonely Hunter* is a quintessential depiction of quiet desperation and pure loneliness. Read *Reflections in a Golden Eye* to better understand the human condition.

- **Henry Miller:** One of the most dynamic men of his century, whose comments on writing, conversation, love, and women are invaluable. *The Rosy Crucifixion* trilogy is among his finest journeys.

- **Magnus Mills:** Who knew he used to drive an autobus in England? Try the laconic, brooding, and droll *The Restraint of Beasts*, and move on to *Three to See the King*.

- **Haruki Murakami:** Popular Japanese author whose panoramic stories of love and introspection are a distinct pleasure. *The Wind-Up Bird Chronicle* is his unforgettable masterpiece, and *Kafka on the Shore*, another rich, sumptuous journey.

- **Flannery O'Connor:** The Southern bell-ringer, a spinner of rugged tales of betrayal and indelicate endings. Pick up *The*

Collected Stories and relish "A Good Man Is Hard to Find" and "Greenleaf."

- **Cynthia Ozick**: A modern writer with a flair for big-hearted humor and religious deprecation. Try *The Puttermesser Papers* to discover what happens when a stubborn mud golem discovers New York and *Heir to the Glimmering World,* about an immigrant family's fame and ill fortune.

- **Charles Portis**: The great, overlooked American writer. *Norwood* and *The Dog of the South* are stellar; *Masters of Atlantis* is wry times two.

- **John Cowper Powys**: A star of the early twentieth century. His booming lectures on literature were so stunning, people were wont to faint and swoon. Try *Wolf Solent* first for a memorable tour through life's contradictions and the quirkiness of desire.

- **Thomas Pynchon**: Murky modern novelist. Tread carefully and labor for your illumination. Begin with *The Crying of Lot 49*, proceed to *V,* then (and only then) to his rewarding tome, *Gravity's Rainbow*. The breezy detective caper *Inherent Vice* is dessert.

- **The Raymonds**: Raymond Carver for his short story narratives, such as *Cathedral*. Raymond Chandler, whose complex Philip Marlowe offers the private dick's perspective of seamy LA; begin with *The Big Sleep*, then the singular *Long Goodbye*.

- **Matt Ruff**: *Power Gas and Electric* takes Ayn Rand, sewer gators, and ticking time bombs to cyberpunk heights. *Bad Monkeys* is a pure summer brainteaser.

- **Jose Saramago**: Wordy, metaphysical, strangely riveting tales written by the late master. Start with *The Double* and *All the Names*. For an unforgettably poignant downer, there's *Blindness* and its wrenching sequel *Seeing*.

- **Jim Thompson:** An able follower of Hammett and Cain, his pathetic characters get squeezed by both dissolute women and their own oversized ambitions. Try *The Grifters* or *After Dark, My Sweet*.

- **John Kennedy Toole:** *A Confederacy of Dunces*. Perhaps the most humorous book ever written (even more guffaws than Terry Southern's *The Magic Christian*).

- **Thomas Wharton:** An erudite writer whose wondrous tales of lost love take us to the desert (*Salamander*) and the glacier (*Icefields*), in search of an infinite book and a crystalline ice angel.

Mix up your playlist with a few classics: Joseph Conrad, *The Secret Agent*; Jack London, *The Sea-Wolf*; Malcolm Lowry, *Under the Volcano*; Mary Shelley, *Frankenstein*; James M. Cain, *The Postman Always Rings Twice*; Constance Fenimore Woolson, *Selected Stories & Travel Narratives*; Edith Wharton, *The Custom of the Country*; The *Letters of Vincent Van Gogh*; Kurt Vonnegut, *Cat's Cradle*; J. P. Donleavy, *Ginger Man*; W. Somerset Maugham, *The Razor's Edge*; D. H. Lawrence, *The Lady Who Rode Away and Other Stories*; James Hilton, *Lost Horizon*; John Steinbeck, *A Winter of Our Discontent*; Gustave Flaubert, *Madame Bovary* (Lydia Davis trans.); Frank Norris, *McTeague*; and revisit Poe before and after Halloween.

THEMATIC READING

Summertime calls for a literate whodunit and other portable pleasures, but blustery winter calls for a large classic to curl around, preferably a Russian novel that's thick enough to stop a small-caliber bullet. A hardback copy of *Crime and Punishment* in the breast pocket has saved many lives from gunshots and other existential crises, and the more modern Victor Pelevin has twisted his share of readers' intellects. The following are some of the finer atmospheric novels.

THEME	ENTICING TITLES
BASEBALL	Philip Roth, *The Great American Novel* David James Duncan, *The Brothers K* Bernard Malamud, *The Natural*
MAN ON THE EDGE	Merle Drown, *Suburbs of Heaven* James Lasdun, *The Horned Man* J. Robert Lennon, *Castle* Paul Quarrington, *The Spirit Cabinet*
LITERARY SLEUTHING	Tim Davys, *Amberville* Jedidiah Berry, *The Manual of Detection* Michael Chabon, *The Yiddish Policeman's Union*
DRUGS & BOOZE	T. C. Boyle, *Budding Prospects* Augusten Burroughs, *Dry* Hunter S. Thompson, *Fear and Loathing in Las Vegas*
MAGICAL REALISM	Nicholas Christopher, *A Trip to the Stars* Stephen Dobyns, *The Wrestler's Cruel Study* Mark Helprin, *Winter's Tale* Karen Russell, *St. Lucy's Home for Girls Raised by Wolves*
SEARCH FOR TRUTH	Umberto Eco, *The Name of the Rose* James Ball, *Samedi Is Deafness* Ignacio Padilla, *Shadow Without a Name*
AMBITIOUS & REWARDING	Fyodor Dostoevsky, *The Idiot* (Peavear and Volokhonsky translation) John Barth, *The Sot-Weed Factor* Philip Roth, *American Pastoral*
HISTORICAL VIBES	Daniel Mason, *The Piano Tuner* Sarah Hall, *The Electric Michelangelo* Richard Flanagan, *Gould's Book of Fish* Kazuo Ishiguro, *An Artist of the Floating World*
ROMANTIC ODDITIES	Edmund White, *Hotel de Dream* Nani Power, *Crawling at Night* A. L. Kennedy, *Original Bliss*
CUBA	Rachel Kushner, *Telex from Cuba* Graham Greene, *Our Man in Havana* Leonardo Padura Fuentes, *Adiós, Hemingway*

FOREIGN RAPTURE	Nina Fitzpatrick, *The Loves of Faustyna* Stephano Audeguy, *The Theory of Clouds* Milan Kundera, *The Unbearable Lightness of Being* Howard Norman, *The Museum Guard*
SHORT STORIES	Steven Milhauser, *Dangerous Laughter* Aimee Bender, *Willful Creatures* A. M. Homes, *Things You Should Know* Nicholai Gogol, *The Collected Tales*
INTERCONNECTED STORIES	David Mitchell, *Cloud Atlas* Donald Ray Pollack, *Knockemstiff*

POESY

Long days and short commutes leave little time to digest full chapters. Instead of going bookless, nibble on some verse to feed a lyric-starved intellect and hear what Rilke called the primal sound. For a concentrated, ass-kicking dose of anticubicle ethos, attend a poetry slam or dive into Rimbaud as Zappa plays on the hi-fi.

Know well one dead poet and one living poet, yet leap over eighth-grade-anthology fodder and develop your own taste. Scan a clever woman's nightstand for inspiration so that the next time you read Yeats "at wine-dark midnight," you'll conjure a lyrical brunette lover and not some blue-haired English teacher. As for Shakespeare, at least be able to quote the closing couplet of a belov'd sonnet. Likewise, eschewing punctuation a la e. e. cummings isn't nearly as daring as reciting the "shocking fuzz" of his erotic verse. Among your prose, devote at least one shelf to a diverse group of poets (dead and living) in terms of gender, geology, and gestalt. Don't know *Howl* from *Horton Hears a Who*? Start here:

Beyond the Beats, Brautigan, Catullus, Hugo, Larkin, O'Hara, Millay, Neruda, Rumi, Schuyler, Sexton, and Teasdale, sniff out under-the-radar regional poets and these living luminaries:

- **Ai,** *Vice:* Raw and visceral multiracial feminism that's not exclusionary.

- **Kim Addonizio,** *What is this thing called love:* Deconstructs love with modern vernacular in classic forms.

- **Sandra Beasley,** *I Was the Jukebox:* Provocative personifications, sardonic humor.

- **Ciarán Carson,** *Collected Poems:* Solemn, erudite Irishman uses wordplay to capture love and strife in Belfast.

- **Cornelius Eady,** *Hardheaded Weather:* Jazzy insights on the ironies and injustices of African-American life.

- **Tony Hoagland,** *What Narcissism Means to Me:* Quirky, witty contemporary observations.

- **August Kleinzahler,** *Sleeping It Off in Rapid City:* Gruff, edgy, voice-driven non-MFA poetry.

- **Thomas Lux,** *The Street of Clocks:* Singular moments illuminated with meticulous language.

- **Adrienne Rich,** *The Fact of a Doorframe:* Sexy with solid syntax.

- **Robin Robertson,** *Swithering:* Scotsman who writes sensual, precise verse best read aloud.

- **Kay Ryan,** *The Best of It:* Glib, tweet-length poems that make you double back.

- **Frederick Seidel,** *Poems: 1959–2009:* Unapologetic rhymes on death, breasts, and politics.

- **Richard Siken,** *Crush:* Breathless, daring collection tinged with panic and obsession.

- **Dave Smith,** *The Roundhouse Voices: Selected and New Poems:* Prolific, down-to-earth Virginia poet who paints with words.

- **Patricia Smith,** *Blood Dazzler*: Slam champion's chronicle of Hurricane Katrina's ruination.

- **Gary Snyder,** *Regarding Wave:* Sublime, cosmic, staccato lyrics.

- **Matthew Zapruder,** *Come On All You Ghosts*: Brooklyn-born poet with long narrative form that is charming, hip, and hopeful.

Not every man is a bard, but make it a habit to pepper your texting and email prose with some poesy. What man cannot clack the occasional romantic stanza, filthy limerick, or Twitter haiku? The strictest difference between prose and poetry is the latter's use of end stops, so hit the return key

now

and again

if only to keep

intimates

      on

            their

                  zen.

CLASSICAL MUSIC

There's a world of medieval and renaissance music that existed before the "best of" two hundred or so years of the classical Western music tradition (1700–1920). Claudio Monteverdi provided a pivotal moment in 1605 with his *Fifth Book of Madrigal*, which contained unheralded dissonances and other modern touches. The original score included a written essay declaring a break from the accepted rules of music for expressive purposes, akin to Martin Luther's nailed theses at Wittenberg. Mark the straight shot from Monteverdi through Beethoven and Wagner to the twelve-tone modernists like Webern, Berg, and Schoenberg that put traditional tonality mostly to bed in the early twentieth century, capped off in 1967 by Jimi's masterful use of the strident Devil's Interval in "Purple Haze."

Classical music is nice on the radio, but after a few minutes, it can become little more than a pretty accompaniment to rush hour traffic or dishwashing. To truly experience the emotional carnival ride, attend a symphony, string quartet or piano recital. For the non-Juilliard set, approach symphonic music like fine Scotch or bourbon—sip, stop, and appreciate, and don't expect proficiency upon the first gulp. Once the aromas are deciphered, the complexities and wonders become accessible. Before wading into modernist or minimalist compositions, start instead with the crowd-pleasing, older canonical works like Sibelius's *Symphony no. 2* or Rachmaninoff's *Second Piano Concerto*. Be on the alert for dynamic guest conductors, artist débuts, or visiting collectives, like the impressive Russian National Orchestra.

Dress for symphony hall and soak in the tuxedoed professionals on stage. Leave upper respiratory infections, sputum production, and smoker's hacks at home, as well as crinkly wrapped candies and activated cell phones. Preserve the experience and don't be the stumblebum who blows into the auditorium thirty seconds before the opening note, only to be ushered outside to wait. The Medieval Italians felt that the arts were best appreciated with a mixture of the rational and the heart, so for a touch of musical foreplay, arrive early to scan the playbill notes. These little digests are typically written by a musicologist and discuss the composer's life and influences and the work's notable passages and historical significance. Listening blindly to a piece of music without knowing its context is like performing cunnilingus without knowing where the clitoris is—large swatches of lost looks with occasional lucky bursts of delight.

Not unlike the rock'n'roll heartthrob who humps the mic stand, the maestro drives the performance, sometimes with feverish arm-pumping and hair-whooshing swoons à la popular conductor Gustavo Dudamel. Though good orchestras will actually ignore conductors they don't respect; watch for the occasional mismatch where even an éminence grise conductor is flailing in vain as the orchestra goes on autopilot. When in doubt, follow the standing rituals and bravo calls of those around you. Don't mimic the clodpates who applaud between movements of a concerto or sonata—the pause is part of the piece. Wait for the conductor to put his arms down before erupting.

The following are some works and periods to pique your newly-found philharmonic fancy:

1. **Beethoven:** If TV cameras were present in nineteenth-century Vienna, Ludwig might have turned Cassius Clay and bellowed, "I am the greatest" . . . and he would have been right. His *Symphony no. 5* is often considered the best ever written. Listen beyond the first movement as the master resolves the cruelty of "fate knocking at the door" in the opening chords with the triumphant C-major fanfares of the final movement. If the *Fifth* is perfect, then what is Beethoven's *Ninth*: the masterwork that helped reshape the symphony, a clarion call about the decline of Enlightenment ideals,

the masculine expression of oncoming sexual impotency, or a little of all three? If the Old Testament is Bach's *Well-Tempered Clavier*, the New Testament is Beethoven's piano sonatas. How about a late Beethoven piece like the *Hammerklavier Sonata*, op. 106, which was written over the course of a year, like a symphony? On the other side, the incomparable *Violin Concerto*, op. 61, is guaranteed to elicit a tear of joy by the close of the final movement's cadenza.

2. **Berlioz**: *Symphonie Fantastique*. This French composer prefigured modernism by fifty years while representing the excesses of the Romantic movement. This symphony is about his drug-inspired, suicidal musings of love for an Irish actress (whom he actually invited to the first performance to win her hand). Highlights include his "march to the scaffold" in punishment for his love and a Satanist Sabbath with tolling bells and damnation—all 150 years before AC/DC.

3. **Tchaikovsky**: *Symphony no. 6, Pathétique*. Stirring, portentious masterwork. When first performed in Saint Petersburg and conducted by Tchaikovsky himself, it received little fanfare. Tchaikovsky died nine days later (the cause of his death remains a mystery; some suggest an accident; others, suicide by arsenic).

    Incidentally, though Tchaikovsky's *1812 Overture* and its cannon explosions are a familiar accompaniment to Fourth of July festivities, the Russian composer wrote the piece to commemorate Napoleon's retreat from Moscow, not America's little skirmish with the Brits.

4. **Mahler**: Not for the faint of heart, this fin de siécle Austrian Jew-turned-Christian composer remains hot hot hot in musical circles since his profundity was "rediscovered" by Leonard Bernstein in the 1960s. The uninitiated dare not start with anything but his *Symphony no. 1*, which is infused with enough neurosis to

fuel a ten-year psychoanalysis. It also has moments of exquisite beauty and affirmation, as well as a third movement with borrowed "Frère Jacques" strains in a minor key. Mahler believed a symphony could encompass the world—the scintillating *Fifth* spans everything from funeral march to sublime *adagietto* to boisterous rondo finale. His *Third*, the longest standard symphony ever written, opens with eight horns in unison representing stony nature and ends with a chorale that answers the human question of "What Love Tells Me."

5. **Wagner and Liszt**: Wagner's Ring Cycle lasts sixteen hours through four operas, while Bugs Bunny's sublime "What's Opera, Doc?" is only seven minutes—yet neither are subjects to build an evening around. Instead, check out *Tristan und Isolde*. Its opening chords shoot an arrow through tonal organization and resolution, and its duets between the doomed lovers will induce hot flashes even in balding, "manopausal" schnooks. As for Liszt, enjoy the *Damnation of Faust*, *Mephistophelean Waltz*, and *Hungarian Rhapsodies*, all the product of a virtuoso pianist who used his compositional skills to woo at least as many women as Magic Johnson during his Lakers "Showtime" heyday.

6. **Baroque**: Begin with two composers born in 1685, J. S. Bach and Handel—then add Vivaldi. Even a jaded Manhattanite might temporarily melt at hearing Bach's *Brandenburg* concertos; if you thought Rick Wakeman's Mellotron and Moog prog rock stylings on Yes's *Close to the Edge* were the pinnacle of keyboard improvisation, check out the *Fifth Concerto*—sinsemilla enhancement optional. Handel is more than just choral music and Christmas *Messiah*s. In fact, he was the first rock star, famous in England and a member of the royal court, where he hid his probable gay sybarite tendencies behind a corpulence that was legendary. Can

you resist the horn trills in the *Water Music*? What's better at an outdoor gala than his *Royal Fireworks Music*? Why settle for the well-worn chestnut of Vivaldi's *Four Seasons*—melodies often thieved for the soundtrack to irksome diamond commercials—when you can listen to the rest of his twelve-part cycle, *Il cimento dell'armonia e dell'inventione* ("The Contest Between Harmony and Invention"), in which he places one instrument (violin) forward as hero to mirror the reborn importance of the individual in society?

7. **Tilting Toward Modern**: Holst: *The Planets*. Probably our recommendation closest to "date" music. Best listened to outdoors on a clear summer evening (initiate first affections during the light-hearted "Venus" and "Jupiter") or while reminiscing about the destruction of the Death Star (Boba Fett junkies should spin "Mars" to hear the influence on the Williams soundtrack). Similarly, if Respighi's "Pines of the Appian Way" from *The Pines of Rome*, with its representations of the triumphant Roman army returning to the city, doesn't nurture an erection, text your urologist stat for a refill of Levitra, to be washed down with a mighty swig of house Chardonnay. Moving east, we recommend you sample the musical grace of Shostakovich, the most renowned Soviet composer. His stunning *Fifth Symphony* was composed in response to an article in *Pravda* (purportedly written by Stalin himself) that panned the composer's most recent modernist opera as indulgent and vulgar and implicitly stated that if his next work didn't herald Mother Russia, there was a lifelong opening with the Siberian Philharmonic. The *Fifth* is triumphant, yet the ending is a pastiche of every final cadence style—is this ironic, celebratory, or a big Nyet You to the authorities who sought to mold his art?

JAZZ

[keys]

[horn]

[mouthpiece]

"Do you know what it means to miss New Orleans?" Louis Armstrong mused way before Katrina hit the Ninth Ward. Whether it's Charlie Parker on a lolling Sunday morning or a hip quartet chomping bass in a low-ceilinged club, it's jazz, and it makes your foot twitch.

Jazz's allure spikes when seen live and late into the night. Break up the usual and breeze into a small jazz club. Sample the host of genres, from down-home brass bands to modern quintets. For new-comers, get to know the greats and work your way modern. Choice liner notes enlighten, as will documentaries like *The History of Jazz*, *A Great Day in Harlem*, and *Let's Get Lost*.

What follows is a short list of singular recordings often over-looked, both new and old. As the oozy Quato said to the preelection Governator in *Total Recall*, "Open . . . your . . . mind."

- **Dave Douglas:** Heady postbop sound, but so modern and mul-tifaceted. First, listen to the tight, lyrical quintet on *The Infinite*, or even better, *Meaning and Mystery*, with the deft Donny McCaslin replacing Chris Potter on tenor sax and showing off his own lustrous phrasing on "Culture Wars" and snaky cool on "The Sheik of Things to Come." Then, slip into a silk shirt for his "Keystone" electronic sextet (*Moonshine*). It's a record boasting improvisation, song craft, fusion, DJ funk, and even a hint of rock to make your head bang and your foot tap.

- **Miles Davis:** *In a Silent Way*. Bridges the gap between the last great quintet (*Miles Smiles*, *Nefertiti*, Wayne Shorter as songwriter) and the later polarizing output. The album consists of two super kaleidoscopic songs, not so stylistic or melodic, but still compelling. Great for me time—yoga even. If only for the sound (exceptional for its time) and the star power (don't expect star turns, though), this should be the third handful of Miles to check out, after his first two quintets. Note, this is not your parents' predictable "We're still sorta hip" Miles careening over the $2,000 surround-sound system during another snoozer dinner party with the Levines.

- **Chris Potter Underground:** *Follow the Red Line*. A funk jazz band, and all without a bass. Craig Taborn fills the gap on the Rhodes, playing counterpoint to his own vamp on the epic "Arjuna," while later the drummer eggs the timid guitarist into the solo standout of the album on "Pop Tune #1." Plus, there's Potter killing it as usual on this great slice of New York jazz. Like any good live album, it *sounds* like the venue it was recorded in, and if you know the Village Vanguard, you can really hear the walls on this one.

- **Grant Green:** *Idle Moments* and *Green Street* are perfect for an intimate porchside gathering or cool solace following a night of overmedication, not to mention the sublime *Complete Quartets with Sonny Clark* (their "Airegin" will stay with you all day). Beyond these essentials, sneak into the rotation those funky '70s live discs, like *Alive!* (recorded in Newark, New Jersey) and *Live at the Lighthouse*. Green may be cranking out some recycled riffs, but the band is on fire. Check out both eras—one for before dinner, one for after.

- **Herbie Hancock:** *Maiden Voyage*. Possibly the purest example of the expressive/transcendent possibilities of jazz music; difficult to convey with words, easy to understand with one spin. With its predecessor, *Empyrean Isles*, *Maiden Voyage* provides a one-two punch that seeps into your DNA. On to *Head Hunters*. What the falafel am I listening to? Sip your scotch and it'll soon make sense. Accept the cheezoid keyboard textures and almost-grating intro-vamps in stride and you will be rewarded by at times stunning and atmospheric solos in each song. Desire a plateful of both eras? Check out *Flood*, the live-in-Japan disc Herbie dropped in the latter part of the Headhunters period.

Incidentally, for a round of giddy courtship, have you heard Ahmad Jamal's "Poinciana"? Not worth the price of the full disc for new fans, but patently worth a 99-cent download from the *Live at the Pershing* collection. Keep your ears open to hear the occasional glass rattle and swinging door open.

Hank Mobley: *Soul Station*, *Workout*, *Roll Call*. The Blue Note sound, squared; the great underappreciated tenor. Play these gems alongside the Shorter records and marvel at the consistency in sound. Quintessential hard bop, straight ahead, never frothy, satisfying as a French dip at your favorite café. The players on his records comprise the panoply of dizzying '50s/'60s luminaries (Art Blakey, Freddie Hubbard, Sonny Clark, Lee Morgan).

Willis Jackson: *Nuther'n Like Thuther'n*. Roll-out-the-rug soul jazz to accompany your third gin southside at cocktail hour. At its lowest points, it sounds like organ music between innings at a ballgame, but the high notes bring to mind Jimmy McGriff's *Groove Grease* and might spur a sprightly spin in your alligator shoes. This collection was compiled from a pair of Rudy Van Gelder–produced records, one of which is titled *More Gravy*. Need you more incentive? For more soul jazz, go beyond the iconic *Somethin' Else* and the hoppin' *Cannonball Adderly Quintet in San Francisco* and play the Cannonball Adderley Quintet's *Mercy Mercy Mercy*. The lead track, "Fun," promises a set full of joyful music and great in-between-song patter by Adderley himself. Applaud with the crowd at the end of "Sack o' Woe."

- **Wayne Shorter.** *JuJu, Speak No Evil.* Some of the best examples of the classic Blue Note sound. Shorter's compositional skills are on display in these exciting, emotional, thoughtful pieces. *JuJu* gives us epic eastern mysticism a decade and a half in advance of Steely Dan's *Aja;* the gorgeous, loping "House of Jade" is the album's solo forum, giving way to blues-based tunes, both ebullient ("Yes or No") and muted ("12 More Bars to Go"). *Speak No Evil* is full of darker, intricate songs wrung out by an amazing band.

  Incidentally, go Shorter and noir. Check out "Teru" from *Adam's Apple* and conjure Jake Gittes sitting cliffside, bandaged nose, smoking as the sun goes down over the Pacific. For brighter thoughts, download the rendition of "Teru" on Nicholas Payton, Sam Yahel, et al.'s tribute disc *Mysterious Shorter* (if you can find it).

- **Chuck Mangione.** *Feels So Good.* A staple of late '70s lite jazz and radio crossover, this brilliant set . . . [yecchhh] just kidding!

- **Tito Puente's Golden Latin Jazz All-Stars.** *Live at the Village Gate.* This disc will amuse the boys and have the girlies in heels dancing in the kitchen by the first break. Recorded live at the defunct New York club and sounding like the timbale is in your living room, this hot date delivers an omnibus lesson about Latin/Afro Cuban in one little jewel box. "To blazes with Tito!" you may exclaim—"I'm into Mongo Santamaria!" Hold on until track 4, and Tito's got you covered with MS's spirited version of "Afro Blue." Other highlights include the barnstorming "New Arrival" and nods to trad-jazz with "I Loves You Porgy" and "Milestones." The authors grant a host's sly skip of "Oye Como Va," but the pretty skirts in the kitchen may object.

- **Bill Evans Trio.** *Sunday at the Village Vanguard* and *Waltz for Debby.* The former was recorded live just weeks before bassist Scott LaFaro's death. LaFaro melodies are gorgeous on "Gloria's Step," Evans solos beautifully, and Motian is solid (on a good system his cymbals will sound nearly three-dimensional). For a different take on the piano trio, sample the rich, swirling sound and hot drums of Vijay Iyer Trio's *Historicity.* You're hooked by the opening title track.

   Incidentally, after listening to "Some Other Time" from *Everybody Digs Bill Evans,* drop "My Way" and "Free Bird" from the eulogy-song finalists to make way for this monster, a tune that'll have even the cousins-in-law bawling in the aisles. Added bonus: preinstruct the mortician to print the song title in the souvenir booklet for maximum tear-jerking irony.

Nice (rounding) touch: After the fusion of Billy Cobham or the Five Peace Band, dip into Nu-Jazz with Rudder and their many iterations. Revel in the sound of guitar, Fender Rhodes, and the meteoric drums by Keith Carlock, whose shifting meters and fiery beats are a small-jazz-club goer's very damp dream. If you have a music geek in the house, take him to a show and that former Rush fan will revere you for contributing to his musical growth.

FITNESS

After a night of indulgence, isn't a bike ride up Alpe d'Huez or a football toss in the park more beneficial than the #19 Chow Fun

MSG special? Life is a continuing cycle of rebirth and destruction, pruning and renewal. Toss a disc, walk a dog, eat a fruit salad, and get in the game.

Staying fit after thirty requires disciplined time management. Lunchtime gym jaunts, evening workouts, or other sporting activities at least thrice weekly stave off the degeneration into a disproportionate size-40 gut that resembles a hairy, jiggly aspic. Whether you train for triathlons out of vanity, vitality, or competitive fervor, the exertion will strengthen and defog. Confidence is the foundation of sexual aptitude, and a gentleman should feel uninhibited without a shirt. A good body is contagious—as your muscle tone increases, watch compatriots untangle their jump ropes. Despite their own drooping pecs, most men demand that a lady be trim. Before pinching your lover's inch, develop your own routine of strength training and cardio.

Nonlinear fitness is more fun: think prison-cell pull-ups off the top bunk. Besides the usual treadmill and Nautilus circuit, fine-tune your breaststroke, corral a squash partner, hit the heavy bag, and earn that *shvitz* in the steamroom. Water and snow skiing, mountain biking, and spelunking build tone without the claustrophobic ennui of gymnasia. For the perpetually lazy, go with a gym buddy to keep a regular schedule and mix it up with different routines and classes. Eventually, missed workouts will cause guilty uneasiness and a jonesing for the addictive endorphin high. In lieu of a sedentary hobby like ship-in-a-bottling, step into nonlinear pursuits that activate your flesh and your mind: fox hunting and sporting clays, fly- or deep-sea fishing, kayaking, sailing, survival and bush craft.

Incidentally, the home presents too many distractions. Buying personal workout machines will only make some future online bidder happy when your stationary bike goes for $20. Why not get out and meet like-minded people at the health club or the jogging trail?

YOGA

Fad diets, orgone boxes, and light tar cigs are relatively new phenomena for achieving enlightenment, but yoga, in one form or another, has been around for several thousand years. Those with tight hips and a spiritual curiosity might try a class and embark on a lifelong practice for balance and poise on 11.3 sq. ft. of natural rubber (FYI: buy thinner, nonspongy mats made of natural fibers to avoid sliding on sweaty feet). Each type of yoga has a different focus: Hatha (concentrated poses, less movement); Vinyasa (fluid movement + mediation; good for the easily distracted); Ashtanga (rigorous series of specific asanas for intermediate and advanced students); Kundalini (advanced breathing techniques and postures that channel sexual and creative energies upward); Restorative (gentle poses for the hungover or pregnant set, since the only sweat broken is the anxiety of wondering when class will end; good for a postworkout cooldown); Bikram Yoga (proprietary, copyrighted set of poses at 105°F = big fun?). So take off your socks and breathe; yoga is not a competition to see who can bend the farthest or commune the deepest with the cosmos. If practiced with true meditative intent, after a time you'll marvel at the mind's clarity and the body's magnificence. There is an unexpected bonus: yoga classes have a five-to-one female/male ratio of illuminated, well-rounded souls who see fitness as more than twenty minutes of iPod-induced treadmilling.

Points to consider as you sweat to the oldies:

- Whilst waiting to use an occupied machine, don't hover like a vulture. When a patron appears finished, ask, "Can I work in?" Also, know how to spot (or when to call for one) and interject a few coaxing phrases to spur that last bench-press rep.

- Fitness requires no record keeping. Plot your progress in a spiral notebook only if Chuck Norris is an uncle and you sprinkle Creatine on your low-carb toast.

- A witless fool clangs dumbbells after each repetition.

- Technical running gear, coordinating workout clothes, and season-specific getups are luxuries to be earned with sweat equity. Slowpokes don't need track shoes or *un maillot jaune*; no lavish spending until you're a toned regular.

- For tasteful peeking at others, take advantage of the wall mirror's magic properties of incidence and reflection.

Green touch: Respect for your body and the planet should coincide, such that a gentleman needn't use one towel for showering, another to dry his hair, and still another to drip on—never mind three Q-tips to remove nonexistent ear wax, two separate plastic bags for barely soiled shorts and sneakers, a tossed plastic water bottle, a disposable cup for a shot of mouthwash, and a noisome spray of sport fresh deodorant for everyone's bronchial pleasure.

SOOTHSAYING

[the all-knowing   magic 8-ball]

A gentleman needs the occasional snake-oil rubdown. Keep your eyes peeled for unexpected theophany or more subtle visions of grandeur. Like I-95's lonely stretches of kitschy south-of-the-border billboards, life is littered with karmic signposts, some (Nostradamus) more reliable than others (Miss Cleo). When it feels like fourth and

long, Notre Dame's "Touchdown Jesus" or an upright horseshoe will
align your lucky stars.

What She Said Would Happen	1958	World War III breaks out.
	1967	Cure for cancer found.
	1995	Rush Limbaugh forced to go on welfare; Whitney Houston marries Mike Tyson; Peter Jennings is the first journalist in space.
What Actually Happened	1997	Psychic Jeanne Dixon dies.

MAGIC 8-BALL

If you're at loggerheads and have forgotten what comes after "eeny
meeny miney," consult an old sage, that ultimate plastic Solomon—
the Magic 8-Ball. The magic orb is more decisive than Indian leg
wrestling and rock-paper-scissors for settling group disputes.

Good: "Should we call in sick and play in bed all day?"

Bad: "Should I still go into the office with a honkin' case of
swine flu?"

Somewhere between fortune cookies and audiences with Edgar
Cayce Institute mediums, the 8-Ball awaits your vibe. Shake it awake
to summon the voodoo within. While "Outlook not so good" hints
at "No," "Ask again later" and other ball uncertainties require more
devout persistence. Thus, if encumbered with "Cannot predict now,"
bring in the hot hand. No need to wait the maternal twenty minutes
before taking another dip into the occult. Don't let a doubting dilly
muck up the works and question the ball's authority. If bubbles or
cracks are impeding cube legibility, resort to more basic problem-
solving solutions, like a show of hands or a logical discussion.

Incidentally, as for Ouija, do you really think you can obtain authen-
tic, high-grade enlightenment from a Milton Bradley board game?

FORTUNE COOKIES

Only killjoys deem these nuggets of wisdom mass-produced tri-flings. Rather, they are personal telegrams from the Fates. In a tale of two cookies, Tesauro follows five steps: (1) silently pose an issue before the cookie; (2) crack in half; (3) chew one hemisphere while unfolding the Confucian advice; (4) nibble upon the remnants; and (5) digest its meaning.

Nice touch: For a bit of that finding-a-crumpled-ten-spot-in-the-dryer sensation, stow a shrewd fortune in a jacket pocket for later discovery.

MAN CYCLE

Few men are ignorant of a woman's hormonal tides when she's "on her moon." What about the man? Men are moody, too, and often their sine-wave gyrations are tied less to the pituitary gland and more to local teams' playoff woes or a toothpaste error on the tie. Indeed, like thirty days on the NASDAQ, a month in the gentle-man's life is plotted with peaks and valleys.

CRESTING

When the cards are lucky, up the ante and push the pot. Hot bio-rhythms are functions of serendipity and positivity: traffic lights are green, favorite songs litter the radio, a whole week of good-hair days unfolds, and bank errors are in your favor. When you're on, impossi-ble billiards combos drop and romantic approval ratings hit all-time highs. Looked-up words are spotted in a single flip of the dictionary, and front-row parking spots divinely materialize. This esteem spike is not license for rash expenditures at the track, rather a chance to invigorate flagging friendships, write letters under the influence of joy, ask for a raise, or tackle that garage cleanup with an indelible spirit. Nevertheless, like a nitrous turbocharge in a souped-up hot rod, these unbridled blasts are not sustainable. So don't waste them on the couch or glued to a laptop with The Sims: Livin' Large.

SLUMPING

It's a narrow fjord between fortune and infelicity. Yesterday, conversation was packed with profound, poetic truth. Today, your marble-filled mouth is bumbling, cranial fog preventing even a hint of wit. As the cycle turns, expect bouts of moodiness and binges of unhealthy behavior.

Polished shoes and fenders are scuff-prone, red wine gravitates to white shirts, and romantic kismet falls like an overcooked soufflé. Lesser men thrive when the dice are friendly, but gentlemen are adroit in stormy weather, too. Don't panic—like Biblical scourges of locusts, droughts of glee are unlikely to persist. Usually, a lover's note in the lunchbox or peppy call from Mommy will help mitigate the doldrums. Beware an advancing devil-may-care attitude, which can snowball from a few bad breaks into a reckless bender of stubborn melancholia.

Final note: "I'm PMS-ing" will never describe those times of the month when a man is bloated with blues and misfortune. Yet, like the modern lady, a gentleman faces some days with impenetrable bliss and others with a mild heaviness. Maximize the sprints, shorten the stalls, and preserve an overall baseline of optimism. A gentleman who evenly negotiates travails and triumphs will spend more time making small course corrections and less time recovering from colossal swings of fate.

ME TIME

A man owes himself more than stolen moments of solace. Weekly whiles alone are essential. When inner trouble is burbling, alight to a solitary meal for midday introspection or clear a night's social calendar and take yourself out. "Me time" is therapeutic and efficient. Wash the car, hit the gym, open the diary, and purloin "me time" without turning into a scruffy troglodyte. Remember: not every Saturday evening must be a raucous group affair. Don't fear a phone that doesn't ring with invitations. Little bespeaks the meek like a man who can't muster the self-love for an unaccompanied weekend movie or sandwich in the park.

FONZARELLI MOVES & LEGERDEMAIN

Aaaayy. Shark-jumping feats aside, the Fonz and his motorcycle-revving greaser look is still out of vogue, yet at least a shred of wisdom lives on from his *Happy Days* reign. While ordinary buckos will never master telepathic prowess over diner jukeboxes, a sharp eye and a deft hand can transform the mundane into magic. Graceful mannerisms and dexterous control over objects make up one's sangfroid, an effortless imperturbability that is the hallmark of any gentleman's cool. Cultivate a wide natural habitat and remain poised, even in unfamiliar surroundings.

The success of Fonzarelli moves is less about what's done coolly and more about what's not performed awkwardly. Learn to drive in reverse, swim the butterfly stroke, throw a tight spiral, unfasten a bra in two seconds with three fingers, secure the boat with a flawless cleat hitch, and carry two full martinis without sloshing. Lesser men are boorish; make it look easy. For the advanced, add a sum of numbers (division is more impressive), scratch your name in an Etch A Sketch, or slide down a brass banister without cranial mishap. On the other hand, an unflagging bag of tricks is like wearing too much make-up. Behavioral hocus-pocus is no cover-up for hebetude.

Other worthy sleights of hand:

- After others have failed, be the one to open an irksome jar. Open bottled beer with a lighter, spoon, or cell phone.

- Practice long-distance, no-look wastebasket shooting. Likewise, demonstrate eye-mouth coordination by tossing grapes blithely into the air and catching them in your chops.

- Execute a one-handed parallel park into a tight space with three precision anglings of the wheel; crack an egg one-handed.

- Give a pinball machine just enough hip to nudge the silver ball without tilting.

- Toss fragile objects (glasses, melons, phones) with such an expert touch as to shift blame to the catcher if dropped.

- Fix a colleague's computer crash with three keystrokes, two registry deletes, and one restart.

- Drain behind-the-back pool shots and hone your bank shots. If you truly feel the love, call your backgammon roll.

TAIL SPIN

• Gin • Sweet vermouth • Green Chartreuse • Dash bitters • Lemon twist • Olive •

Chapter Five

APPEARANCE & STYLE

SARTORIAL SAVVY

[shoelaces]

[sole]   [tassel]

Clothing is the gentleman's external reflection of mood and mode. Embrace the meritocracy that is style; money can buy quality, but taste is free. Expression and experimentation are wonderful, yet mild adherence to tradition and seasonal conventions never tarnish a first impression.

A gentleman selects from a wide array of styles and seldom purchases fad apparel. If the far half of the closet is cluttered with once-worn garb, it's time to update. Building a wardrobe is akin to amassing a music collection. Pick up the goes-with-all-occasions basics (black dress slacks, sharp blue shirt, dark blazer, smart pullover) and diversify from classics to funk. Strip the store-window mannequin; preassembled outfits are fun on occasion, but beware mass fashions likely to be copied by packs of mall rats. New pieces that complement old clothes won't leave you with sartorial pariahs that go with nothing else. For example, the orange velvet cape is ideal for Halloween and New Year's Eve, but the dark silk shirt dresses up for work or down with jeans.

Before you explore advanced techniques and boutiques, Phineas recommends finding a niche for personality and budget by browsing finer department stores. After you build a fashion foundation, Tesauro ballyhoos stepping outside the pinstriped lines into ateliers, haberdasheries, and vintage shops. Shopping jaunts for uptown staples and downtown one-of-a-kinds outfit the gentleman for both work and play.

CARE

Pressing makes for impressing and touch-ups at home prevent last-minute wrinkles on the town. Yet handier than the iron is the steamer. In the time it takes to properly draw a double espresso, the steamer is puffing at the ready to smooth out your duds without the tedium of negotiating sleeves and buttons. Whereas an iron flattens fabric for a crisp effect, steamers fluff-up fibers for a clean, soft look that lasts longer and requires fewer dry cleanings. Another useful tool in the closet is the electric pill shaver. Like scraping soot off the Sistine Chapel to reveal the fresco's vibrant colors, shaving your sweaters restores luster and adds years of life. Moreover, if you don't know the cold-water care of delicates, call Mom or stick to permanent press.

Incidentally, plain undershirts aren't fashion, rather a protective layer between naked skin and fine clothing. At dress-up affairs, don't casualize a smart open shirt with an exposed white crew neck that peeks above the top button.

VINTAGE CLOTHING

Vintage clothing is like an old home. Often, there's evidence of a former tenant: a resewn button, the handiwork of an expert tailor, or an inked monogram courtesy of Sir-Marks-A-Lot.

Thrift stores like the Salvation Army are meccas for inexpensive basics such as black pants, work shirts, or the rare treat of a classic paisley tie or shoes that fit. Another spot for nifty thrift, Army/Navy stores are best browsed for pea coats, boots, and gear for start-up militias. The choicest vintage shops resemble top-dollar designer boutiques chock full of mindfully chosen gems, picturesque polyester, and well-aged denim; hands down, the place for purchasing economical and unique accessories. Introduce yourself to the shop-minding boulevardier and ask him or her to point out unusual acquisitions.

Antique studs, cuff links, crossties, and pinstriped pants are best found here. Occasionally, treat yourself to a few boutique binges and nix the secondhand penny-pinching, lest overindulgence in the discount bin brands you an outdated, sloppy fop.

FOOTWEAR

Shoes last countless years with periodic maintenance and repair (resoles, reheels). Mild care is sensible and cheaper than buying a new pair. Shoehorns ease slip-in and prevent premature erosion of a shoe's backstay and lining. Caught on the go? Use the end of a belt as a substitute. Rotate your footwear, so as to evenly wear soles over time. For days of deluge, footwear needs protection. Wear rubbers or nominate dress shoes in disrepair for rainy commutes. After traipsing through a storm, lay your shoes on their sides to allow the leather to dry out. Cedar shoe trees, mandatory for fine footwear, preserve shape, absorb moisture, and eliminate odor. The three-dollar shine conditions leather, redarkens outsoles, and is a simple pleasure that feels like a decadent luxury. Shoe shines are for gentlemen what weekly manicures are for ladies. If the shoeblack does a fine redye of the outsoles or provides a relatively unfingered porn magazine to peruse, an extra tip is a louche imperative.

Reserve cross-trainers for sporting activities, smart sneakers for bouncing around, and relegate comfy boat shoes to Saturdays on the poop deck or chores in the garage. On the shoe rack: sturdy black leathers, brown bucks, shiny oxblood wing tips, and throwaways to handle muddy tasks. Branch out into monk straps, split toes, slip-ons with pricey tassels, suede wing tips, and jazzy two-tones. Be footwear-frivolous and keep two pairs of nightclub-only treads and winter or cowboy boots. Once you appreciate the handiwork of a toe puff or a heel stiffener, step up to handcrafted shoes. It's an investment that comes with your own selection of leathers, liners, stitching, and punch-cuts. The top of this quality pyramid are bespoke shoes made from a custom "last" (wooden carving of your foot).

Incidentally, before you slip toe-ringed phalanges into a pair of expensive kicks, stock up on proper socks. Take the cue from your trou: socks matching your pants create a seamless silhouette down the leg. When in between tones, generally opt for the darker hue. Once you've mastered the basics, slip into argyles and coordinating patterns that evince fluid style when you sit down or remove shoes for airport security.

BUSINESS ATTIRE

Dressing for the office isn't all bad. Two rules: neither the Saturday night funk nor the Sunday afternoon frump. Still, well-coordinated play clothes double as desk and datewear when paired with fine fabrics, smart accessories, and shined shoes.

Dress Shirts

Diversify your holdings, as even mediocre clothiers stock non-white shirts in a host of stripes and patterns. Beware discount rack brands that are nearly translucent; test by jamming a finger under the fabric and checking for unacceptable thinness. Svelte gents should avoid baggy-armed dress shirts cut for corpulent desk jockeys and seek out shirts designated Slim or Athletic Cut, or go custom-made. Don the spectrum, closeting several shades of blue, ecru, and other earth tones with smart designs. Expand your hues: variants of lemon, lime, and lilac to brighten warmer months. Unlike the monsignor, vary your collar styles—the button-down collar is the least formal, and the surest way to downplay an otherwise dressy outfit. Both point and spread collars accentuate broad shoulders and allow ties room to flaunt their patterns and dimples. Tab collars provide a closer fit and confidently showcase a gentleman's tie. Wait until you've been complimented on your dress before venturing into contrasting collars or rounded French styles requiring a collar pin. A short-sleeve shirt with a tie demonstrates kinship with door-to-door vacuum salesmen.

Incidentally, once you've accrued a few pairs of classic studs and cuff links, slip French-cuffed attire into workday sport coat ensembles.

Suits

Every business professional's closet includes the old IBM-mandated classic blue suit, but true sartorial savvy means that you're dressing up beyond the corporate code. To rock the threads without going into hock, maximize permutations and look for groupings that turn a small bounty into a well-stocked walk-in closet. Your suit is the picture frame and your shirt and tie are the picture. Buy a purple suit and you can wear it the first Monday after you get it, but not again for another couple weeks. Yet a solid grey or charcoal frame can go several days in a row: blue shirt with a blue and gray tie, pink shirt with pink and gray tie, white shirt with gray plaid or burgundy stripe. Besides your secretary and your live-in, no one's the wiser. Less costly than new suits are blazers (solid-colored jackets) and sport coats (jackets that are patterned—stripes, checks, herringbone) that mix and match to fill in the gaps between Power Suit Monday and Casual Friday.

Beyond color, match button style and subtle piping with body type and appearance. Chestnut or olive suits agree with darker features; three-button or four-button models allow for more expression and are perfect for taller gents. Add a vest and your suit becomes a jazzy three-piece that looks sharp without a jacket. Rules of thumb: skinny suits, side vents, and two buttons higher up are ideal for endomorphs, and bigger guys must avoid wide stripes or windowpanes that accentuate girth. Always hang suits after use to breathe and unwrinkle; if done faithfully, pressing and dry cleaning are but a rare occurrence. Pressing a suit without dry cleaning is verboten.

Bespoke

The zenith of men's dress is the bespoke suit. An English word interchangeable with "custom," "bespoke" describes the art of making something to order. Chalk stripe, windowpane, sharkskin, and seersucker ought to be part of the Modern Gentleman's vocabulary. Bespoke garments include extras that bespeak personality: the pick stitching, the drape, the feel, the luster, and the ego fulfillment when you open a jacket with your name sewn inside. Customize by tweaking button stance, gorge of the lapel (how the notch is cut in), vents (center, side, or none), pleats (or flat-front), pockets, and pocket flaps (straight or angled). If you're not ready for the 100 percent handmade suit, at least pony up for tailoring that makes a prêt-à-porter suit look perfect. With conscious costumery, bespoke or otherwise, your wardrobe has consistency; instead of looking for that favorite outfit for an important meeting, every suit is your go-to suit when left to a professional clothier.

Nice touch: When your suit features surgeon's cuffs/functional buttonholes on the sleeve (unlike off-the-rack models with decorative buttons), undo the button nearest the cuff as a marker to other fancy Dans that you too appreciate craftsmanship.

SWEATERS

Own a few basic cable-knit sweaters for splitting wood at the cabin or huddling on the beach in November. V-necks are casual enough to funk up with bright colors and jeans, but to mix things up at work come cooler climes, wear cashmere or merino wool over a lighter shirt-and-tie combo with or without a jacket. Argyle dresses up an untucked button-down and makes a handsome sweater vest for the classic prep-school look that's great for the golf course or under the reading lamp, but not for a night out with the rugby squad. As for turtlenecks and mocks, honor the fallen Yankees Boss, but mind whether a giraffe-neck fold-over gives the impression of George Steinbrenner or a whiplash recoveree.

OVERWEAR & UNDERWEAR

The traditional raincoat (tan or olive green) never goes out of style. Unless a proper street flasher, don't actually tie the belt around your waist. Instead, loop it around back, clasp together, and allow it to hang harmlessly. When the arctic cold front hits, wear a midthigh-length black or navy wool overcoat and a stylish muffler. A fine cashmere or wool blend scarf also accommodates workplace or evening jaunts. For transitional weather, loop a scarf about the neck even without a coat. In the sunny months, a summer linen scarf in white or pastel tones accents a flowy shirt, protects the tender jugular from nippy sea breezes, and punctuates swim trunks with a hint of St. Tropez.

Beneath the polished veneer, it's up to each gent to stow his mask and snorkel how he deems fit, whether boxers, colorful briefs, or hybrid cuts. Just as those with resting heart rates below 60 qualify for pro-grade athletic gear, gents with chiseled physiques are cleared for low-rise briefs and thongs. As with socks, holey or elastically challenged undies must hit the waste bin.

TUXEDO
· · · · Gin · Sherry · Dash sweet vermouth · Dash bitters · Lemon twist · · · ·

ACCESSORIES

Don't wear trinkets, shirt-pins, finger-rings,
or anything that is solely ornamental. . . . Don't be a "swell" or a "dude,"
or whatever the fop of the period may be called.
—CENSOR, *Don't,* **1880**

Highlight your extremities with a dash of élan. The dresser top is a handy residence for Pop's old tie tacks and other vintage trimmings. Transform an ordinary Dixie-cup, vanilla-scoop sport coat into a sundae suit by sprinkling on some sterling or gold garnishes. The investment in an array of silk handkerchiefs and sturdy studs will upgrade a wardrobe for years to come. A quality pair of cuff links, for example, should set you back; substandard accessories stick out like baseball caps with a tuxedo and demean a handsome ensemble.

Digital watches are for triathletes on the go, but dressier or funkier models are the gent's functional jewelry. If so inclined, carry a pocket watch to keep forearm unencumbered by weight or tan lines. Tucked away, a pocket watch protects against pedestrian inquiries of the hour; it also leaves the gent at liberty to ask a spry lady for her time.

Incidentally, belts should extend past the buckle but not snake and loop down to the crotch. Rather than driving nails into a closet or bending wire hangers, invest in an anchor-shaped belt rack that hangs on the rod.

POCKET SQUARES

A white cotton handkerchief elevates style and costs next to nothing. Finish dressing—don't neglect a bare breast pocket, or worse, stuff in a hard pack of smokes. This is not a bow tie—cummerbund set; the best pocket squares complement but don't match exactly. Your pocketful of silk is a quiet flag akin to international semaphore spelling s-t-y-l-e. Contrast texture and tone: muted linen squares with flashy ties, patterned silky handkerchiefs with solid-colored ties. Master the four folds: (1) the conservative square-ended or Presidential fold; (2) the classic one-point triangle fold; (3) the elegant multipointed Cagney fold; and (4) the dandier puffed or Cooper fold, typically worn with colored silk and handlebar moustaches. If you can produce a paper airplane, the pocket square is within reach. Visit a men's shop or the Web for a fold-by-fold tutorial.

Incidentally, a man carries two hankies: a silky one in the breast pocket for Her . . . and a standard-issue "tissue" in the pants pocket for Him. A plain white handkerchief is standard-issue for the non-naked man and serves primarily to dab foreheads or clear a schnozz, but in a pinch, a clean one can be a peep show towelette, champagne saber polisher, or crime scene cleaner-upper.

BILLFOLDS

A wallet should fit comfortably in a front, back, or breast pocket without upsetting the smoothness of clothing. Except for full-serve Hess station attendants and gentlemen's club regulars, it is unnecessary to carry a bulging sheaf of bills. Purge the inner folds of old business cards, pay stubs, receipts, and long-lost nudie shots.

A billfold's style is as serious as that of a gentleman's everyday belt. Brown or black leather is a timeless selection, in regulation size or the longer, Southern, checkbook length. Velcro models are reserved for sporting activities or for the hopelessly wealthy. If your wallet is old, faded, and cracking, retire it. For a more subdued look, seek a money clip in sterling silver or gold. This is no place to clench a weak wad; fold in at least as much as the clip is worth.

Nice touch: Stash a few stamps behind your ATM card for last-minute mailbox drops. When traveling, remove ancillary wallet materials and stick with what's utilitarian on the road. Do you really need that "buy ten, get one free" hole-punched deli hoagie card in El Segundo?

KNOTS & CRAVATS

Along with boxer shorts, neckwear is one of the most telling articles of clothing. A colorful litter parallels weather and mood. Brighter ties emerge in the sunshine, sedate hues mirror the nimbus clouds. A handful of conservative dot or striped ties should fill out your (non-motorized) cedar tie rack. Most ties match white and blue shirts, but not all stripes or patterns. When shopping, pull a few styles from the fine-shirts department for comparison to prevent a glut of strictly primary colors.

Around a swinging rack, one distinctive silk gem leers from behind discount clutter, causing a great stir in your charge card. A great tie, like a vintage car, snatches the eye and calls for attention, sometimes in a whisper, other times a shout. Develop this radar. If a tie doesn't move you, don't buy it. If you can't recall the last "nice tie" compliment, ask a well-dressed sales clerk to assist among the silks.

KNOT KNOWING

Let the width of your collar guide you: spread collars showcase wide knots and thick fabric, narrow collars require slimmer knots and thinner materials. The consequence of reversing this formula leads to either tiny knots abandoned in a wide expanse of collar or bulging knots crowding the collar and displacing the collar points.

The schoolboyish Four in Hand was fine for your salad days, but now 'tis time to widen your cravat vocab to include the Victoria, a six-move knot that makes an extra revolution 'round the center for added bulk; the Plattsburgh, Tesauro's seven-move go-to fave with spread collars that produces a broad, sharp triangle that requires no dimpling; the Windsor, a conspicuously elegant eight-move knot; and the Grantchester, a nine-move knot that starts with the tie turned seam side up.

In the world of quick assessments, ties are a Geiger counter of character (see chart). No limp ties, except if you are allergic to silk or compliments.

TIES THAT (DON'T) BIND

FIRST IMPRESSION	PERMANENT CHARACTERIZATION
Small dots and diamonds, bland color, or uninteresting collegiate stripes; button-down collar.	Classic conservative. If the Constitution had permitted, third time's a charm—Reagan '88.
Computer-generated entropy design with no discernible dimple.	Likely a shut-in; plays Magic: The Gathering.
Thin, older model; drab paisley; seemingly leftover from the prop department on *Hunter*. Tie tip never reaches the navel.	Lazy, dispirited. Barring that company memo, sweatpants would be a casual day option.
Nonholiday-time Loony Tunes design or other novelty.	Take one step back—lunched on a Happy Meal today and kept the toy prize.
Really tight knot the size of a pinhead.	Pinhead.
Obscenely ugly, abstract, essentially low-grade Pollock puke. Crooked, hasty, four-in-hand knot; tie drapes down over 501 button-fly jeans.	Deficiency of taste: litter box smell in bedroom, thinks Kenny G is "soulful."
Smart design, sturdy swatch of silk, instantly (but casually) eye-catching, secondary colors, properly arched knot that speaks to the shirt (and stays fastened to it with a tie bar or tack).	The Modern Gentleman, of course.

BOLO

• • • • • • • • Rum • Lemon or lime juice • Orange juice • Sugar • • • • • • • •

ASCOTS

For those who disapprove of tight collars or full-time jobs, the ascot is a sound alternative. Four out of five *flâneurs* recommend it over the conservative cravat. It is for loosely sophisticated affairs when a *soupçon* of swank and *Playboy* is not inappropriate. The ascot zests up pyjamas, fancies a cocktail hour, and elegantly denotes a frisky host. A black or white ascot is quite versatile as social lingerie, either for public gaming or intimate affairs. It remains fast to the neck with a modified four-in-hand knot or a tie tack.

Incidentally, Fred Jones, the blond *bon homme* from *Scooby Doo*, is at least a semigentleman. He wears a distinctive red piece of neckwear, singly knotted, with pointed ends over his white sweater. Hanna-Barbera classifies this as an "ascot." In reality, it is merely a "cravat." In his 1978 classic, *Dressing Right*, Charles Hix clearly states, "The true ascot, sometimes seen at formal daytime weddings, has wide, usually squared ends that are worn, after the neck has been looped twice, folded diagonally one over the other and held in place by a jeweled or plain stickpin." A cravat, like a scarf, is wrapped around the neck and looped once in a single knot without a tack. Ergo, Fred is wearing a cravat, not an ascot. No squared ends + no stickpin + a single knot + a silly sweater = cravat.

At the end of the workday, too many unknowing gents wantonly strip their tie from a shirt, trawling it around the neck band, stretching and twisting the silk back and forth like an older brother's Indian burn. Turn up your shirt collar and untie by retracing the steps of knotting gently. Then, drape the fatigued tie back on the rack.

BOW TIES

Ranging from professorial to formal to funky, the bow tie is the hand-tied benchmark of gentlemanly virtue. Unlike a straight tie, which isn't undone until undress, a bow tie is fidgeted with and reknotted throughout the day. Take a moment of "me time" to fiddle and retie when caught in a slow elevator. The undone bow is a subtle beacon; onlookers know it's a manual, not a prefab clip-on. Indeed, a bow tie is quite phallic. With deft manipulation, it stands soft yet turgid, puffing with stiffness or leaning askance.

You already have the clothes to go with a butterfly, or bat-winged bow tie: it goes with almost any collar, except the tab collar, and it's not just for tuxedos or stuffy sport coats with elbow patches. It goes with most any suit and in a pinch doubles as formal wear. Still, a knotted bow tie paired with a lackluster oufit thrice accentuates a nerdy lack of style.

Knot a bow tie only so tightly that it may be undone by a lover's gentle tug. As Frank Sinatra hinted, attempt a keen bow no more than three times. After that, leave it . . . it's jazz.

PYJAMAS

Amongst appropriately intimate company and especially when alone, slide into a pair of pyjamas. In the warmer climes, collarless lightweight cotton is preferred. Try on simple patterns and prints, as opposed to shorties and pairs with childish choo-choo themes. Essentially, don't be too casual; pyjamas shouldn't seem incongruent with a snifter. For the kinds of nightcaps that are poured rather than worn, keep a sleek set for chic repose. As the nights grow long and frosty, swap for flannel and lounge by the fire. The more mature should seek out faux cuffs and buttons as opposed to snaps. A third pyjama pair should be kept as a spare or reserved for guests. Additionally, a men's size small makes a clever hint and splendid gift for a playful love or platonic gal.

Pyjama tips:

- Flashy polyester can double as urban club wear. Once, spend the night at a lover's metropolitan pad and ride the subway home in pyjamas.

- Host an intimate affair where pj's are required attire.

- For extra credit, find out what really goes in the breast pyjama pocket: a sawbuck for wagers and dispatched errands; ear buds; snuff; contraception; paraphernalia?

Nice touch: Spin pajamas in the dryer for a toasty transition from a shower or to ease a lover out of bed on a glacial morning.

ROBE DE CHAMBRE

An antecedent of the dressing gown, the robe is an undervalued article of gentleman's clothing, not merely hotel pilferage. Don't let Tabernacle choirboys, Majesties, Supreme Court justices, and Jedi Knights monopolize the garment's virtue. Ranging from dragon-print kimonos to shiny satins worn by ringside welterweights, robes are more than a bolt of terry cloth worn after a soak. There are bathrobes, usually in thirsty cotton weaves, meant strictly for post-bath comfort and cover. In the stickier months, sporty designs are casual, light, and short as a green-belt's judo gi. In the wintertime, don a calf-sweeping model. If dashing across snow to a gurgling hot tub, employ something hooded. Finish with fuzzy slippers, but no pink floppy ears or anything purchased at the hospice gift shop.

EYEWEAR

[frame]

[arm]

[lens]

It is polite for a gentleman to have 20/20 vision, but it is not rude to require prescription oculars. Until LASIK surgery is scheduled, myopic gentlemen should sport sensible and stylish frames. Accentuate cheekbones and dark lashes without resembling Mr. Magoo or Waldo. Glasses are worn front and center, so spare no extras: purchase featherweight, scratch-resistant, high-index lens for a sleek fit and de-smudge them with a microfiber cloth. Even wear-with-a-hangover-and-allergies spectacles should suit a business meeting or happy-hour date. Regular wearers should stock at least two to three motley pairs: dark, workaday goggles, brownish on-the-town metropolitan specs, and other-colored très moderne glasses for snazzy, jazzy (but not spazzy) nights. No matter what, edgy frames must fit your face and charisma, lest your glasses be cooler than you. To anyone with perfect vision who sports wild frames as a fashionable accessory: may the ghost of Oedipus poke your eyes out. Shame on you, you myopic poser.

FRINGE-WEAR

A monocle, on a chain or floating solo, is a fine Austrian accoutrement; Colonel Mustard, diamond appraisers, and Baker Street antagonists shouldn't have all the fun. Balanced upon the bridge of the nose, the armless pince-nez (excellent with a vintage bow tie) was hot with Woolworth's counter-backers and nineteenth-century accountants. Lorgnettes help you get an eye on faraway arias at the opera. An eye patch is a niche accessory with its own ecstasy, though, only those named Von, Erich, or Von Erich may regularly employ one for nonmedical reasons.

Incidentally, the triathletic gentleman might own sport sunglasses. However, wrap-arounds and anything endorsed by Olympic volleyball players should not leave the sand and may never accompany a business suit. Remember, goggles are for the slopes, racquetball, chem lab, motocross, and Lakers starting centers only.

HATIQUETTE & UMBRELLA POLICY

After perusing the pyjama shop and fine-footwear department, nestle an uncovered head into a hat and discover the gentleman's answer to a lady's shoe fetish. Little so sparks attention at an affair as a gentleman in a fine hat, dressed appropriately and well-fitted from brim to toe. A hat doesn't create gallantry, but a gent's aura and crackle is noticeably enhanced with the right tilt of a lid. When traveling, nothing restores the fancy to trains and airplanes like a man in a slim hat. However, there is a fine line between looking foolish and looking enviably dapper in a hat. If you are in the latter 10 percent, hats off. For the remaining crop of gentlemen, there are sombreros in Tijuana and hard hats for safety.

STYLES

Let a haberdasher show you around. The brim shades sun, and the band holds a feather; the crown covers the head, and the crease is how the hat is indented or protruded (center or pinch, for instance).

For yachting and election night, try an Italian straw boater. For slipping into a zoot suit or anticipating a night of jazz, try a felt fedora or homburg. Chauffeurs like tweed driving caps, and Bond villains enjoy classic derbies and bowlers in wool or fur. The beaver fur or silk/satin collapsible black topper is a must for the opera.

Matching hat style with the occasion involves seasonal considerations as well. Winter demands lamb fur, pigskin suede, wool, and cashmere, and never calls for novelty hats that turn your dome into a cutesy alien, court jester, or stegosaurus. Summer hats keep a head cool with weaves of straw, corn, and coconut. Poplin hats repel April showers. Nearly indestructible synthetics like Mylar take a drenching and pack without a hatbox.

Incidentally, leave the sunglasses at home when donning a hat. Not only does a hat shade the eyes, the full circumference of shadow guards against sun glare and misjudged infield pop-ups.

HAT CARE

If a proper hatbox (slightly larger than the hat) is unavailable, hang your lid on a hook or rest the hat on its crown. Always store the hat with its brim upturned, then snap it back into place when ready to wear. Unlike its shoddy cousins, a well-made hat retains its shape after years of wear. Regular brushing with a soft bristle maintains luster. For the best chapeaus, invest in a hat jack, which preserves shape like a shoe tree.

Famous doffers P(hineas) T. Barnum, Frosty the Snowman, and the Mad Hatter melded style with manners: (1) removal when a lady enters an elevator, when sitting indoors, or during a funeral procession; and (2) lifting after performing an act of courtesy, when passing in close quarters, or in offering up one's seat.

UMBRELLA POLICY

Umbrellas are like lighters: everyone owns one, but few have ever actually purchased one. There are two types: those routinely left in taxis and finer *parapluies* meant to be cherished. Black, push-button styles are fine for commuting and routine errands. A "disposable" $3 street-vendor model is ideal for rainy barhops where the chance of precipitation and a lost umbrella both approach 100 percent. An archcriminal's stick also doubles as an automatic weapon or quick getaway whirligig, à la Penguin. Stash one in the office for an unexpected early-evening cloudburst, but go without one for a misty mizzle or snowstorm. Snazzier stick or malacca-handle models are for formal outings and fine duds and may serve as an escort's parasol during outdoor summer festivals.

Do not drag your umbrella on a sidewalk or hardwood floor, nor furl a brolly in the house. Only the anal-retentive poke a pointy ferrule at discarded cigars on the pavement. And nothing proclaims a city dweller to be a self-important wanker more than monopolizing sidewalk airspace with an elephantine golf umbrella bearing a corporate logo from a defunct investment bank.

Incidentally, prohibitions against premature affection are suspended in the rain. Drape an arm over her shoulder while sharing a pocketsize 'brella. Even in monsoons, however, early "ass-patting" is still out.

TATTOOS

Perhaps a night with the boys in Nuevo Laredo or a wrong turn off Bourbon Street left its indelible mark. The gentleman's code includes the decorated crowd. Who wouldn't say that a gent with a three-piece suit and a forearm skull and crossbones is at least indefinable?

One cannot be too patient in measuring instant gratification against permanent liabilities before getting tattooed or pierced. As with musical and sartorial choices, you might eventually "grow out" of a tattoo, but learn to appreciate the moment of youth instead of scrubbing nightly with a Dobie pad in a vain attempt at ink removal. Lest you experience pallor in the parlor, answer the three key questions:

Motivation: Is it for a lover, entrance into a subculture or fraternity, personal expression, or mere frivolity? With modest tattooing and piercing almost commonplace, a single tattoo is no longer rebellion, though a colorful "sleeve" or an ear gauge is still a kick in The Man's onions. Recognize a tattoo's immediate upward glamour and inexorable decline on your wrinkled, mottled, sunburned hide . . . but getting old was never pretty anyway.

Medium: Art or text, color or not. Colored tattoos hurt more, since quality work requires several visits. Don't discount snippets of poetry, lyrics, or prose packed with personal metaphors; investigate the proper font for elegant presentation.

Location: Depending on lifestyle, personality, and pain threshold, some prefer the safety of the Corporate Zone (that is, meaty areas not seen when wearing short sleeves), while others want the attention that comes with decoration. Before choosing the latter, imagine explaining your ink about ten thousand times to decades of curious onlookers. On the flip side, with a touch of charm in your pocket, expect a bowlful of easy conversation starters with prospective mates and unabashed stroking of your inked extremities.

A second-glance discovery under rolled shirt cuffs is more furtively exciting than a center-stage Illustrated Man neck display. To engage in blatant exhibitionism for the sake of shock or entertainment value is not an example of unflappable confidence, though it might land you a freak-show job on Coney Island or earn you a bummed cig outside the punk club from a kohl-eyed lass. Similarly, ill-conceived and unimaginative art demonstrates a lack of depth on the body's sacred canvas. Avoid the terribly banal—trendy Chinese characters, the latticed bicep ring, lovers' names, and any styles found on top NBA rebounders—though perhaps celebrate irony with an inked Hervé Villechaize or the word "Innocence" marked on your inner thigh?

Before getting inked, seek out a recommendation from a satisfied customer and visit a tidy parlor to peruse the artist's entire portfolio. Look for bright, crisp, lasting colors and sharp, thin lines that evince a skilled pro worth the tariff. A session feels like a thousand stabbing needles, but the pain hopefully settles into a bearable backdrop. A prelude Pabst might take the edge off (though reputable parlors won't mark an intoxicated patron), and Tylenol eases the dull prickly pain without affecting blood clotting. Afterward, follow the care instructions and appreciate the impermanent permanence.

HAIR, HYGIENE, & HABITS

[brush]

[shaving soap]

[cup]

Like that biannual visit to the dentist, perform a crown-to-sole inspection of your appearance. Once the thirties have sprung, contemplate modern issues in hygiene and habits concerning exfoliation, cavities, regularity, and squamous cell carcinoma. A gentleman's outward presentation starts with management at the bathroom sink.

HAIR

Long hair will make thee look dreadfully to thine enemies, and manly to thy friends:
it is, in peace, an ornament; in war, a strong helmet; it . . .
deadens the leaden thump of a bullet: in winter, it is a warm nightcap;
in summer, a cooling fan of feathers.

—THOMAS DEKKER, *The Gulls Hornbook,* **1609**

This is not an employee handbook: your coiffure can venture past
the shoulders, swoop into your eyes, or even depart completely via
electric shears; regardless, be wary of chain-store salons run by
beauty-school dropouts. When the follicles are in serious retreat,
shave your noggin and step into grooming minimalism. The hopelessly Caucasian have two choices: remain clean shaven and resemble
a very large infant or grow facial hair to balance out the chrome
dome and add a touch of apparent ferocity that improves business
negotiation and damsel protection skills. Expect the odd request
to rub your bald pate, which, like a ball python's skin, is surpris-
ingly smooth. The clean look is especially chiseled when you're tall,
well-dressed, and in shape, otherwise you're channeling less Andre
Agassi and more novelty heavyweight Butterbean.

Facial Hair

In 1972, slugger Reggie Jackson arrived at spring training for the
Oakland A's with a fat stache, breaking the clean-shaven ethic of
baseball. The team won a World Series with several furry-lipped
stars, featuring Catfish Hunter's cookie-duster and Rollie Fingers's
sleek handlebar. Forty years on, facial hair is the most purposeful
ornamentation, usually grown out of laziness, a misguided attempt
to hide a fat face, or shame (think postelection Al Gore circal 2001).
The majority of women fancy ear lobe—length sideburns or modest facial adornments, though if your main squeeze repeatedly asks

others' opinion of your vaunted "vacation" beard, that's a quiet way of saying, "I hate it. Please back me up."

A chin souvenir prefaces a man's proclivities and style. A plain moustache will generally be associated with careers in the trades, construction, police work, and professional wrestling. A thicker one suggests aptitude with an axe or the wild idea that "Burt Reynolds's star turn was never better than in *Sharky's Machine*." A full beard is often a curious stopover from the smooth chin life and is hastily removed at the first itchy, humid day. Anything wilder suggests a creative sort, a freelancer, or a hard-lucker without enough scratch for new blades.

Hirsute points along the mustachioed continuum:

- **Handlebar Moustache:** Meticulous academic; part-time surrealist; craft bartender.

- **Pencil-Thin Moustache:** Emits a John Waters–esque, charmingly pervy air (which most can't pull off). Wrap it around the chin for the old hip-hop look.

- **Sculpted Sideburns:** The most nondescript way to evince nonconformity ("You must know I'm way cooler than my button-down work outfit").

- **Mutton Chops:** Rocker/biker/roadie/Shaft/ironic hipster. Laughable on the nebbishy set.

- **Goatee/Van Dyke:** Long the 1990s generic coverall for weak chins and Rogaine rejects, it has been replaced with the innocent soul patch or a thatch of undifferentiated chin music signaling a hint of shaggy rebellion.

- **Chin Curtain:** Civil War reenactor, Amish, family bible on bookshelf, speaks of "redemption" with utter seriousness.

- **Full Beard**: A full beard adds years, but trimmed stylings offer avenues for youthful exuberance. A mottled nest denotes Steppenwolf rockers, fixie and lamplighter bike enthusiasts, homebrewers, or Jesus, post-Galilee.

Decisions, decisions. How does a gent portray an unshaven artistic verve and still arrive at the office looking as professional as God? Once in the department's good graces, hair can creep here and there as long as your work attire measures out in the top 15 percent of your firm. Slyly, a trusted employee might return from a two-week vacation with a hairy setup that almost appears preordained.

Whiskering
Who needs to shave but thrice weekly? Purchase a quality touch-up electric razor and buzz right after a proper razored shave, and then again that same evening. Barring those cavemen who seem to sweat stubble, a gent will remain appropriate on odd days, leaving extra time in the morning to scan the paper or realign the sock drawer. If you dare, venture into the straight razor. Paired with a mug-'n'-brush set, leather strop, styptic stick, and a Med-Alert bracelet, this well-honed steel cuts so close that you won't get five o'clock shadow until next Tuesday. In unpracticed hands, it's also capable of Chinslaughter in the First Degree.

Nice touch: During engagement, full-bearded grooms-to-be ought to shave it off as a gesture of disclosure to the curious fiancée.

Secondary Fur
Trim neck hair with clippers or a disposable razor. Wandering unibrows must be plucked until the follicles wear out (shaving actually encourages growth). Like prescription antidepressants, tweezers

will be in your medicine cabinet for a long time, so purchase a precise instrument, not a bargain model. A copse of chest hair should be hacked back monthly to a manageable length, especially around the aureole and navel regions. Similarly, snip underarm overgrowth as it begins to peek out the sides.

Tertiary Down
Don't ignore it, especially during the warmer seasons and most active periods of libidinous exchange. Much like a lady's flowerbed, a gentleman's boscage should be pruned monthly. A light trim around the edges will usually do, but one is free to express any latent creativity in manner and pattern. Whether you prefer the natural or sculpted look, one shouldn't go Brazilian or Xoloitzcuintli and play on a completely bare surface or rub in foamy mousses around the lower latitudes.

EXTREMITIES

Are your soles and palms unsightly, cracked bricks in need of a pumice stone or callus remover? Avoiding this is no small feat during harsh winters and sweaty sandal season. Biweekly clipping, filing, and general care of toes and fingers is sufficient for most men. For those whose career or social habits require meticulous presentation, treat yourself to regular manicures and/or pedicures. Powder up with talc in the summer to ease humid cling; look for it at department stores or haberdasheries, not on the drugstore shelf next to medicated foot sprays. Though a slap of scented baby powder offers a quick fix for a ripe gent running out half-asleep for brunch. As for ears, cotton swabs were designed for make-up removal, not daily drilling of the delicate auditory canal.

CLYSTERING

Ah, the internal cleanse. Similar to clearing gutters at signs of the first robin or a good neti pot session, spa enemas are a great adjunct to spring cleaning. There's nothing awkward about a gentleman in a comfortable room, covered in a sheet, experiencing the healthful effects of a high colonic. After a brief enem-etiquette tutorial on the ins and outs, you are left in a private chamber upon a special table with control of water pressure and temperature. Like a hygien-ist probing your tartar-flecked teeth, the attendant should be trusted to regard your dignity in this vulnerable moment. A home enema is a milder, less intrusive Roto-Rooter for detoxifying after bouts of drink, junk food, or the in-laws.

COMPLEXION

Crow's feet, age spots, and sagging features are successfully post-poned for a few more birthdays with studious application of sun-screen and postshower moisturizer (and hopefully no more zit cream). Wrinkles might be dignified on a salt-and-peppered gentle-man, but saddlebags under the eyes and elephant skin around the joints look more neglectful than distinguished. Yearly, gift yourself with a day of beauty that a lady would envy. A body wrap, cleansing facial, and deep massage are more restorative than a cigarette after sex. No matter how much lumber you cut, keep hands soft for prac-ticing basic sensual massage techniques on a ready lover.

BRONZING

Compliments of Apollo, sunshine is a gift to melanin fiends and photosynthetic flora. For your own freckled hide, purchase sun-screen at SPF levels at least triple the middle-school grades and select products according to protection and waterproof durability first, pleasing coconut scent second. Dark tanning oils with near-zero protection are for vain ozone disbelievers and rump roasts cooked to well done. During sunscreen application, don't neglect forgotten corners of the forehead, collarbone, feet, and earlobes. Left to the elements, the neck will wither into an unsightly, corrugated "rooster neck" before age forty.

The all-weather, all-season, steel-belted-radial tan is overkill. If you want a little color in your wheyfaced cheeks during barren winter months, place the flush-inducing *Secretary* or *Belle du Jour* in your Netflix queue. If a wintertime business boondoggle calls to warmer climes, soak in the rays like a hungry hippo lazing at the wading pond.

Tanning salons, or "sun centers," are for the hopeless, heliocentric sort. If you require extra Vitamin D, drink milk; if you favor UV lighting, step into a stoner's closet. Though melanoma is sidestepped, many sunless tanning creams and commercial spray tanning booths produce an irradiated orange glow that's acceptable only if Syracuse should make the Final Four.

ORAL FIXATIONS

Gum is a once-in-a-while treat that makes an appearance when the gentleman is sour-mouthed and out and about. No exploding gum "Chewels," juicy "Freshen Up" squares, or gum tape. Likewise, no Big League Chew unless you are DH'ing in a Saturday stickball game. Chiclets are for senior citizens, and Pop Rocks are dangerous killers. Don't be caught eating Chuckles. It's not funny.

Black licorice is an acquired taste akin to anisette. Go natural and savor the herbal flavor with a seasoned, mature tongue. Swizzle the occasional red Twizzler, especially as a straw to slurp up an ice cream soda.

COTTON CANDY

Hearken back to Sundays at the state fair. Even if your prized sow, Petunia, didn't win best shank, there was always cotton candy. Unless trailing a favorite niece, mind the following tenets:

- Cotton candy has two recognized hues: white and pink, not Smurfette blue or Grape Ape mauve.
- Like the Benihana shrimp special, the good stuff is produced boothside. Get it from the spinner, collected on a white, conical stick.
- Cotton candy is not attic insulation—steer clear of the prepackaged, plastic-wrapped swag that is injected with enough preservatives to cure the meat of an eight-point buck.

The volatile mixture of too much fantasy and not enough play leads to bad pickup lines and nervous habits. Shy away from the person who always sucks mints or hands out Certs like religious leaflets on the subway (listen for the telltale Altoid shake). Beware these Freudian tics, indicating stunted oral-stage development or a miserable month on the dating calendar: persistent ice cruncher, pen-cap mangler, pencil biter, label peeler, nervous belt aligner, Styrofoam-cup teaser, phone tapper, swizzle-stick mutilator, cocktail-napkin baler, earring twirler, macho triceps massager, or maniacal ball shifter/pocket-pool player.

Incidentally, honor thy orthodontia. Straight white teeth are the gentleman's best accessories. Floss, gurgle, and brush so you don't piss away years of braces, headgear, and pink retainers.

LOLLIPOP

• • • • • • Green Chartreuse • Cointreau • Kirsch • Dash maraschino • • • • • •

DOMESTICITY

DOMESTIC POLICY

A gentleman's living quarters bespeak a well-landscaped personality. A soulless home lacks framed photographs and a dictionary for looking up tough crossword clues. The archetypical bachelor—with only an old can of Schaefer, a half-empty bottle of relish, and an onion in the crisper—has fallen out of vogue. Modern touches, art on the walls, select vices, and flourishing flora affirm vitality.

Outfit your space properly. If you are using a butter knife in place of a flathead screwdriver, invest in a small toolbox or designate a kitchen drawer. Candles—unscented and in holders—are vital mood setters and furnish soft ambiance. A candy dish filled with European mints and ginger chews fills out the living room, but skip the bowls of starlight mints, caramel squares, or butterscotches—save these bundles of sunshine for your grandmother's high-rise apartment.

THE STRONGBOX

So you've accrued the requisite credits and think you're ready to matriculate? Are you actually prepared to relocate your valuable documents from an under-the-bed shoebox to something more substantial? Enter the strongbox, that fire-proof alloyed container built to shelter one's dearest effects. Small, chic, and portable, the strongbox securely houses the family's cherished costume jewelry without the bother of a behind-the-painting wall safe. To qualify for a strongbox, the gentleman must be a policyholder insured for more than his auto, or he must have executed a will. Once you've met these basic requirements, toss in passports, love letters, sensitive media, paraphernalia, and anything you want to flee the house with during the next hundred-year storm.

THE KITCHEN

Be your own health inspector. Dish sponges shouldn't be emissaries of germs consigned to double duty: nominate one for the sink, another for counter tasks, and microwave them periodically to disinfect. Stow a fire extinguisher for flambé gone awry and marital flare-ups. Go Southern: pick up the versatile cast-iron skillet and learn to season and care for it. Those with perfect parade lines of copper cookware should be culinarily proficient, able to pronounce demi-glace and whip up spinach *crespelle* in a jiff. If you cannot produce even a bachelor-fridge 4 a.m. scramble for a booze-flushed bedfellow, you are hopeless. However, city dwellers are forgiven when the quick tap of an iPhone delivers bountiful goodies to the door at any hour.

A stocked refrigerator exudes balance, good health, and self-sufficiency. Like Bronson's Mr. Majestyk, fight for your watermelon and other produce. If you find that you have vastly more boxed or canned food than fresh vegetables, post an ad for roommates with rolling pins. TV dinner nostalgia aside, never be caught with more than one prefab selection in the freezer. As far as Lean Cuisine goes, if nutrition and caloric intake are at issue, wheel on over to the produce section. Rotate the perishable stock and reserve eye-level storage for daily comestibles. You shouldn't have to move the capers to get to the cranberry juice. Keep a jar of unsweetened applesauce chilling in the back of the icebox for near-death hangover experiences in which the colossal pain makes you realize, rather sullenly, that last night's revelry inflicted irreversible biotic damage.

Incidentally, do not hoard take-out condiments. Moreover, electric can openers are for the meek, who shall not inherit the hearth.

DISHWASHING

The anal-retentive sock drawer is arranged by color and rayon content, yet the dishwasher remains an open forum of expression. No worries, you can safely desegregate knives and spoons to commingle in the utensil compartment. On occasion, even a glass from the top shelf can elope with a wayward mug to the lower dish level. Still, there are some rules to observe. Silver plates, wooden spoons, and sex toys are not top-shelf dishwasher safe; wash these delicates by hand (in a liberal household, the last can be aired in the drying rack). And take it from Tesauro: use phosphate-free products, toss in a rinsing agent for extra-gleaming glasses, and never substitute sink-top liquid dish soap for dishwasher detergent lest you have a foam party on the floor worse than any syndicated "zany" 1970s family sitcom.

VITTLES

[steam]

[toasted rye]

[lever]

How is it that some men can replace spark plugs, decipher schematics, and fiddle with circuit breakers, but can't follow a recipe? If you've spent more time with *The Joy of Sex* than its tamer cousin, *The Joy of Cooking*, you might be intimidated by the prospect of folding an egg white or grappling with a double boiler. Enroll in a few cooking classes and master a menu of tasty recipes—but befriending off-duty chefs or rolling meatballs with Grandma are the part-time culinarian's surer path to proficiency. Don't sweat it if you cannot dress a leg of mutton. If you've got a generous hand with good olive oil and have traded Morton's for rare gourmet sea salts reputedly sourced from Lot's wife, all you need is cracked pepper and common sense to chow well at home.

Indeed, simple, delicious food—an herbed omelet, grilled fish, summer fruit salad—leaves no place to hide the flaws and works best with top ingredients. Take the BLT test. Whip out the lily-white bromated bread, smoke-injected bacon, and bland tomatoes atop iceberg leaves with whipped dressing . . . and taste failure. Assemble an all-star local line-up of fresh bread, thick-cut butcher shop bacon, garden tomatoes, local greens, and homemade aioli, and you've arrived. This same mind-set works for simple sides such as homemade hummus, guacamole, olive tapenade, sundried tomatoes, a quick-whisked vinaigrette, or well-orchestrated threesomes on a bed of satin.

Tastiness aside, don't allow your foodie credo to impinge on a fit frame. Gourmandizing on wine, olives, charcuterie, cheeses, and hearty breads will lead to not only foie gras apathy, but also a prosciutto gut that says well fed but not necessarily well bred.

Cooking entails more than broiled meat doused with prefab marinades. It's okay to cheat and buy bakery carrot cake, but create the entrée yourself. Log some range hours and develop a few signature dishes that can be whipped up to perfection without recipe cards. With enough butter, cream, and eggs, even amateurs can speciously impress; the real goal is to achieve tasteful weak-kneed decadence without the Alfredo death factor. Instead of drowning veggies in oil at the sauté station or deep-frying fish, feed your friends from the grill. When dining out, steal ideas for winning plate combos and quirky garnishes.

Incidentally, a dessert fruit salad is transformed by a splash of brandy or Triple Sec. Turn heavy cream and a splash of liqueur into a Class I fetish.

BREAKING BREAD

We will not linger on the basic table manners Mom reinforced by raps upon your knuckles with a spoon or spork. Instead, brush up with our bibliography and remember when setting the table that the fork goes to the left, the knife is turned to cut the plate from the right, and the spoon rests adjacent. A butter-flecked knife is not welcome in the jam, nor a wet spoon in the sugar bowl. Ask someone to pass the peperoncini rather than running the wine-stem gauntlet or beer-bottle slalom by reaching an outstretched arm across the table.

BREAKFAST AND LUNCH

It is not impolite to show appreciation for a fine bowl of Cocoa Puffs by raising it to your lips in sugary brown communion. Use the four-finger bowl hold with thumb-clasped spoon, instead of the double-handed, shivering, soup-kitchen sip. At home, a used knife may return to the warped butter log—loose toasticles are signs of comfort. Whilst breakfasting, note the waffle-square neurotic who meticulously drizzles equal syrup doses into each chamber. As an out-of-town guest, partake in available foodstuffs; only finicky ingrates disparage non–New York City bagels or non-Vermont maple syrup. Any meal can be taken in pyjamas, but only breakfast should be taken in pyjamas.

Sandwiches are instantly enlivened with a diagonal cut, a toothpick, and a green olive. Go beyond ham and Swiss with clever combinations that include green apple, Brie, grilled eggplant, avocado, hummus, sprouts, or broccoli rabe and smoked mozzarella. Weather permitting, take a lunch in outdoor solace. For an occasional pick-me-up, treat yourself to a lime rickey or other old-fashioned fountain drink. Lastly, workday fast food promotes daytime productivity akin to that of a socialist state; if your recent lunch history can be plotted with McDonald's promotional game pieces, go healthier or consider a cabinet post in the Mayor McCheese administration.

QUAFFS

The predominant household quaff is filtered tap water, yet sometimes the weather calls for something tangier. To date, lemonade is still made from just water, sugar, lemon juice, and grated lemon peel (sprig of mint optional). As for hot tea, invest in a sturdy tea ball and loose teas by the pound; similarly, no self-respecting Southerner sips instant iced tea. Ideally, whip up a batch of sun-brewed tea and chill it over ice. A home juicer produces a bubbling, organic creation for twice-a-week health kicks and rocky Saturday mornings. Toxically speaking, Quik's artificial chocolaty goodness should not be discounted, especially when a heaping tablespoon of powder is dunked into milk and eaten like a muddy cookie.

Mass-market soft drinks are saccharine sludge, so join the carbonated renaissance. If you're not lucky enough to have a main street soda fountain shop or seltzer delivery man, stock up on regional pops and oddities: New England's Moxie cola; the Carolinas' Blenheim ginger ale and Cheerwine dark cherry cola, Brooklyn's Manhattan Special espresso soda, and Sioux City Sarsaparilla for hardened keglers and devotees of The Dude.

MILK

Whole milk is for coffee and babies, not for mass consumption. For those with crystal-wearing Woodstock moms, try soy or vanilla hemp milk. Two-percent milk, like an unregistered Democrat, demonstrates a distinct fear of commitment. If you are torn between the fatty, womblike goodness of moo juice and the blue-tinted, waterlogged taste of skim, consider 1 percent. Those few saved grams of fat may be traded in at the end of the month for an extra serving of duck confit or a Double Whopper with cheese.

FARMERS' MARKET

Tender pea shoots, spicy arugula, earthy morels, and creamy pawpaws: once a week, urban totebaggers gather to hunt and gather, gossip, and go local over a gourmet gallimaufry pulsing with local vitality, flavor, and respect for the land. At the farmers' market, expect a farm-to-table rendezvous point for purveyors who are delighted to talk about the provenance of everything from grassfed bison to linden honey to raw sauerkraut. Revel in the fleeting delights of the growing season and practice the Japanese art of *shun*, the knowledge of when a food is at its seasonal peak. Connecting to the edible earth around you doesn't require a vermiculture box in the bathroom or a total renunciation of ice cream sandwiches; though after munching on local pears and farm-fresh yogurt at breakfast, it's tough to return to the geometric representation of diabetes known as Pop-Tarts.

Whether it's a ramshackle roadside veggie stand or a multitented fairground, this hotspot gives "meat" market a new meaning. For singles looking beyond the bar scene, nothing says cool and healthy like trim gams and a canvas bag full of fiddlehead ferns, spring ramps, or winter crosnes. Plus, all those innocuous opening lines:

- "I see that parsnips are finally in season . . . how do you like to prepare them?"
- This is enough bok choy for two . . . we should practice conservation and make dinner together."

Now that you've watched *Food Inc.*, googled Alice Waters, feasted on Michael Pollan and Mark Bittman, and eschewed high-fructose corn syrup (except maybe the occasional Mounds bar), gravitate toward localism and fruit without PLU stickers. Whether motivated by carbon reduction, neighborhood economy, or increased probiotics and antioxidants, one should support local farms, eat less red meat, and steer toward the perimeter supermarket aisles away from the processed middle. Local and organic don't always equal ecologically perfect, and farmers' markets may be prohibitively expensive for lower-income gents, so save your elitist scowl for your former guidance counselor who sized you up for a fast-food apron instead of a corner office.

After stocking up at the market on Saturday, one might make a big dish that can last until midweek and munch on snacks and salads for the remainder of the week. All in all, a typical workweek might find a home-cooked meal two nights, dining out another two nights, and one night of take-out, leaving two other nights that depend on the social calendar and whether you've got a steady mate or a kegorator in the basement.

Incidentally, until your own modest garden plot sprouts a bounty, consider joining a CSA. Community Supported Agriculture establishes "shareholders" in farm production. In return for committing greenbacks prior to the growing season, members receive a weekly share of the greens. For steadies not yet living in sin, splitting a share is a way to keep close and field-test domesticity without actually signing a lease.

SHELL GAME

Viticulture is all about terroir, but oyster aquaculture is about merroir, or where in the water it's found. Recognize the mild rockiness of the cooler East Coast oysters like Wellfleet, Malpeque, or Bluepoint, or the earthier, sweeter West Coast varieties like Emerald Creek, Olympia, or Pearl Bay. Just as sashimi buffs are sparing with the soy sauce and wasabi, be light on the mignonette and ditch the bottled cocktail sauce.

- Deep-cupped bivalves indicate that they're from higher in the water column and typically less gritty than flat oysters harvested from the seabed.

- That oft-uttered dicta to eat oysters only during months with an "r" was apt in the age before serious refrigeration, yet know that oysters are a tad thinner and less flavorful during the May-to-August reproductive season.

- Opening oysters with nothing more than a short, blunt knife and an old dishtowel bolsters the oyster's aphrodisiacal qualities with raw bar machismo.

- When partying down in N'awlins, besides a crawfish boil, nothing fills an empty stomach better than a scrumptious oyster po'boy (fried oysters, spiced mayo, lettuce, tomato, on Louisiana French bread).

MAGI MOJO

Like a custom clothier, the butcher, the baker, and the fishmonger are three wise (wo)men who belong not far below Uncle Harry on your speed-dial. Befriend your neighborhood butcher and seek out the best grass-fed beef, roaming chickens bought whole (or rabbit, which is leaner, more interesting, and higher in protein), regional game, and housemade/cured bacon and charcuterie wrapped in white paper. "Best" meat, however, does not equal "choicest" cuts—rather, the ideal cut for the method. Burgers, for instance, are better from the fatty shoulder (aka butt) than the lean tenderloin. For braising, stick to cuts like brisket or flank; on the grill, the doubly flavorful skirt is half the price of New York strip, and the big, slow-cooking vacio makes a great party steak.

Whereas supermarkets stock up on the usual swimmers (tuna, salmon, bland talapia), reel in some Arctic char, bluefish, cobia, and escolar ("white tuna" on sushi menus). A fishmonger not only knows what's fresh off the hook but also keeps you informed about sustainable aquaculture and imperiled species, so that tonight's special isn't Endangered Bluefin Tuna Tacos. Experiment with roasted whole fish, too, which makes for a beautiful presentation and lets you bone up on your deboning skills. Lastly, don't sop up the juice of *moules frites* or make a Dagwood sandwich with some sad loaf jacked up with preservatives and bastardized flour. A weekly visit to your local baker is the greatest thing since sliced bread.

CITRUS MISTRESS

When the ROYGBIV spectrum has been shrunk to a dull gradient of grays, there's always one notion to brighten a brunch, salad, or cocktail . . . the blood orange. Sadly, just as verdant spring returns, the *Citrus sinensis* season runs out. Yet from December through March, engage in a juicy affair with blood oranges and other edible tropicalia. Counting food miles? A chilly man needs a zesty grapefruit, and it is rightly said that in the dead of winter, many an overzealous locavore dies of scurvy.

SACRED GROUNDS

Bloom, Fair Trade, latte art, microfoam . . . savoring coffee goes far beyond the delivery method of caffeine. Thanks for the percolated Folgers memories, but modern gents have secretly replaced commercial coffee with microroasters chock full o' passion. Even if Starbucks is the gateway for char-roasted jolt, it's not the Promised Land. The coffee cognoscenti ought to drink local and step away from the flavored syrups and ersatz Frappuccinos—those who "milk and three sugars" a cup of joe to a candied demise are not the people quality roasters stay up all night for. Craft batch roasters lay expert eyes on hand-sorted, triple-picked "cherries" or "berries" and liken the buying process to trading pork bellies on the commodities market.

At home, remember that percolators are for punks (and camp stoves); a coffee press or Chemex is as essential in the kitchen as a wooden spoon and spatula. Grab a cup from a Clover coffeemaker or Cona vacuum pot if you get the chance; these wonders brew up singular smoothness and unadulterated flavor. And if you can't swing that battleship-sized espresso machine, ask Santa for an illy caffé espresso machine for the countertop. For unfuzzy commuting, percolate your own workaday morning coffee and fill a stainless steel thermos.

Buy whole beans and grind fresh each time. Around-the-world tips: Ethiopia: aromatics; Central America: sweetness; Brazil or India: bitterness and body; Tanzania or Kenya: acidity; Asia: rich mouthfeel. Also note: arabica is the good stuff; robusta is inferior and often used for decaf (which Phineas declares can be sipped without reproach, iced or hot). Also, light roast = more caffeine, dark roast = less.

Incidentally, a gentleman skips instant coffee except when holed up in a country cabin or on an ice-fishing junket. Still, drink Sanka twice a year. You'll know when.

ESPRESSO 101

If a dry martini is the ideal expression of gin's character, espresso is such for coffee. Don't fear the demitasse—there's 40 percent less caffeine in a single espresso than in a 12-ounce mug of drip coffee. Surprise others with your preternatural Our Man Flint powers and discern a quality espresso by the pour. When the barista presses the button, count: five seconds until the first flow (faster/underextraction = weaker, slower/overextraction = more bitter). The whole process lasts twenty-five to thirty seconds and ought to produce a rich, nut-brown "crema" (a silky layer of tiny CO_2 bubbles) with a mottled, reddish "tiger skin." Bypass the silly lemon peel, as it's a remnant from the bitter days of bad coffee, and turn in your gentleman badge and ascot immediately after sullying an immaculate espresso with a sprinkling of artificial sweetener.

Nice touch: Cappuccino, so named because it matched the coffee-colored cloaks of the Capuchin Order of monks, is solely an a.m. quaff (though, if on the pivotal "Casanova or Bust" romantic third date, save your know-it-all caffeinated tutorial for the morning). When it's time, though, put that steam wand to use for home entertaining. Like knowing one quality card trick, two guitar chords, and the three jewels of The Tao, a single perfected pattern of latté art (such as the rosetta leaf) is always impressive.

AFTER-SUPPER COCKTAIL
• • • • • • • • • • • **Apricot brandy • Curaçao • Lemon juice** • • • • • • • • • •

SINGLE SPACE

Your bed is a sacred place that projects strength, style, and intimacy. Avoid a cavelike retreat of dim and dingy repose by investing in down pillows, high-thread-count sheets, and a handsome duvet. Odysseus and Penelope had the most historically significant bed, featuring an olive tree as one of its posts. For those residing outside Ithaca, a lush bedside plant should suffice. A framed mattress and box-spring set is standard; the minimalist's futon rests on the floor, as long as it's not the bleak centerpiece of an ultramodern blank-walled mise-en-scène. A wrought-iron or basic, nonsqueaking bed set with a headboard does nicely for the bachelor, poster beds for the monogamous.

YOU (HAVEN'T) MADE YOUR BED

Phineas finds daily bed making time-consuming, unhealthful, and reminiscent of some conservative, call-your-dad-"sir" household. Meanwhile, Tesauro knows how to bolster pillows, fold a fitted sheet, and delight in the nap-tempting allure of straightened bedclothes. Both find the mitered military tuck and constricting hotel cocoon quite unacceptable.

Certain accoutrements reside near the gentleman's bed. Within arm's reach: fire, water, candles, and the makings of mild bedside activities and orated poetry. A house vibrator soaking in blue Barbicide on the nightstand is too colorful; massage oils, condoms, and other instruments of vice are housed discreetly within an adjacent drawer or box. For smoothness, check remote-control angles to ensure the stereo can be operated horizontally from the bed and that your hi-fi setup is wireless or else shrouds an unsightly nest of twisted coaxial cables. For the nightstand library, Gideon's Bible may be filled with miraculous bedtime stories, but isn't the Bhagavad Gita more enlightening?

What about the rest of the room? Original artwork, personal photos, and black-and-white prints show you're not a week-to-week lessee. Garnish corners, empty spaces, and windowsills with cacti, pottery, or heartifact curiosities. Mood lighting is a must: be eclectic but subtle. Save dreamy lava lamps and glaring neon signage for cookie-cutter cocktail lounges. A full-length mirror reflects the fashionable gentleman, though feng shui might dictate a different location lest spirits within disturb your sleep. Recycle any rusting Chock Full o' Nuts coffee cans and procure a vintage candy dish for loose change and miscellany.

Localize clothing clutter to one armchair near the closet. Mimic four-star inns and keep a steady supply of after-tubbing towels plush enough to soak up Noah's deluge. The room should look lived in but not camped in. Leftover snacks and empty glassware call for a kitchen bus tub. Motivational plaques urging perseverance received from misguided family members rest comfortably in closeted mildew, next to Cub Scout merit badges. Likewise:

- No telltale lotions near the bed unless you have a serious skin condition, like leprosy.

- Aside from an absinthe-drunken whim, no gypsy-beaded doorways to your "den of love."

- Do not "accidentally" leave financial statements or stock reports on your bureau. Secure confidential and sensitive materials out of plain view.

- No collegiate sporting equipment (baseball spikes, lacrosse gloves) displayed in the corner to dupe unsuspecting visitors about your former athletic prowess.

- The gentleman's room shall contain no "furniture" that could be used to ship Vitamin D milk or start a retaining wall. No more than one "expensive looking" particleboard bookshelf or rattan end table shoddy enough to be splintered by a white-belt's karate chop.

HEARTIFACTS

Everyone from the noble landowner to the train-hopping hobo carries a few near and dear mementos in the personal bindle. Life is a collection of memorable events, but what's a gentleman to do with this heap of romantic ephemera and other folderol? If any keepsakes have made the cut of a multiapartment shuffle or vigorous spring cleaning, perhaps they are worthy of classification in the gentleman's archive. How does a gentleman determine the real value of long-held odds and ends? Put your mementos up against the following criteria, and then plot them on the graph to see whether they end up in the display case or recycling bin.

MEANINGFULNESS

Is the object directly related to the event or is it a secondary prop? Milestone objects that signify growth and development merit consideration—letters from first flames, diplomas, and keys to your first house.

Tone of Experience: Tokens may harken back to simple events with strong reverberations: for example, the room-service bill from a long-ago weekend getaway.

UNIQUENESS

Sometimes nonmeaningful objects are worth saving for their originality. For instance, a friend behind the Iron Curtain sent a bottle of Georgian vodka. Drink the booze, keep the label.

Collective Association: Particular objects quantify aggregate events. An engagement ring symbolizes not the night of proposal, but the entire courtship; a fraternity sweater, the entire hedonic four years.

FAMILIARITY

Regardless of meaning or uniqueness, certain items latch onto you unnoticed, from dorm to apartment to the home junk drawer.

Obligation: Some ornamentals are devoid of meaning and actual retail value, yet still garner a corner in the utility closet behind the ironing board. These knickknacks are usually leftover Chanukah gifts, wedding presents, or hand-me-down family gimcracks kept out of politeness.

ARC OF ARCHIVABILITY

The Arc of Archivability sets a threshold of worthiness to justify retaining mementos. To avoid the bin, an object must surpass it on at least one of the three axes. For a passing grade:

- An object must be at least as meaningful as . . . a good first date or a farewell token from an ex-coworker.

- An object must be at least as unique as . . . a commemorative cup.

- An object must be at least as familiar as . . . something you use monthly.

THE VALUE VECTORS

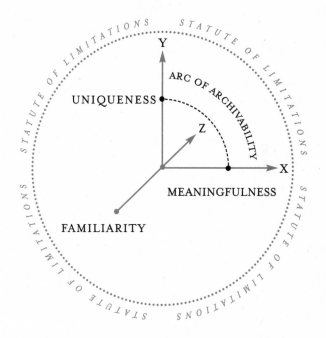

Heartifacts must be plotted on three axes before they
are allotted shelf space in the den.

X-axis . . . How meaningful?   ◆   Y-axis . . . How unique?
Z-axis . . . How familiar?

CLUTTER

Even if you live in a stately manor, practice a small apartment mind-set to curb the agglomeration of mass-produced gewgaw. Eliminate LPOs (large plastic objects), dusty small appliances (sayonara, rice cooker and ice cream maker), unessential serving platters, and those free-form piles of arcana that seem to propagate like wind-driven spores. In the future, avoid home emporia superstores that peddle eye-catching schlock; these middle-class lickpennies can drain the wallet faster than ten minutes in a buddy booth in Chelsea. Spend your moolah on noncluttering goods like quality media, travel, a friend's happiness, and disposable pleasures like wine, dark chocolate, and novelty phallus-shaped gummi bears (for her). Down to the comfortable essentials (that is, minimalism + 2), revel in sunlit, airy rooms unstuffed by forgettable objects and embrace an anticonsumerist weltanschauung that's easier on the psyche and the planet.

A quarterly digital housecleaning is as satisfying as detailing the roadster: denude the desktop of worthless icons; defrag the hard drive and empty the recycle bin; delete long-dormant phone contacts and vagrant emails loafing around the inbox and create new folders for increased organization; and toss redundant backups, now that your data is on an external device or in the cloud.

STATUTE OF LIMITATIONS

The Statute of Limitations is a function of decreased value over time. It surrounds the entire graph because even the most meaningful, unique, or familiar keepsakes ultimately fall prey to decades of growth and change. Your first-place summer-camp equestrian ribbon had importance, but it faded with dust mites and adolescent neglect. Though objects of the highest meaning or uniqueness transcend this statute: antique family heirlooms, ancient love letters, and the Magna Carta.

To illustrate:

- A sibling mails a touching poem written on a napkin. The uniqueness of a napkin is nil, and the item is not yet familiar, but the meaningfulness rates high on the Arc of Archivability.

- One manual can opener has shepherded you since your twenties. During a decluttering clean, you consider tossing it. Upon deep reflection, it returns to the drawer for another ten-year stint of opening canned yellow cling peaches in heavy syrup. The meaningfulness is questionable and there is nothing unique, yet the item passes the Arc on merits of familiarity.

- Your ex-roommate scoops up a bagful of infield dirt from Fenway Park and ships it to you on a whim. If you dislike baseball, the meaning is low, but the uniqueness makes this gift worthy of a discount urn.

- You come across an old store-bought holiday card from an adjacent cubicle-mate. Keep it? The item is unoriginal, lacks profound meaning, and isn't a familiar fixture. Toss it.

- Rummaging through the attic, you stumble upon a junior prom commemorative Champagne glass from which you once sipped Champale with Mindi. Years ago, the flute was especially meaningful and the screen-printed glass seemed unique. Now Mindi's married and so are you. Pour Natty Boh brew in the glass, take a last swig, and toss it into the fireplace . . . the Statute of Limitations has run on this item.

TOILETIQUETTE

Let's to the washroom. Do not disrupt the dignity of sparkling porcelain by behaving like an ogre in the bathroom. We provide a lavatorial primer, from hand towels and soaps to nomenclature, for both home and on the road.

MAINTENANCE

Neaten the restroom. Purchase only quality toilet tissue, and don't store bare spares on the windowsill. Blue toilet bowl inserts are unthinkable, unless you're operating an airplane lavatory. If the bathtub is ringed and clogged with filth and fallen hair, it has been too long since your last languid soak. Keep glass cleaner in the bathroom cabinet for cleanup in a jiff when unexpected guests or romantic interests stop by. Be the first to hit the bathroom to spray the smudges off the mirror, whiskers off the sink, and dried crud off the bowl.

Incidentally, be conversant in flush-mechanism repair and light uncloggings. Know when to plunge, jiggle the chain, manipulate the ball cock, or walk away and call the plumber.

FOUR FLUSH

· · · · · · Rum · Swedish Punsch (or spiced rum) · Sweet vermouth · · · · · · ·

· · · · · · · · · · · Dash grenadine (or simple syrup) · · · · · · · · · · ·

HAND TOWELS & SOAPS

Bathroom towels come in two varieties: functional and ornamental. Workhorse cotton models are for regular use. Ornamental towels—often found well hung on a brass rack, with frilly lace or holiday patterns—are for admiring, not manhandling like a dishrag. However, at times the only hand towels available are worth more than your monogrammed gingham broadcloth shirt. Faced with this emergency, delicately pat your hands dry on the backside to preserve the neatly folded façade.

Similar rules apply to dainty European soap leaves, papers, and soaps carved like angels or flowers. Despite your faith, don't befoul a decorative toilet-top nativity scene. If no other cleansers abound, give the angel's wing a light swipe for minimum melt.

DECIBELS

Little has been written on water-closet etiquette, leaving the gentleman to cope with such unnerving beasts as the off-the-living-room head or the dreaded everyone-can-hear-what-you're-doing-in-there half-bath. For rare times when decreased volume is desired, rim aim is vital. Further dilute decibels with wads of tissue or sit down to shush a tinkle's tintinnabulation. With more serious matters, make sure the fan is whirring, otherwise trickle the faucet for wet white noise when outsiders are in close proximity.

Nice touch: Infrequently enjoy the freedom of al fresco toiletiquette, especially when taken hands-free in the countryside or between the slats of a beach house deck railing.

NAMING IT

A gentleman's broad vocabulary makes it unnecessary to invoke vulgar language when announcing a trip to the donicker. Must it be announced at all? A simple "Won't you excuse me" is rarely rude. Words such as "potty," "loaf" and "little wrangler's room" are no better than "crapper" or "throne," and certainly no one cares that you "have to urinate" or "do number two." When asking for directions, stick to innocuous phrases: "Gentleman's room, please" or "Where may I wash up?"

THE HOT SEAT

Elimination at the inopportune moment is execrable. Scenario: you have stopped at a lover's house to meet the parents and have refreshments before dinner. Suddenly, you feel a tremor. What is the proper course of action? For pressing engagements, go; this is not fourth grade anymore. Yet, if there is wiggle room, a grave decision awaits you, much like Kennedy, Khrushchev, and the Cuban missile crisis. Provided your business can be resolved expeditiously, quicker than an ATM "Fast Cash" withdrawal, proceed. The clock is ticking, however. If you sense an unpleasant, difficult half-hour logjam, grit and tighten up (like Archie Bell & the Drells).

In accordance with matched consideration, do not sit down unabashedly on a new lover's toilet until you have experienced this person in a congruent state of informality. Breaches of privacy force your partner to cross bridges of intimacy prematurely. Tinkle manners are generally more relaxed; the bathroom door starts out tightly latched but progresses to slightly cracked then utterly ajar as relations familiarize over time.

A word on the medicine chest. Avoid burrowing about the pharmacopoeia of another. Curious cats who can't resist a peer into an unlocked vault of vulnerabilities should at least avert eyes from prescription medication. Preserve privacy and enjoy the mystery—what's wrong with a little psychopathology these days?

Incidentally, at an intimate gathering, if the user before you (or you) befouls the toilet rim, don't walk out without first offering a swipe with paper. Otherwise, you will be labeled a foul sprayer, a piss-creant for the ages, because these are the types of things couples talk about after everyone leaves the party.

SPITTING, HICCOUGHING, & OTHER EXPULSIONS

Spitting is sometimes necessary, perhaps for watermelon seeds or the jettison of medical nuisances. Nonetheless, this act need not be accompanied by a nasal-cleansing hack that echoes about the Alps, unnerving poor Heidi and countless mountain goats.

Do not try to squelch a sneeze and emit a short, girlish squeak. Emissions happen; forget your guilty religious upbringing. Use a closed fist or assume the Dracula sneeze pose to temper germ transmission. If tickles persist, simply leave the room; if coughs continue, go in for a lung biopsy.

HICCOUGHS

Be vigilant and don't make the record books. Charles Osbourne began hiccoughing in 1922 and didn't stop until 1990, dying a year later. Hold your breath, have a drink of water, and cure hiccoughs quickly. For yogis and the mentally limber, practice mind-over-body control to end spasms. Otherwise, head for the bench away from the action. Those unlucky souls with cartoonish, crescendoing reports should expect good-natured ribbing and name-calling.

Incidentally, for humor's sake, collect a few hiccough-curing old wives' tales—tongue pulling, sugar swallowing, lemon biting, tummy rubbing, or brown bag hyperventilating—as desperate people will agree to do anything when afflicted. If at the cinema, suggest the hiccougher overstuff his mouth with buttery popcorn until breathing is labored and then insert one Milk Dud for good measure. While this procedure may prove ineffective, it is delicious.

GASEOUS EMISSIONS

Flatulence should generally be ignored. Don't accentuate the effect with "whoops" or wild exclamations, unless humor of the moment dictates. Always attempt to blame any odor on a hapless pet, nearby restaurant dumpster, or faulty catalytic converter. Note that it is acceptable for auto passengers to dispel spirits by efficiently rolling down the window and just as quickly rolling it back up. Lastly, in mixed company never adjust body posture more than ten degrees to accommodate dispersion.

VOMITUS

Most of your technique was likely perfected in college, along with a well-honed Spidey-sense auguring its onset. For an adult, expelling is a truly rare event. As a guest, have the decency not to unload on white carpets, fluffy bath mats, or sleeping pets. To prevent supreme embarrassment during formal, open bar events, maintain a full belly or temper intake after the first restroom break, as there is nothing so hapless as a lush spewing in a tuxedo. In public, exorcise amidst shrubbery or in the shadows between two parked cars. When a morning after in the cubicle takes a turn, use the hallway slop sink/mop closet for ultimate privacy.

part three

The
POTENT
GENTLEMAN

So? Who's in a hurry?
—ROBERT BENCHLEY, when told that drinking
and smoking are "slow poison"

Chapter Seven

VENERABLE VICES:
ALCOHOL, TOBACCO, & FIREWORKS

SPIRITS

The true inability to drive safely or complete a sentence is impolite, but the appreciation of liquors off the usual depth chart is rather gentlemanly. Most college graduates matriculated with a major in malted barley studies and a minor in Russian appreciation. There is no reason to stop slurping vodka or knocking back craft brews, but the blooming palate and keen mind mandate an extended tour through the higher spirits. Know the proper time for an afternoon Lillet, between-the-acts Armagnac, dessert Porto, or late-evening Madeira.

The following is a short list of underexplored, remarkable favorites and the easiest ways to indulge in them. For home-bar enthusiasts, these spirits are remarkable favorites that keep your decanters brimming. Put your flask to task, guided by the noted portability factors, from zero to five stars. Percentages refer to alcohol by volume (A.B.V.).

CHARTREUSE (YELLOW OR GREEN)

Unlike the Colonel's 11, Chartreuse is distilled by Carthusian monks with 130 herbs and spices. In 1605, François Hannibal d'Estrées bequeathed to the Carthusian elders an ancient manuscript entitled "The Elixir of Long Life." Brother Maubec undertook the task of deciphering the complexities but died before finishing. On his deathbed, he disclosed all secrets to Brother Antoine, who finished the translation in 1737. During the French Revolution in 1789, the monks fled the monastery with the manuscript and the secret formula. Napoleon's henchmen, the Secret Remedies Commission, captured the document but rejected the recipe as too complex. Besides Waterloo, this was Napoleon's silliest mistake. Only three monks from this silent order know the secret formula.

At 55 percent, the beguiling green Chartreuse is minty, spicy, intensely aromatic, and gets its distinctive color from chlorophyll. In 1838, yellow Chartreuse was produced; its color is derived from saffron. This milder Chartreuse, at 40 percent, is sweeter, lighter, honeyed, and more viscous. Vieillissement Exceptionnellement Prolongé (V.E.P.) is an extra-aged version of green or yellow Chartreuse and is the most mesmerizing liquor these authors know. Drink it with nothing but rocks. And although unavailable in the United States, the Élixir Végétal is a 71-percent ABV medicinal worth tucking deep within your luggage upon return from overseas as a cure for jet lag.

For the uninitiated, sample either yellow or green Chartreuse over ice with or without soda, perhaps with a dose of cranberry. Next, move to the Alaska: yellow, gin, dry vermouth, and bitters, with a touch of soda and a cherry. The Bijou is a cool-weather classic: green, gin, sweet vermouth, bitters, and a cherry (and some juice), with a twist.

Flask factor ★ for Green, ★★ for Yellow, ★★★ for V.E.P.

RHUM AGRICOLE

Most rums are made from molasses, a dark, gooey by-product of industrial sugar production and quite delicious on biscuits. French Caribbean rhum agricole is made from freshly squeezed sugar cane juice (think first-press extra virgin olive oil). The best dark or amber rums get their color from barrel aging. However, if a mass-produced rum is very dark, caramel color was likely added. Rhum agricoles don't beg for the cover of cola; they are bright and shiny, with inviting caneyness, florals, and fruitiness. Younger rums are best mixed with juice, carbonated beverages, or a slice of lime; aged rums should be taken like whisky.

Flask factor ★★, needs a chill.

SINGLE-MALT SCOTCH

Go beyond Dad's Chivas. Single-malt Scotch is so named because it's the product of a single distillery. Malted barley used for single-malt Scotch is double distilled and not blended or vatted with other whisky. (Blended whiskies are typically the product of several single-malts from different distilleries assembled into a smoother, lighter blend.) The Highland peaks supply much of the water—the coveted lifeblood of Scotch that wends over granite, peat moss, and heather. There are five notable Scotch-producing regions: Speyside (home to over half of the country's whisky distilleries), Highlands (balanced, firm, dry), Campbeltown (full-bodied, peaty), Islay (pronounced "EYE-luh;" heavy peat, powerful), and Lowland (light in color and flavor).

All Scotches are made from sprouted barley dried in kilns fired by peat and coal, which infuses the whisky with smoky characteristics. Color comes from wood aging. Most casks are retired bourbon barrels; others are leftover from sherry and Madeira houses.

A few stylish examples: the Glenrothes Select Reserve (Speyside—nicely balanced fruit, vanilla, heat, mild smoky factor); Highland Park 12 (Highland—malty, heathery, understated smokiness; exceptionally smooth); Auchentoshan 10 (Lowlands—light and zesty, with lemongrass and vanilla); Springbank 15 (Campbeltown—salty, dry, malt-rich, and complex).

Single-malt demands to be drunk neat or with a diluting splash of water, but one ice cube is fine. For Scotch and soda, stick to blends.

Flask factor ★★, ★★★ *if you bring a second flask for branch water.*

ARMAGNAC

Cognac's tawdry older sister from southwest France, this full-flavored brandy dates back to fifteenth-century Pays d'Gascogne (Gascony). Many of its producers are still rural artisans, not behemoth corporations. Made from a blend of distilled grapes, Armagnac is continuously stilled and aged in black oak, a method that yields a more rustic character than does the pot-still process responsible for Cognac's smooth richness. Armagnac is more intense, with jagged flavors of chocolate, wood, and fruit. Since caramel isn't added, Armagnac is paler than Cognac. Look for quality and age demarcations: "V.S." (very special), "V.S.O.P." (very special old pale), "X.O." (extra old, over six years). Enjoy it at home with a cigar.

Flask factor ★★, *pricey and meant for glass, not metal.*

CALVADOS

Too cold to grow grapes, Normandy's Pays D'Auge is not a land of applesauce, but the home of Calvados, a prized apple brandy. Quality is denoted according to oak aging. On the label, "Réserve" indicates three years, "Vieille Réserve" or "V.S.O.P." is four years, and "Hors d'Age" is six years or more in wood. Younger Calvados exudes more *pomme* fruit forwardness; the aged versions are imparted with the oaken characteristics of vanilla and spice. The bouquet is intoxicating, the mouthfeel is soft, and the finish is warming. Fans of cider open to winter exploration should drop their schnapps and pull up a nose.

At 40 percent, Calvados is a sipping spirit. Réserves belong neat or on the rocks. With younger bottles, try the inimitable Dick Molnar: Calvados, Swedish Punsch and fresh grapefruit juice, grapefuit twist garnish, served straight up)

Flask factor ★★★★★, *the height of wintry flasking.*

SHOCHU

Shochu, a regional firewater from Japan, is a clear, distilled spirit (25–45 percent ABV) made from various local materials. Some favorites include *kokuto* (black sugar), which plays like a dry rum; *imojochu* (sweet potato), more full-bodied and complex; or *awamori* (rice), the wonderfully crisp elixir from Okinawa. After rice-derived *shochu*, graduate to wheat or barley, which offer a vodka-like cleanliness with exciting hints of earthiness and wild mushrooms. Most *shochus* are best drunk on the rocks, with a splash of hot water, or mixed as a highball with fresh fruit juice.

Flask Factor, 0—needs cubes.

OPORTO

Ruby, tawny, and white ports are aged in oak casks and blended for balance. Ruby is bottled fresh and fruity; the name is derived from its color. Tawny is so named for its color, too, as years in wood turn port a golden brown. Made from white grapes, white port is a rarer style and perfect as a chilled aperitif. Vintage port is the best of its kind. Declared vintages occur only a few times per decade (for example, 2007, 2003, 2000, 1997, 1994, 1960, 1945); rather than a blend of different years, a vintage port is made up of grapes from one harvest. Aged in the bottle, not in wood, vintage ports require simple decanting skills to separate wine from sediment. "L.B.V." (Late Bottled Vintage) is a wine that was left in its cask for most of a decade and then bottled for immediate consumption. Most great ports are less sweet than you think.

Nice touch: Pouring, a port punctilio: port is passed to the left. In the formal setting, the host fills the glass to his right, fills his own, and then passes the bottle clockwise.

Flask factor ★★★ (nonvintage), port-able sophistication.

MADEIRA

Port gets all the press, but Madeira is what the founding fathers drank when they signed the Constitution. In the 1600s, ships from the East Indies stopped at Madeira, a small island southwest of Portugal. Ships were loaded with wine that would often spoil due to heat exposure and the turbulence of long voyages. Madeira, though, improved with abuse. Today, *estufas*, or large, outdoor hot rooms, mimic those squalid conditions. Four distinct types of Madeira are produced: Sercial (light, pale, and nutty); Verdelho (medium dry and smoky); Bual (medium sweet and raisiny); and the nearly indestructible Malmsey (full-bodied, dark, and rich), which can last a century. Poured like port, drier Madeiras make excellent aperitifs, and the high acidity pairs splendidly with food. Older Madeiras are a graceful end to a sensual meal.

Flask factor ★★★★, *ten-year-old Bual, especially.*

Incidentally, other sipping wines to serve as dessert include Banyuls (a must with chocolate), Marsala (not the cheap swill that goes with veal), Sauternes, Trockenbeerenauslese, and Hungarian Tokay.

SHERRY

A fortified wine, sherry isn't just for cooking or for Grandma's liquor cabinet. True sherry comes only from the Jerez region, a small triangular area in Andalucia, Spain, between the cities of Jerez, Puerto de Santa María, and Sanlúcar de Barrameda. A sherry's quality remains constant year after year due to the Solera System, which requires mixing new wines with older vintages. It's said that new wine gives the old some freshness as old wine teaches the new its character.

Drink these varieties before or after dinner: fino (light and very dry; serve chilled), amontillado (darker and nuttier), Manzanilla (pungent, yet delicate), oloroso (sweeter and potent), and Pedro

Ximenez (sweet, lush dessert accompaniment). Sherry is considered by some to be the greatest value in all of wine.

Flask factor ★★★★, try amontillado on Edgar Allan Poe's birthday (January 19).

ORUJO

Finish a meal in Italy, and they hand you an entrancing eau-de-vie made from grape pomace. Spain's digestivo of choice is *aguardiente de orujo*, distilled in copper pots. Producers typically offer three *licors*: blanco, herbas, and café. Delicate and lovely, chilled or neat, orujo is best appraised by rubbing several drops between your palms to release the aromatics. Bring your hands to your face and inhale complex floral notes and herbaceous richness behind the 40 to 42 percent alcohol. Keep a bottle on hand for when foreign nationals pop in for a nightcap.

Flask factor ★★, not as tasty without a tummy full of grilled pulpo a la Gallega.

BEYOND & TONIC

[the whimsical   drink umbrella]

Spicy conversations and saucy companions warrant something more titillating than fill-in-the-blank and tonic. While there's nothing wrong with the ol' familiar, don't let a highball of habit leave you stuck in a single-minded rut. An interesting order makes a barkeep reach beyond the insipid speed rail of cliché cocktails and house-brand liquors.

Wetting one's whistle should be celebrated for the experience, not merely the effects. Ever had Fernet Branca? What goes with tequila besides a shot glass? How's that local small-batch rye? Read a vintage cocktail book, study some labels, and sate bottle curiosities with frequent doses of experimentation. Write down a few recipes and buy bottles for mixing yourself; it is difficult to remember drink recipes without having made them firsthand. And with every metropolis boasting a neo-speakeasy with serious barkeeps and homemade bitters at the ready, craft bartending is but a secret knock away. If you see the proper ingredients, politely ask the bartender to make your quizzical drink; if your call for a Monkey Gland meets with a blank stare, recite the recipe and proper garnish. After pouring the thousandth vodka-and-tonic that night, a bartender will be happy to learn a new drink for the repertoire; tip extra for the cooperation. However, this is no time to play "Stump the Bartender" or assume the joint is stocked with egg whites or orange flower water, especially when the bar is jammed six deep with low-brows screaming for Lowenbräu.

Just as drinking rookies seek out the anodyne properties of vodka (liquor so versatile it goes splendidly with tonic, juice, and most flavors of Vitamin Water), home-bar pretenders eschew the shaker for tepid prefab mixes that require little more than ice. The booze-crafty gent takes charge of fixing, mixing, and pouring and makes deft use of distillates in imaginative concoctions that eschew Mr. and Mrs. T for the real deal.

Guests appreciate a snappy Scotch and soda, but why not bestow a novel drink? Hand off living-room hosting to an able first mate so you can wrestle in the kitchen with tools that sound like Batman villains: the muddler, the jigger, and the strainer. No matter how cold the frosty shaker, grip with vim and hold on like a wing walker. You've arrived as a home concoctionist when a tumbler full of drinks requires service of the reamer, lemon spout, citrus stripper, or bar spoon.

THE ROSETTA STONE

Intuitive cocktailing is as easy as XYZ. The mysterious XYZ Cocktail is the simple combination of dark rum, Cointreau, and fresh lemon juice, the mirepoix of mixing. Substitute brandy for rum (plus a curlicue lemon twist off the side of the glass) and you've created the venerable Sidecar. With gin instead and an egg white shaken to frothy goodness, a White Lady appears. Don't know what to do with those lazy cordials? A splash of Grand Marnier in the lead leads to a St. Clementine.

	XYZ Cocktail	Applecar	Hoopla	After Supper
1 ½ oz.	*Dark rum*	*Calvados*	*Brandy & Lillet*	*Apricot Brandy*
¾ oz	Cointreau	Cointreau	Cointreau	Cointreau
½ oz	fresh lemon juice	fresh lemon juice	fresh lemon juice	fresh lemon juice

Incidentally, moonshine endures in the Southeast and dovetails nicely with the farmers' market food ethic, since nothing's more local than a still in the woods behind the garage. With distillers still turning out courtin', sippin', sellin', and fightin' whiskies, don't turn up a snobby nose to a trusted pal from Dixie or a dedicated home brewer offering a Cherry Bounce jazzed up with genuine hand-cranked corn whisky. Skilled artisans do sell quality popskull, but the truly bad coffin varnish descended from corner-cutting Prohibition-era recipes is still around, so get your tangleleg from a trusted source.

THE HOME BAR

The home bar evolves from an above-the-fridge cabinet to a specially appointed furnishing or buddy-built bar with matching stools. An outlay of $250 will open your home bar for business. Start with your favorites from our list of essentials: reputable bourbon or rye, boutique gin, noncommercial vodka, sipping Scotch, generic Triple Sec, blanco tequila, Barbancourt rum, apricot brandy, and one sexy cordial (Grand Marnier, Armagnac, or Calvados), and Angostura and Peyshaud's bitters.

Besides the staples, stock some festive accessories: themed cocktail napkins; picks, straws, and stir sticks; jarred garnishes (olives, cherries, onions); and wacky drink umbrellas. Silicon ice trays create the ultimate square cubes for Euclidean precision. Antique and thrift store decanters beautifully display your premium liquors.

═══ SODA SIPHON ═══

King of the "big three" mixers, club soda is new-car fresh and crisp as a laundered collar, an easy cocktail topper and dimmer switch for adjusting potency. Classic recipes routinely urge a leaden pour, short on mixers: assuage the sting with a touch of club. Short out of the tumbler? A jazz of soda at the top of a Collins glass keeps the garnish from languishing unseen below the rim. Stumped for mixing ideas? Fine liquors over ice with club soda are a simple, rare-miss creation. Soda regulates mood and mode. Depending on crowd impairment and lateness of evening, adjust high-octane drinks with a splash of soda, added after shaking to preserve effervescence. A hot, lingering afternoon begs refreshing, bubbly quaffs. Hesitant imbibers need a lighter hand; the first drink of a long night should allow the palate to soften. Lastly, club soda with lime is an acceptable lunchtime alternative to iced tea and makes a presentable hand-filler for the teetotaler.

MIXERS & MISCELLANY

Fresh juices, especially citrus, compensate for any recipe imbalances by smoothing out a distillate's rough edges. Sweeten the bracing pucker of sours with a splash of orange juice or tip the jar of maraschino cherries into a drink that needs some color. While high-end or homemade tonic water tempers stiffness, too much quinine is an Amazonian clear-cutting of taste. Despite fitness proclivities, diet cola and energy drinks are not proper mixers. Ginger ale (particularly fashioned from your own ginger syrup) makes a fine companion to bourbon or rye. For expert play, especially when working with citrus elements, add an egg white to the ingredients and shake to form a creamy froth. Then add the ice and finish as usual.

When shade is a commodity or activity is furious, a tray full of Manhattans is the wrong cure. Instead, look to the fruit bowl for tonier ideas and colorful medleys involving crème de violette. Muddling is the best method of rescuing the last two strawberries and other fruit refugees trapped in the crisper. Don't limit yourself: watermelons, lychees, peaches, and greengage plums form the perfect base to gin or rum muddling expeditions. Freshly plucked mint ignites late-afternoon revelry every time, whether in Juleps, Southsides, or French 75s.

Nice touch: Enliven any home-bar experience with a snappy soda siphon for a lovely accent of fizz pizzazz. Dedicate a second one for carbonating fresh summer juices. Put specific gravity to work and learn to layer liquors into striated concoctions like the pousse-café.

THE TESAUROPOLITAN

There is the joy of a finely crafted cocktail. But there's also the glee of a spontaneous original punch from odds and sods, particularly when standing before a friend's liquor cabinet holding a forgettable fifth, a sticky bottle of blue curaçao, a near-expired can of fruit cocktail, and a Fresca. Cheerfully enlist a Tibetan singing bowl and the stem of a flashlight as muddling apparati. Despite these sparse, legal aid–like resources, the concocting gent prevails with a Tesauro-politan tropical martini accented with muddled pineapple cubes, halved cherry, or drizzle of local honey. Indeed, certain liquors are amenable to loose experimentation—vodka, rum, gin, triple sec, apricot brandy—as well as citrus, grenadine, bruised melon, and the classic fizzers. Whatever your concocted poison, steer clear of Long Island Iced Tea clones, lest you forget that gin + Ouzo + spiced rum + Goldschlager = revolting, not visionary.

BLOODY MARY (SERVES I, IN A 24-OUNCE MASON JAR)

3 or more shots mid-class vodka (gin, for a Red Snapper) • Fill glass halfway with tomato juice • $^2/_3$ tsp. spicy yellow mustard, stir vigorously • Several healthy splashes Worcestershire sauce • Large lemon and lime wedges wrung and dropped in glass • Repeated splashes Tabasco to taste • Healthy sprinkling celery salt (the vital ingredient) • Light dusting black pepper • Stir and sniff to gauge strength and amount of ice or juice needed for dilution • Top with tomato juice and more ice, if necessary • Stir with a firm and fresh celery stalk; leave in glass • Final splash of dry sherry, if available. Caught short of supplies with a living room–full of overnight guests suffering from a collective katzenjammer? Our pick when 100 percent from-scratch is unlikely (or head-poundingly impossible) is the incomparable Demitri's Bloody Mary Seasoning. All you'll need to hunt and gather are quality tomato juice and garnishes.

TESAUROPOLITAN #3

• • • • • • Gin • Crème de Violette • Cachaça • Domaine de Canton • • • • •
• • • Squeeze of fresh Meyer lemon juice • Squeeze of Navel orange juice • • •
• • • • • • • • • • • Top with soda • Pinch of cayenne • • • • • • • • • • •

THE SOLITARY DRINK

I like bars just after they open for the evening.
When the air inside is still cool and clean and everything is shining
and the barkeep is giving himself that last look in the mirror
to see if his tie is straight and his hair is smooth.
I like the neat bottles on the bar back and the
lovely shining glasses and the anticipation. I like to watch the man mix
the first one of the evening and put it down on a crisp mat and
put the little folded napkin beside it. I like to taste it slowly.
The first quiet drink of the evening in a quiet bar—that's wonderful.
—RAYMOND CHANDLER, *The Long Goodbye*

Frequent consumption of cocktails with only the company of Jack, Jim, or Johnnie is worrisome. Nonetheless, the occasional solitary drink, or two, in the taproom in the late afternoon is a solid, gentlemanly prelude to a bustling evening. Where else can one check out the afternoon baseball scores and Tour de France stage results, or inhale the atmosphere of screwdriver-swilling pensioners amidst the ether of generic cigarettes?

Steer clear of trendy brewpubs or restaurant lounges: the ideal afternoon is spent among struggling actors and service staffers, with just the right touch of atmospheric grunge. If you hear strains of idling Allman Brothers songs or potluck R&B, step right in. After a lazy half day of work, recline and order a bottled beer or a sipping bourbon. The bar is probably empty, save for a few school teachers decompressing and gossiping. Pocket the flirtation and steal some "me time."

This is a great time to pen a letter or prepare an upcoming best man speech. Stretch out with a hobby magazine or tabloid. Recline unabashedly, savor the surrounding sights: the peeling liquor labels, a leather-jacketed woman chalking her pool cue, and later, the restroom-stall prose. Treat this thirsty sojourn as your little secret, like that late-night soft-core adult feature you ordered on the last business trip.

OENOPHILIA

Don't say too much about the wine being "sound" or "pleasant":
people will think you have simply been mugging up a wine-merchant's catalogue.
It is a little better to talk in broken sentences and say, "It has . . . don't you think?"
Or, "It's a little bit cornery," or something equally random like, "Too many
tramlines." I use this last phrase because it passes the test of the boldly meaningless.
—STEPHEN POTTER, *One-Upmanship*

To drink wine is to sip of the land and its time. For the youngest wines, like Beaujolais Nouveau, pouring a glass means quaffing juice that's a mere few weeks old. In the oldest bottles, wine is a time capsule that offers vintage mouthfuls of long-past decades. It is astonishingly poetic that one can read the Declaration of Independence while drinking liquid crafted in the same year.

Trips to a vinous retailer bolster confidence the next time a waiter drops the wine list in your lap. Brush up on wine vocabulary and be specific—light or full bodied, fruit or oak driven, soft or crisp? "I'm baking a ham for my anniversary," offers far more clues than, "I dunno, something good and red." This is not an auction (yet), and if budget's a concern, say up front how much you're willing to spend. Give the pros a chance to point out the best values.

CHOOSING

Though it is the oenophile's onus to distinguish the nonpareil from the dreck, nothing is better with a region's cuisine than its own wine. Outside of food, season and mood dictate selections. In the cool climes, bold, rich reds warm the belly. Dip into big Rhône styles from France and Australia for a deep taste of Syrah/Shiraz, Grenache, and Mourvèdre. Barolo and Barbaresco (Nebbiolo) and Amarone (partially air-dried grapes) are Italy's answers to a blustery night. California offers young, ripe-now wines like Zinfandel for connoisseurs who can't wait ten years for a bottle to mellow. Bordeaux blends and Burgundy deliver old-world complexity and character when the professor's in town for a steak dinner, and Spain's lush Rioja (Tempranillo) and age-worthy Priorato (Garnacha, Cariñena) beg for nights of flamenco and tapas. For value, uncork up-and-coming cabs from Chile, Argentine Malbec, and South African Chenin Blanc. Languedoc-Roussillon's Carignans and Pacific Northwest Pinots earn impressive marks without inflated prices.

For whites, appetites are best whetted with crisp, minerally Loire Valley Sancerre, New Zealand Sauvignon Blanc, Austria's Grüner Veltliner, and dry sparklers. Spicy foods and hot conversations love aromatic, spicy whites: Gewürztraminer and Pinot Gris from Alsace, Viognier from the Rhône, and Albariño from Spain. The "ABC" rule of "anything but Chardonnay" is good advice when you want to avoid mismatching creamy, full-bodied whites with casual porch sipping and a delicate ceviche. For grilled swordfish, white Burgundies from France are a finesse-oriented class of Chardonnays; for buttery notes, head to California and Australia.

A note on off-dry wines and the misconstrued rosé: little in the world of wine is as pleasant on a mid-July afternoon as a glass of Tavel. Dry rosés offer gorgeous hues ranging from salmon to cinnamon, and refreshing fruit. The low alcohol and clean finish of saignée rosé from Lirac, Provence, or Spain pleases the palate without weighing down the senses. Off-dry whites are lovely alternatives to tart wines with bracing acidity. Wander through bottles of Vouvray, German halbtrocken, and Argentinian Torrontés for a grapey, honeyed fix.

BUZZ FACTOR

When selecting a wine, pay attention to the alcohol percentage. The difference between 12.5 and 15.5 percent may look like only 3 percent, but it's really a 24 percent difference in the total ABV, thus important when drinking at lunch, lubricating a love interest, or tiptoeing around an extant DUI on your record.

Incidentally, wine isn't all France and Napa Valley. When in Long Island, try the white blends; in New York's Finger Lakes, dive into Riesling. In Virginia, discover that Jefferson was right about the local terroir as you sip the best Viognier and Cabernet Franc in the U.S. And don't miss a riverside detour out of St. Louis into Missouri wine country, where indigenous American grapes and intriguing hybrids are hidden gems.

OPINING

Feigned wine smarts are transparent. In the store, demonstrate knowledge and interest by asking questions ("How about something from France's Jura region?") or referencing a recent article. In the dining room, avoid being the talky bombast; however, friends appreciate the quick dossier of a wine or region. If uneducated, treat wine like museum art and use your creative senses. Comment on radiant hues, aromas, or how the wine feels on the tongue. While an untrained nose might not discern Müller-Thurgau from Puligny-Montrachet at ten paces, a humble enthusiast can still spot richness of color and taste, and voice a sensation. To train your mouth, practice the BJ method: drink *blind* and keep a *journal*—blind tasting calibrates your palate's taste memory, and wine journaling logs your progress.

ICEWINE

Icewine is a bright dessert-style wine traditionally made in the wilds of Austria and Germany and the chilly confines of Canada. Like a mucus-freezing northern Wisconsin winter, icewine harvest must wait until the grapes freeze and temperatures hover near a gelid $-10°C$ ($14°F$, $263.15°$kelvin), often requiring an outdoor night harvest in the extreme cold to ensure no ice melt . . . the Polar Bear Plunge of winemaking. This labor of frigid love explains icewine's intense flavors and typically higher prices. Sip it as you would a wine or pour it into cordial glasses, eliciting a warm belly feeling not felt since Mom Fedexed brownies to your freshman dorm.

SCRATCH 'N' SNIFF

In restaurants, the sommelier or steward announces the bottle to confirm your selection—check the year against the vintage you ordered. No need to be a thermometer-wielding fusspot, but if reds are too warm or whites numbingly cold, ask the server to fetch or remove an ice bucket. Examine the cork with a squeeze: a moist cork halfsoaked with wine is better than a dry, brittle plug, although neither is a definitive sign the wine is sound or flawed. Ordinarily, there is no need to smell the cork, but historic and otherwise interesting bottles might warrant a sniff. As for alternate enclosures, screwcaps and synthetics, like Internet dating, lost their stigma ages ago.

The short pour that follows is the real test. Swirl to volatilize the esters and release the bouquet, and then smell the wine. Most times, a deep sniff is enough to detect a fault. If still unsure, take a sip. This is not the scorer's table with tableside spit buckets; the initial pour determines the wine's potability, not likeability. A gesture or kind word signals acceptance ("Yes, it's lovely"). Rounds of table wine don't necessitate a glassware change, but insist on fresh stems for remarkable bottles. Instead of brimming glasses, ask for modest pours so that you can appreciate how aroma and character develop with each refill.

B.Y.O.

For special occasions, it's a delight to pack a bottle you've been maturing in the cellar. For tiny trattorias without a liquor license, toting a smooth Brunello di Montalcino is encouraged. Call ahead and inquire as to the corkage fee. Gladly fork over a ten- to fifteen-dollar tariff for the right to import your own gem, but never show up with a substandard bottle or one that's already on the list. This option is for expressing taste, not whittling down the tab. Offer the server a glass from a hard-to-resist vintage and often the fee is waived.

SENDING IT BACK

A delicate deed, sending back a dud is by no means taboo. Approximately three in a hundred bottles are faulty. Look for clues: a raised, moldy cork or leaky capsule indicates heat damage. White (tartaric) crystals, sediment, and harmless crumbs of cork are not faults, but beware strong scents of Madeira or sherry in unfortified wines, which point toward noxious oxidation. Musty, wet-newspaper vapors indicate undrinkable corked wine. When suspicions arise, summon the steward and offer the glass. "What do you think?" is more polite than an acerbic rejection.

Incidentally, if the sommelier recommends a bottle based on your stated preferences, sip early before a poorly matched wine becomes an albatross on your table.

EQUIPMENT

The impassioned wino enjoys the accoutrements of enthusiasm. Nevertheless, don't gussy up a limp wine collection with state-of-the-art lever pulls and hydraulic cork extractors. A decent opener with a rim fulcrum and knife will do. Bottle coasters and neck rings protect table linens, and a decanter is de rigueur for older gems or young upstarts whose tannins need tempering. An ice bucket is a must for the avid champagne drinker or frequent host. As for glassware, what a travesty to see a fabulous bottle poured into a substandard vessel, with no room for the wine to breathe! No, you shouldn't scoff at quaffing wine served peasant-style in juice glasses, nor should you afford a stem for every possible varietal. Yet once you get into serious wines, you'll want to invest in a temperature-controlled wine fridge and proper crystal.

Incidentally, never clean delicate glasses if your BAC is above the legal limit or it's after 1 a.m. Instead, when an infantry of stemware has formed ranks at night's end, pour a dollop of water into each bowl to prevent a red crust from forming and then off to bed, or more.

BUBBLY

Swirl the sparkling wine in a thin, tulip-shaped flute and appraise the star-bright color—does it register in green hues or bronze tints? Take a generous sip, swish it around, and feel the prickly tingle. Note the clean acid, fresh fruit, and soft, foamy mousse. Admire the hint of chalk and balanced aftertaste. These are the distinctive sensations of champagne.

Champagne is a region in France; thus, other sparkling wines must be called by another name. In Spain, it's Cava; in Italy, Franciacorta, Prosecco, or Spumante; Germany makes Sekt; other countries simply call their bubblies "sparkling wine." All champagne is made according to a traditional process in which still wine, aided by the addition of sugar and yeast, undergoes a secondary fermentation in the actual bottle. The *prise de mousse* (capturing the sparkle) ensues as yeast activity causes carbon dioxide bubbles to form in the bottle. How do you get the sediment out without losing carbonation? Over the next eight weeks, spent yeast cells are collected in the bottle neck through a laborious process called *reumage*, or riddling, wherein the bottle is slowly inverted by hand. Later, the neck is dipped in ice-cold brine; the sediment is frozen and disgorged out of the bottle, propelled by trapped carbon dioxide (*dégorgement*). Finally, the winemaker tops up with the dosage, a solution of still wine and sugar that determines sweetness and compensates for spilled wine lost in the dégorgement. The bottle is recorked and, voilà, there is sparkle. To find a bottle made in the same style as Champagne, look for "méthode champenoise" on the label.

Given the cool climate, producers are forced to blend wines from different years to create palatable nonvintage champagnes. Two or three times a decade, however, an exceptional vintage is declared good enough to stand on its own. Stellar years to look for:

1995, 1996, 2000, 2002. Prestige Cuvée designates longer aging and a house's top bottling. However, household names like Veuve Clicquot and Moët et Chandon are owned by giant conglomerates and blend grapes from scores of growers. For artisanal quality, look for a tell-tale designation on the label: "RM" (Récoltant-Manipulant) indicates independent grower-producers making small-batch "farmer fizz."

Champagne labels are, by law, quite descriptive:

Blanc de blancs: "White from white," meaning that only chardonnay grapes were used. Lighter, more floral; best for beginners. Vintage versions have great toasty richness.

Blanc de noirs: "White from black," indicating that only black grapes were used. In Champagne, this means a *cuvée* (blend) of Pinot Noir and Pinot Meunier, although outside of France other grapes are used. Fuller bodied, with more fruit and spice.

Rosé: Either red wine is added or color is extracted from red grape skins. Don't serve to the uninitiated, who might mistake the pink stuff for the house schwag at the Hotel California. At best, rosés are rarer wines with beautiful hues and charming summer-fruit qualities.

Master your opening technique lest you lose precious wine (or an eye) in a Grand Prix gush of fizz. Despite the appeal of a climactic pop of a fresh bottle, it is correct to ease the cork out gently. A deft touch leaves the bubbles unagitated and sounds of a lover's sigh. Pour slowly: a steady trickle thwarts clumsy overflow. Tough corks may warrant champagne tweezers, but advanced users should employ a ceremonial champagne saber or the back of a cleaver to festively behead bottles of bubbly.

Nice touch: For indoor *sabrage*, careful *sabreurs* ought to affix a length of ribbon or kitchen string to the wire cage with the other end tied to their wrist or belt. Then refasten the cage to the cork above the lip. The string keeps the cork and intact glass from launching into chandeliers, stained glass, or down-range décolletage.

Champagne that costs less than a pair of movie tickets is non-existent. Fortunately, there's inexpensive sparkling wine. Delicious Prosecco and Crémant are priced for liberal pouring that requires no more reason to celebrate than a gathering of two over figs and prosciutto. South Africa is getting into bubbly production, and New Zealand has a suitable climate for great sparklers. Australia's sparkling Shiraz has fruity, oaky appeal.

- Don't destroy a delicate cuvée with spurts of OJ. Use everyday sparkling wines (under $12) for mimosas and yacht christenings.

- Stay the fizz: a bottle stopper preserves pressure for several more days.

- As an aperitif, bubbles lighten moods and crisp acid whets the appetite. Caviar, oysters, and a hotel key: bubbly at the raw bar is decadence.

WORKING WITH A HANGOVER

Maintain integrity with your employer by arriving daily in a salable condition. To be sure, an incredible evening should never be cut short for the sake of prudence, but set a sensible curfew of about 1 a.m. on school nights. This witching hour allows for adequate fun, six-plus hours of sleep, and a rock-solid gregarious reputation.

Carousing with unimpeded cohorts, career slugabeds, and agenda-less *flâneurs* is fraught with danger. Invariably, actors and freelancers boogie deep into the night, staging the inevitable poesy-filled, guitar-playing be-in. This is quitting time for you; otherwise, five beers, two tokes, and three hours later, when dawn is spawning, you will still be there, confused.

Quit dribbling the snooze button. Before age thirty, if more than two sick days per year are logged in the name of party overdose, get on the UNOS liver transplant list or drink more water before bed. If necessary, glide into work an hour late with a medical excuse (upset stomach) instead of missing the entire day with a falsified doctor's note.

The key recovery period is the precious, fuzzy hour of morning ablutions. Hydrate, pain-relieve, and swallow some B12 or load up on antioxidants with a honey-ginger smoothie spiked with prickly pear cactus extract before a restorative shower. Don't forget to shave, as the stubbly face/baggy eye combo is the telltale mark of an overindulgent sot (twentysomething earners coasting in disposable McJobs are exempt). During the commute, quell queasiness with a lightly caffeinated beverage and something egg whitey and croissantlike.

At work, acquaint yourself intimately with the water cooler and keep a low profile. For the advanced, pack a snuff. As residual rottenness evaporates, ride this energy boost from 10 a.m. until 2 p.m. Place important calls, write urgent letters, and draft more substantial documents while the life force is still rising. Despite the ache to build a pillow-lined fort under your desk, don't squander this artificial spike. Undoubtedly, the late-afternoon outbox will be barren from 3:00 p.m. until closing; the hangover itself likely receded before lunch like a soul lightening, but will reemerge like a fever sore. Do your best to endure excruciating yawns and involuntary chair slouching. Have a nice day.

Incidentally, if instead of the beeping alarm it's a mewling tot disturbing your convalescence, learn to occasionally parent with a hangover. Like a PC booting up in Safe Mode, turn on only the required systems, honor thy responsibility to feed your progeny, and then look to the telly (low volume, preferably educational) for salvation.

THE ETHIC OF ALCOHOL

Don't get the idea I'm a boozer. Setting out deliberately to get drunk is pathological. I like to drink just enough to change the temperature in the brain room. I'll turn to less mainstream substances if I want to rearrange the furniture.

—TOM ROBBINS, *Fierce Invalids Home from Hot Climates*

Drinking usually evolves from a curiosity to a cultivated appreciation. Early on, beer is a shining amulet, the quaff of mystical older brothers and those with a fake I.D. For a teenager, drinking turns card games, movie rentals, or hangouts in the woods into joyous rebellion. Into the early twenties, alcohol appreciation widens, hedonistic possibilities surface, and the body becomes steeled to handle the sludge of frequent partying. Then, one day in your mid-to-late twenties, you will wake up with a hangover—not the ordinary Sunday wooziness on the sofa, but a roundhouse blow to your constitution and formerly elastic liver. With head in hand, you ponder the reasons why a mild soak resulted in such a spirit-trampling quagmire. As you gobble painkillers like Pez, you feel like the old gray mare—"I ain't what I used to be."

Following this sober revelation, denial inevitably follows. Feelings of invincibility mute calls for tolerance from your aging body. At some dehydrated point, your body will have a summit meeting, wherein the agenda will be graver than arms control and global warming. The end result is a deal negotiated between two old sharks. Your mind will bargain away the omnipotent hold of peer pressure and senseless excess in exchange for pragmatism, discipline, wellness, and a future first-round draft pick. In the aftermath, you'll acknowledge that getting snookered is no longer a prerequisite for amorous charm or vibrancy. Low-key nights warrant moderation and an early clock-out; one-star yawners might be skipped altogether.

The foregoing is not a self-important essay on temperance. Giggle water is a winning social lubricant for those of sound mind and body. There are singular nights (sometimes, many in a row) in which ferocious incaution is the evening's keynote. Still, evolution is inescapable. Grow up or defend your lifestyle to those with country cottages and healthy relationships. Be a refined tippler—the part-time, lovable degenerate. Impetuousness ripens into spontaneity, impatience into timely verve, unbridled energy into charisma and élan. Instead of floundering into slurred oblivion, aspire to be "the man who can hold his liquor" as opposed to "that old, pathetic drunk." Get in touch with your chakras and vitality; the venerable vices are not an intrusive competition, but a limbering stretch of control. The ethic of alcohol is about acknowledging personal limits, even as you intentionally step past them.

TOBACCO

Smoking is a most divisive vice, cleaving Southern states from the Union and restaurants into demarcated dining zones. The cash crop of yesteryear, tobacco has a contemporary stigma that requires a gentleman to consider more fashionable sins. Nonetheless, for those who disregard well-known warnings, puff rarely, if at all, and do not sully an otherwise vigorous lifestyle. Compare the raspy one-packer who fires up in bed to the weekend ring-blower who shares a couple of rollies with pub mates. Do not fear the onset of vice when enjoying a celebratory cigar, pensive pipe, or college football—game chaw.

Since the decline of the first Playboy empire, most homes have nonsmoking policies and are not equipped with room-to-room ashtrays. Whether the host digs nicotine or not, acceptable receptacles do not include drinking glasses, houseplants, or the house toilet.

Tobacco has many delivery methods; choose wisely for each scenario. Whipping out Capri 100s at a campfire will raise eyebrows, as will puffing nicotine vapor from a creepy e-cigarette. Likewise, having a dip or chew at the opera is crass, even if spitting during intermission into the lobby's brass cuspidor.

Nice touch: Bummed a smoke from a kind soul in a bar? Later, buy your own pack, reapproach, and offer a return gesture. Get caught short-cigged too often? Quit panhandling for menthols, you mooch.

Stretch your sophistication and employ the cigarette holder while in a dark lounge, bubble bath, smoking jacket, or incognito. For the infrequent smoker, tote a handful of smokes in a vintage cigarette case. As with the flask, do not put cheap fags in a silver case. To thwart an assassin's bullet, position said case in your breast pocket. For a change of pace and a wicked high, go to a Middle Eastern hookah joint for tea and tobacco with an eccentric group or date.

Note to the smoker: Pleasure smokers can regularly go two weeks without a cigarette. Persistent ash tappers, on the other hand, look foolish huffing after one flight of stairs. Where's the pleasure in shivering outside an office building in 25°F December because you have been banished, like a leper, from the lobby?

SNUFF

Heralded as one of the safest forms of tobacco in ye olde England, snuff was routinely toted by the Union blue during Sherman's march to the sea. Infused with flavors such as anise and mint, snuff is tobacco ground finely as espresso and sold in a box or tin. To use, simply take a tiny pinch and sniff lightly; a pleasant aroma and mild nicotine rush immediately stimulate. Look for the authors' preferred tin: Wilsons of Sharrow Crumbs of Comfort. Caveat: over-snuffing leads to persistent nasal drip and mistaken identity as a Fauvist-era, tights-wearing dandy.

SIXTY-SECOND CIGAR PRIMER

Choosing. The wrapper leaf is the most important feature to notice when selecting a cigar. An oily, uncracked appearance means it was correctly humidified. In general, dark wrappers indicate sweeter, richer smokes than lighter ones. Length and ring gauge (diameter) determine burn time and flavor: long cigars burn slower and cooler and the extra length diffuses heat for a cooler smoke. Block out some time for longer cigars; you'll need at least forty minutes to enjoy a seven-inch Churchill. If faced with unfamiliar names, bands, wrappers, or blends, take the Robusto for a spin. If that mainstay isn't solid, chances are the more exotic smokes aren't up to snuff. Once a brand passes muster, however, *figurados* (general term for odd shapes) are typically rolled by veterans with seasoned hands.

Ritual. There's no hurry in a cigar. Practice suave legerdemain when drawing a premium stick: examine the veined wrapper (unbroken, oily leaf, supple to the touch), roll it by your ear, cut, toast, and light. The Hollywood act of running a cigar lengthwise under your nose is only marginally more useful than noting a wine's bouquet by sniffing the outside of a decanter. For the most intensity, put the open end to a nostril and inhale. Sufferers of post-nasal drip are barred from nosing others' smokes.

Clipping. Debate over clipping methods continues, but the Guillotine cut is easier to execute than the Punch, the V, or the Pierce, and exposes sufficient surface for even draw and full flavor. No matter the technique, take care not to lop off too much.

Lighting & Smoking. Hold the flame about half an inch away and warm the cigar until it begins to darken evenly. Always use a butane lighter or wooden match for lighting; cardboard matches and Zippo-style lighters dispense fumes that destroy aroma and flavor. Next, place the cigar in your mouth and draw the flame into the foot. Don't hold the tip over the fire like a prong of roasting marshmallows; rather, pull on the cigar evenly and rotate it until you get a bright-red cherry covering the end. Don't rush the lighting ritual—take at least half a minute. Never bang the ash off a long cigar; roll it off, lest you ruin the even burn of a well-wrapped stick. A long ash also makes for a more mellow smoke, especially when the cigar is short. You should be able to smoke a Churchill in about four ashes and a Robusto in two. When finished, set the cigar aside to extinguish rather than snubbing it out like a mob informant.

Nice touch: Snap off a strip of cedar, often found in sheets within a fine box or wrapped around a single stick in a cigar tube, and light for use as a long, aromatic match.

Humidorable. Few gents require a walk-in, temperature-controlled humidor, but most can afford an elegant desktop/bookshelf model that requires little maintenance besides routine top-ups with distilled water. In a my-other-humidor's-in-the-shop pinch, a resealable plastic bag with a well-wrung-out paper towel will do, but only for the most casual partakers. Not all sticks are stogies—the name is derived from covered "Conestoga" wagons—and referring to one as such can be taken as an insult because "stogie" once meant the cheapies smoked by drivers transporting affluent passengers with fine cigars.

Incidentally, if you dig cigars but not the funk of morning-after mouth, restrict your stick consumption to rosé hours, namely, late morning to twilight, so that there's time to cleanse the palate after

an espresso-strength *maduro* before hitting the rack with rank gums
that even double hits of mouthwash and wholesome prayer can't fix.

PALL MALL

· · · · · · · · · · · **Gin · Sweet vermouth · Dry vermouth** · · · · · · · · · · ·

· · · · · · · · · **Dollop white crème de menthe · Dash bitters** · · · · · · ·

SUBSTANCES

It is imprudent to sample every dish in the narcotic buffet, but a
developed palate for chasing the dragon evinces an experienced
maturity. Don't venture alone or be the surreptitious pill popper;
like the lifter maxing out with four plates at the gym, use a spot-
ter. Sharing with trusted intimates ensures buddied judgment on
proper place or activity. Certain substances are delightful accoutrements to creativity, sensuality, and spiritual exploration—although
they will not "create" creativity. Sometimes drugs are instant stamina
extenders or sensory enhancers for an especial night of dancing and
debauchery. The sniffy set, with less hair and fading allure, believe
that drugs change the serendipity equation and are the best method
to meet "those" type of people.

Caveat emptor: as when stumbling on a suspiciously cheap used
car, beware the seedy lemon. For reliable and safe service of designer
Super Tuscan dope, purchase discreetly from a local bartender,

younger brother, well-greased bellhop, IT guy, or recommended dial + delivery operation.

Treat your body well and abuse lightly. Most drugs have a fall-out effect during the next day(s), so research hard candy before its parlay. Lest they lose the forbidden wonder of an infrequent treat, drugs should maintain their supplemental status and never become necessities. With your prestigious graduate degree in hand, it is now immature to pop Xtasy like Flintstone vitamins or routinely gurgle a postwork bong hit. In fact, by a certain age, if you look for it less, you can say yes more often, the social equivalent of Dave Kingman, boasting a high vice slugging percentage but a low on-(free)base percentage. It takes a cultured sense to know when to plateau booze and other substances and recognize when an espresso will spark the fun more than another dose of meow meow mephedrone. Learn to craft an evening through friends, venues, strolling, food, booze, and surprises, instead of a white pill split in two.

THE GYROSCOPE OF SANITY

When the mind is young and pliable, shaking things about never feels messy. Once you've stabilized your adult mind with consciousness and order, toxicity may be quite hazardous. Introduce a psychotropic parasite into a calm, complex mind and the bizarre skew of reality quickly dispels the romantic myth of drugs. Forming sentences is impossible, sleep is fought for and lost, and old friends awaken to your apologetic messages explaining last night's split of wits. It's now time to kiss the candy-popping irresponsibility of your twenties goodbye and awaken to the more organic highs of jazz, sushi, and vino that don't induce the usual ball-scratching, dry-mouthed morning debility. Remember this the next time a bad trip leaves you wrecked on a sandbar of lost time. Isn't it more polite to keep your shit together? Be fortunate and learn this lesson at the cost of a few hundred bucks of booze bought for strangers or sacrificial objects lost to the cityscape, instead of real inconveniences, like divorce or a ride downtown in a metro cruiser.

LEAVES OF GRASS

Reactions to ganja are a social filter: a polite, comfortable "no thanks" reveals as much as a hungry grin for seconds. Used right, reefer madness brushes away the clouds of confusion after a breakup or bout with traffic and, depending on your grass, can be a light kick. Abused, it's a procrastination pill that makes progress futile and relationships falter. Instead, visit a museum or gallery, write beatnik poetry, or sip Orangina outdoors in pyjamas. Marijuana should not be part of a man's daily utility, although it may creep into your hiking pack, weekend tote, or play-clothes pockets. Great for a spring cookout or a backyard weeding, Mary Jane should be piped in with admission at any planetarium. Pot is a poor cure for whooping cough, better than an ice pack for headaches, and perfect for movie-going, gaming, mini-golf, or bowling (but not archery).

Is the occasional moment of solace at 4:20 or a potluck dinner really a pathology? Abstainers shouldn't spurn partakers on camping trips any more than smokers should stroll around glassy-eyed, looking to score a sack of cheeba. Grown-up tokers with a connection and a two-car garage should invest in hand-blown glass paraphernalia, quality papers, or a vaporizer for esophageal comfort. Those fortunate enough to have translated their chronic insomnia or old "football shoulder" into a medicinal THC Rx should find a respectable dispensary and light up the state's tax revenues.

GAMING

In lieu of dueling at ten paces, feats of leisure are superlatively social and bring out laughter, drama, and drink. When competition is fierce, meet it with skill and sportsmanship. Yet no matter your acumen, do not quash another's zest for the game via a 100-mph serve on the community courts or the Budapest Gambit against an adolescent chess player. Your repertoire should include a host of games that don't require a CPU. Don't be a stick-in-the-mud who eschews board games—the box clearly states "ages 8 and up." Stock your closet shelf with a few classic favorites for rainy days and lazy afternoons (Monopoly, Life, Parcheesi, Master Mind). Visit Internet auctions to hunt down lost obscurities and relive past glories like conquering Dark Tower or finding a mint-condition Electric Football with vibrating gridiron. Travel-sized editions and smartphone apps work nicely for long waits and even longer road trips. Plus, a set of double-six dominoes fits in a glove box or attaché and works equally well on bar tops and beach towels.

Incidentally, Clue fantasies don't end with puberty. Phineas still wants Miss Scarlet with the Candlestick in the Conservatory. Tesauro secretly craves being tied to the Library ladder with the Rope and flogged with tales of Chaucer by the mysterious Mrs. Peacock.

BACKGAMMON

Pastis, side bets, cocked dice, the Lover's Leap, and figs on the deck. Backgammon is excellent for the cat and mouse of flirtation, the rules are simple, and the thrill of chance scintillates. Measure your Man Cycle against the game's capricious dice. Confident play may lure timely doublets, but following the percentages leads to victory. Backgammon exposes a player's persona: the attacker (hits no matter what); the runner (can't wait to flee); the trapper (won't let you out); the stalker (ready to pounce); and the miracle maker (leaves one piece behind to spoil a sure victory). Count using colors and points, rather than tapping out each pip like a sinking ship's SOS. The doubling cube allows you to wager for cash and cocktails, or play for your place or mine.

MAH-JONGG COCKTAIL

∙ ∙ ∙ ∙ ∙ ∙ ∙ **Gin** ∙ **Dollop Cointreau** ∙ **Dollop light rum** ∙ **Lemon twist** ∙ ∙ ∙ ∙ ∙ ∙ ∙

CROQUET

The best use for grass since hula skirts: this game is played on virtually any lawn larger than a badminton court. Croquet is the perfect outdoor social accompaniment and obliges all skill levels. Beyond backyard free-for-alls, there's the elegant chess match that is six-wicket croquet, a finesse game that cares not whether you're young or aged, male or female. Players on a carpet-like greensward shoot hoops barely one-sixteenth of an inch wider than the ball, strategize over the colorful deadness board, cannon opponents, try to make rover, and repair their partners to the nine-inch line. With proper planning, a sporting afternoon of mallets and wickets boasts women in gloves, gents in whites, and all in hats, clutching chilly punch for all-day beak dipping.

CARD PLAYING

Games involving trumps and kitties aren't just for grannies and casino-klatch belles. Be nimble on the cribbage board and master at least three of the following: whist, euchre, hearts, canasta, spades, pinochle, or stud. To sock away bidding acumen for the sedentary golden years, learn contract bridge.

Cracking a fresh fifty-two makes great fodder for staging a small weeknight get-together. Card games are also ideal for family reunions when postprandial café hasn't caffeinated the group to acceptable chitchat levels. Have any fives? Go fish. Most sentient beings with a G.E.D. can follow new games after a few practice hands. For those with steeper learning curves, keep *According to Hoyle* within arm's reach for further instructions—even the box-top undersides of *Payday* and *Candyland* require a quick perusal to arbitrate game-stopping rules inquiries.

══ ANTE UP, INHIBITIONS DOWN ══

Strip Poker, the skinny-dip of parlor tricks, is perhaps the only activity in which a gentleman may cheat, yet it's not the only adult game in town that blurs social boundaries. Truth or Dare never goes out of style—in fact, the Truth option becomes especially provocative once all players are well beyond their got-nothing-to-hide college years—and the Jenga version is customizable to a group's ranging sensibilities. Twister morphs into Tryster when players disrobe, and Spin-the-Bottle is still the juiciest reuse of a recently drained wine vessel. Also, 'tis never taboo to introduce blush-inducing terms to Pictionary and Taboo. For international intrigue, snowed-in couples should turn Risk into Risqué by introducing role-played-diplomacy petting breaks every time the infantries skirmish in Kamchatka. Whatever the mode, aim for fun before fleshliness and keep the mood more soft-core than NC-17.

Upon dealing poker and its progeny, be silly and brash, but not sloppy. Shuffle three times with a smooth bridge method before distributing cards clockwise, yourself last. Boyish shuffling techniques, such as forcing the deck halves together like misfit puzzle pieces or hand-over-hand card flipping, aren't fit for the gentleman's table. Beware the hotshot flicking of cards across smooth tables, risking misdeals or players scrambling to catch wayward aces. With money on the line, ante up without being reminded.

Sprinkle some lingo to liven up the game ("Deuce, six, no help. Jack, king, ace, possible Broadway. And clubs for the dealer. Trio of queens is still high. Six tits, what's your bet?"). Know the poker-hand ranks cold. Asking whether a full house beats three of a kind is poor bluffing technique. Keep poker variations beyond Texas Hold 'Em, such as High/Low, Follow the Queen, and three-card guts at the ready on dealer's-choice night.

Fair-weather rookies are predictable and jump ship with pairs showing. Stay in a few pots with dubious hands to experience the once-in-a-lifetime thrill of pulling an inside straight. Among friends, don't allow betting with paychecks and wedding rings, though hotel keys and promises of hard labor are always acceptable. When the room is quiet and the wagering intense, fair is fair—after all, Lando Calrissian lost the *Millennium Falcon* to Han Solo in a card game.

GOLF

Shelves are filled with paeans about golf's magical places and two-thousand-word fish stories about near-quitting experiences cured miraculously by a tree-and-hazard-defying wedge-in for eagle. Golf is inherently frustrating. Indeed, if the game were easy, no one would spend hard-earned lucre on the newest oversized drivers. Unlike tennis, where mediocrity is attainable, golf is mercurial. Even old pros question their ability and enjoyment from time to time.

Except for retirees and idle law-school students, golf is an occasional treat. Without knowing the intricacies of club selection or Bermuda grass, a novice duffer still appreciates the history and beauty of golf by bringing the right ethic and stance to the tee box. Before unsheathing your three-wood, take in the scene, listen for honeyed thwacks, and cherish the sunshine as it warms gloved hands in plush surroundings.

As long as the atmosphere of play remains positive, a great foursome includes players of differing skill levels. Shooting over 100 won't ruin a day of golf for most sportsmen, but a tiresome, lagging presence will spoil a delightful afternoon with a bad temper and a dawdling pace. Solid play, however, shouldn't include incessant practice swings and needless studying of the terrain. The goal of golf is a gratifying rhythm and a fervent desire to play tomorrow. Wear a plain, collared shirt, even if playing on a public course resembling a vacant sandlot. On most days, don long pants. For repeat players, a pair of water-resistant golf shoes with soft spikes is preferable to sneakers.

GOLF BAG

Show up at the course with your own sticks or call ahead to see if the clubhouse rents bags and irons. Pack ample tees and balls (nonwhite balls aren't kosher). A sleeve of balatas won't last three holes for a novice, so stow a handful of older balls for replacing errant shots into the drink.

For club cleaning, wet one end of a stolen white hotel bath mat and drape it over your bag—the wet end rinses, the dry end finishes. An old travel toothbrush is ideal for scrubbing irons, while matches come in handy for a smoking partner. Pack a few Band-Aids for boo-boos and blisters and a small bottle of aspirin for interminable quadruple bogies. Lastly, stow a sawbuck in the side pocket for clubhouse chews and quaffs.

Nice touch: Even if shot lines appear clean, mark your ball's spot with a buffalo head nickel on the green to avoid hindering others' putting.

PLAY

Golf courses are set up as a zigzag of holes where a strident outburst on one hole may affect play on the next fairway. Unlike arena sports, quiet is required during shot making. After the group tees off, conversation flows freely among course mates, especially when a twosome splinters off to find balls on the far side of the fairway. Although the New York Court of Appeals has ruled that it is not reckless to forgo yelling, "Fore!" to warn others of an errant slice, get into the habit anyway. Rookies might occasionally ask better players for an easy pointer, but a nervous nag who pesters others for advice and swing analysis after every shot is annoying even before the first turn. If dedicated to improvement, sign up for lessons from the local pro. Likewise, accomplished golfers shouldn't puff and offer advice unless asked or correcting an obvious, recurring problem (say, lack of wrist cock).

The worst offenders are those who snail the pace. If a ball veers out of bounds, don't form a posse to rescue it, especially in swampy terrain. After a quick search, take a penalty stroke or, if not scoring strictly or no money is at stake, drop a ball on the fairway edge. Always note ball type and number (for example, Titleist 2) to avoid the ultimate embarrassment of playing another's. Walk onto the green with only your putter, positioning your bag off the green in the direction of the next hole to ease transition after putting out.

COMMON KNOWLEDGE

Tee boxes are arranged according to gender and difficulty. For most of life, use the white tees. If ensconced in a sand trap, no practice shots are allowed, and after cursing your exit shot, rake the sand. As for gauging distance to the hole, look for the colorful markers before conducting a poll. Most courses bear markers in the form of engraved sprinklers or drainage caps, striped wooden stakes, or painted fence posts that denote yardage to the green (usually from three hundred to one hundred yards). Should your pitching wedge send a flying lump of grass on a rainbow trajectory, replace the divots with a light stomp to encourage regrowth; in warmer climes, pour bluish fill/grass seed into the divot (usually supplied in the golf cart). Lastly, if you must relieve yourself, use at least two trees as cover.

Most strapping lads can carry a golf bag for eighteen holes without difficulty or use a handcart, though motorized carts expedite play on courses where the greens and next tees are separated by long, winding paths. Some clubs require the use of a cart and will post "driving rules" to protect delicate fairways. The ninety-degree rule means that the cart is to be driven on the cement path and then turned to enter the fairway at a straight line to your ball. Before walking to your ball, tote all reasonable clubs for the shot. If you think the shot's a seven, for instance, take the six and eight irons just in case.

Nice touch: Pack a deck of cards when playing at a crowded course. A hand or two of poker is more enjoyable than listless practice swings at grass blades before the first hole.

THE PONIES

A brief primer is necessary for those who think that Citation is an old-model Chevy, not the 1948 Triple Crown winner. The call of mud and hooves is usually heeded only for big-name races such as the Preakness Stakes or Santa Anita Derby. To deaden your small-time gambling losses, carry a flask and a fine cigar. If the outing is an all-day outdoor affair, cart your own packed cooler to the infield. Dress smart for steeplechases; for large, daytime gatherings of the local horsey set, stow catered foods and chilled liquor, and drive a large vehicle with accompanying tailgate. Bring two pens (one for the ill-prepared nagging borrower), and if you've had more than a few drinks, write down your bets before approaching the window. Buy a program for knowledge of the field. Scan the medley of stats about prior finishes, handicaps, or sire history. Read the legend or ask a grizzled, cigarillo-smoking veteran for a quick tip. Do not bet over $20 if you do not know what Lasix is.

PARI-MUTUEL BETTING

If you are a rookie, don't fumble with your program and jam the betting-window line with one minute 'til post time. Despite the odds, always place at least a minimal bet on a well-named, catchy-sounding horse. Lastly, horses listed with subletters (Number 2, 2a, 2b, and so on) are grouped for betting purposes. Therefore, if you place a wager on horse "2," then you also receive 2a and 2b automatically.

Speak clearly: race number, bet amount (payouts are based on a $2 bet), horse number (not the name), and desired outcome ("Fifth race, $10 on number 4 to win"). To win, the horse must finish first;

to place, the horse must finish first or second; to show, the horse must finish first, second, or third.

Always "box" exactas (both horses selected must finish first and second in exact order). Boxing is simply two bets covering all outcomes—for example, if your wager was six and seven exacta box, you would win whether the finish was 6-7 or 7-6. A win-place-show bet is three separate bets covering all outcomes. Bet a trifecta (your horses finish first, second, and third in exact order) during a cresting Man Cycle.

Incidentally, You never know about those photo finishes, so don't tear tickets in disgust until final results are posted. Barring something extraordinary, prompting a steward's inquiry, it is shoddy form to comb the ground for winning tickets like metal-detecting beach geezers.

CHURCHILL DOWNS COOLER
• • I jigger bourbon • I shot brandy • Splash Triple Sec • Top with ginger ale • •

Chapter Eight

BETWEEN
THE SHEETS

ROMANTIC RECON

The common adage goes: woman in studio apartment + three cats = single and nonallergenic. But what else can a wide-eyed gent discern about a potential sweetheart upon the first few visits to her pad? Whether a guided tour or the "make yourself at home" walk-through, consider this a license to be curious.

LIVING ROOM

Barren walls speak of a minimalist who values simplicity or a cool kitten who works late or recently moved in. Halted renovation jobs ooze ambitiousness without follow-through, or perhaps a gal who starts hot and then tires quickly of new projects (like you). A Macbook in the corner shouts a creative or techie streak, while art books and Henry Miller novels on the bookshelf speak of a mature provocateuse whose bedroom won't be off-limits to a true gent. Spot any ethnic heirlooms (if she's half-Greek, boyfriends are subject to family approval) or an ego wall of blue ribbons that spotlights who will be the star of this relationship.

COFFEE TABLE

Treat her subscriptions as an inside source for hobbies and future date ideas. Some magazines (*The Economist*, *Vogue*) are status symbols, some are literary (*Zyzzyva*), political (*The Nation*), or edgy (*Zinc*), while others reveal a girl pining for home (*Seattle Met* on an Austin coffee table). Keep an eye out for guilty pleasures—is it Harlequin books with "love sword" underlined on page 34, gossip rags, or something more portentous (*Guns & Ammo*) or half-baked (*High Times*)? Expensive coffee table books are also revealing. Do you spy a retrospective of nude photography or a "seven dry dates and no second base" *Garfield* anthology?

KITCHEN

A colorful array of "Splash & Bash" commemorative party cups and foam koozies marks a sorority pub crawler who can't spell "lasagna." However, if she's got a stack of cookbooks, a rolling pin, and an espresso machine, invite yourself to dinner. Like a coffeeshop bulletin board, her icebox is a hotspot for current events. Beyond refrigerator poetry, officially licensed MLB and NFL paraphernalia indicate sports bar proficiency and ballpark readiness. Look for party invitations, recent snapshots, and artwork by an as-yet-unmentioned four-year-old daughter.

MAIL PILE

A rubber-banded stack of unopened mail bespeaks a busy traveler, while a bevy of gallery announcements and nonprofit mailings signals a cosmopolitan lady with a lefty bent. Window envelopes with FINAL NOTICE in bold print suggest a chick with no oil empire to inherit. What's the addressee's full name . . . is your Millie really a Mildred?

BATHROOM

Gauging femininity (frilly towel sets, tweezers, jars of cotton balls) and peeking behind the shower curtain is allowable. Combo shampoo/conditioners suggest a ready-to-wear kind of girl who makes it to the movies in time for previews. A line-up of hair care "systems" identifies a babe who looks killer on the jetway, but packs a heavy suitcase. Glance askance at the bathroom trash. Signs of birth control method or that time of the month are often in plain sight.

BEDROOM

Take it all in: the sensual Canopy Bed suggests an Arabian night temptress; Sleigh Bed: still believes in Santa; High/Four-Poster: expects to be put on a pedestal; Low/Futon: easy to get in, easy to be thrown out; Twin Bed: check ID. Espy the trappings of a collector, which can be interesting (masks from Bali), querulous ("figurine" anything), or age-inappropriate (menagerie of stuffed animals). Any photographs on the nightstand depict best friends or siblings, you hope—otherwise you're just the rebound schlub keeping her warm until Mr. Smiley pays penance. As for that goodie drawer . . . it's covered under a well-known rider to the Medicine Cabinet Privacy Act of 1988.

PROPHYLETIQUETTE

An armour against enjoyment and a spider-web against danger.
—MADAME DE SEVIGNÉ (1626–1696), on condoms

The cumbersome condom requires impeccable timing and delicate hands. How to broach the subject? Whose responsibility is it? When to don one? Before summoning a hard-line nay, try condoms on for size and learn good manners.

Echoing the ancient Egyptians, Casanova unfurled a reusable linen model. Later, children of the '70s and '80s rode the last train from Woodstock and enjoyed the waning decades of penicillin and promiscuity. Now the game of love is played for higher stakes. Since partners aren't prescreened with a blood test and three references, it's arrogant to think that mere personal selectivity insulates against pesky or deadly diseases.

Modern life affords little sympathy for those who take no precautions against pregnancy. Early withdrawal might garner penalties at the credit union, but it lowers the odds of unplanned fatherhood. Barring statistical anomalies, regular condom use eliminates altogether the need for untimely car seats in your sporty coupe.

PREPARATION

After tattoos are revealed and middle names disclosed, first-time sex looms in the night air like a blimp at a bowl game. If it's your pad, no problem: condoms are stashed nearby. But what if you're on the traveling team? Is it the hostess's duty? No way. Better to impress a new lover by planning ahead than to face an eleventh-hour pickle ending with a sprint to the corner store and a no-frills sheath. On the other hand, whipping out the French tickler before appetizers is clearly crass.

A hosting gentleman offers the basic coital accoutrements for anxiety-free coupling. A cornucopia of wares from an under-the-bed valise is unnecessary, even if presented on a silver tray. Experiment early in your career with different styles before selecting a sock-drawer special.

Glean some insight from a lover's prophyletiquette. Does she keep a cabinet full of flavored condoms, organized like herbal teas? Can she manage the condom as deftly as a boardwalk ring toss? A frank discussion of IUDs and implants deepens intimacy and leads to other conversations. Some fun: "What fantasies do you have?" Some not: "How many lovers have you had?"

LUBRICANTS

Unslippery moments can be a real fly in the ointment. Preferably water-based and paraben-free, a tube of lube restores the unctuousness of natural love. Just as bringing out the toys isn't a comment on your manhood, the use of lube is not a comment about her readiness.

RESPONSIBILITY

If you're intimate enough for sex, you're adult enough to oversee logistics. Whether the worry is paternity or the clap, it is polite to offer the condom option before forgoing protection. A cautious lover shouldn't feel like the bad guy; be proactive and take responsibility, particularly with new partners. Teens and inexperienced Romeos should always buckle up for safety; since the whole gig is new anyway, rubbers are little imposition.

Some gentlemen insist on regular condom use, but consider going bareback under special circumstances, such as in monogamous sexual relations with a long-time lover, especially a spontaneous act in an inconvenient place. Gentlemen past their first love and twenty-fifth birthday might consider weighing the perils of unsafe sex against a lover's lust-hungry waiver. When her crazed infatuation tears at your button-fly and tosses you on the bed like a gunnysack, the mature lady is signaling for immediate action. Permission is still not to be assumed, though. If you can't get a read on your partner's state of mind or bill of health, go to the drawer. Green-light consent must be crystal clear; even if her eyes say yes, let your brain make the final call on usage. Regardless of your well-honed character judgments, this is risky behavior. It presumes enlightened degrees of maturity and honesty best reserved for trusting, sober familiars, not backroom strangers.

Incidentally, by the close of their midtwenties, many women are close friends with the Pill. If a new mate decides to start on it, be patient, as her hormones may not agree with the initial prescription. Merely taking the pregnancy equation off the table doesn't automatically grant every young man who knocks unprotected access to her maidenhead. Whether built by the trust of a budding relationship, an experienced lady's judgment, your social circle's respectability, or your distinct lack of cold sores, the decision to go bareback is her call.

TIMING & DISPOSAL

Produce a condom with dignity and purpose, akin to King Arthur's knights fetching their scabbards. Don't make a stroll to the nightstand a starchless event; infuse it with levity and playfulness.

So now you've got a rubber—what next? Have the forethought to properly equip before the stroke of intercourse. When passions peak past petting, use those hands-free moments to unwrap and unravel, or ask your lover to assist. If the shot clock winds down during fumbled condom retrieval, retrace a few amorous steps before leaping in. Well managed, a condom will not totally disrupt the smooth transition from foreplay to more play.

Do not attempt a walk about the boudoir with a condom dangling precariously, like a wet noodle. A gentleman should tidy up his business in discreet fashion. Wrap spent articles in tissue and toss them in the trash.

Final dicta:

- Lubricated is better than non, and ribbed is indeed for her pleasure. Fruit-scented varieties mask the distinctive odor of used latex. As with beef jerky, stick to name brands and watch those expiration dates.

- Prophylactics redeemed from rest-stop kiosks are like home runs made with nonyellow Whiffle Ball bats. Every score is suspect.

- Asking if her diaphragm is in just before climax is generally impolite.

- Long-term monogamous couples might employ condoms as a role-play prop to redramatize the days of one-night stands.

- If it breaks, be a hero. Either deputize a backup or minimize the anxiety and fake your orgasm.

- Though ineffectual against STDs, lambskin is all right, even for vegetarians.

XXX: PHINEAS'S PHAVOURITES & TESAURO'S TITILLATIONS

Over the course of a healthy physical relationship, a shared fantasy life is a natural extension of intimacy. Embrace the bedroom (and every other room) as a safe space for experimentation. Whatever a lover's fancy, taste without judgment, goad without pressure. In turn, a trusting partner shouldn't have a closed mind. Eroticism is a vast ecosystem of ecstasy, a symbiosis where dominants and submissives, role-play and fantasy exploration, all coexist on the primrose path. Normalcy is not vanilla sex, but acts between consenting hedonists who agree with Ani DiFranco: "I am thirty-two flavors and then some."

Kinky résumés are usually brandished after nervous wooing has passed into playful canoodling under and over the blankets. With whetted appetites, ordinary talk morphs into, "Have you ever tried. . . ." With an open floor, share some favored off-center practices and suggest some Class I and Class II fetishes. After mutual ground is reached regarding tuck-ins, tie-ups, and trapezes, keep raising the carnal bar every sigh session as navels gravitate closer and trust breeds mischievousness. If prudish hesitation chills hot chat, table it until confiding smiles widen with each night spent. Everyone has a vice—even the straight-shooting den mother down the block—so, like dubious game-show host Geoff Edwards, relish the Treasure Hunt.

PORNOGRAPHY

Say *Oui*. Porn is meant to be an infrequent and delectable side dish, never the main course. More than a baker's half-dozen full-length DVDs or downloads suggest a video-onanist, so keep your collection current, but not voluminous. Plucky and filthy selections are encouraged; borderline, scatological choices are for parolees. Store your films discreetly, like fine liqueurs, closeted for discriminate consumption. Unless you still live with your parents, do not stockpile materials under the mattress, though a married gent might keep a basement cache or hidden hard drive folder for smuttier titles.

BLUE STREAKING

Dirty talk finds an outlet during impassioned exchange. The undercurrent is lasciviousness, the tongue ripe with rapid-fire lyric. A mature exploration, blue speak is reserved for near-equal kinksters and is best employed with a measured temperament that does not exceed a partner's tolerance. Nothing complements a stimulated id, healthy power play, or long-distance tuck-in more than choice elemental phrases. While quality pornographic films provide a dragnet for collecting terminology, take care to not borrow text that demeans rather than coaxes. Blue streaking is an advanced stage of intimacy that should gradually and skillfully accelerate the moment. Thus, the use of "slut," "whore," "bitch," and the "C" word should remain on the outskirts of your non-role-playing rotation. Conjure words that connote playfulness, beauty, and primal urges.

OMNIAMOROUSNESS

The consummate epicurean, a gentleman is saturated with a curiosity to sample the feast of sexuality. During formative years, the consequences of dabbling in *délire du toucher* (desire to touch or be touched) are negligible. Before engagements and thirtieth birthdays, experimenting in alternative conduct doesn't threaten masculinity and needn't taint a reputation; a summer course in Greek won't tarnish a major in Latin. The developing gentleman should not forsake a late night *faute de mieux* (serendipitous homosexuality) because of social fears. Hetero or otherwise, boundaries and sexual identity are drawn from an amalgam of experiences with what does and doesn't leaven one's loaf. Whatever your preferences, do so wide-eyed and not yellow-bellied.

NOONER

For a midday pick-me-up, the office's single-cup coffee brewing system has nothing on the nooner. Most romances can't thrive on these minimeals alone, but for worker-bee bed buddies, sometimes it's a nooner or nothing. If necessary, bring a gym bag to the rendezvous to dispel workplace rumors concerning a flushed complexion and freshly showered coif. Whether you eat or fornicate first depends on the couple, but never let a box lunch grow cold on account of a tuna on rye that can be carried to the office in a doggie bag. Unlike tender anniversary sex, nooners are about getting off on the clock; bonus points for keeping shoes laced and ties knotted even as zippers and clasps come unloosed. Nooners are not always equitable, since not all parties may climax. On days off, the nooner can be upgraded with such add-ons as alcohol (salooner), derriere play (mooner), or a quick snooze (spooner). Don't be a nooner ninny: pre-12 p.m. trysts qualify (sooner), as do rainchecks until after lunch (postpooner).

Incidentally, freelancers who can't afford a missed call can proclaim the "phone sex" waiver whereby devices are kept near the sheets. Answer at your own risk, however, because unless previously notified, partners may reengage carnal relations while you take the call.

TABOO

Favor fetish without flaunting it. Enjoy the paradoxical pleasure of wearing a cock ring beneath a tuxedo. Beyond animal acts of sex are respectable lifestyles of lingerie and the whirr whirr of her new "personal massager." The promised land of complete disclosure lies further on, where the bed is a conduit for candid expression. Certain deviances will leave even veterans feeling flushed and prudish. Worry not; a gentleman isn't required to master water sports beyond SCUBA lessons. Still, rent a French Maid outfit for a lover, make dungeon reservations, get tied up in something other than traffic, don some leather, and play "Daddy" (or "Mommy").

ROTE & FOLLY

Not all erotic dalliances entail security clearance and a rope tutorial from the dungeon supply store. In fact, most playful romps involve mind and body, not the toy chest. "Routine" is an evil word in relationships, the surest method to romantic ennui and the early three-and-a-half-year itch. Take the same road to work everyday, but the path to hot love should be a sinuous route from A to Bewitching, sometimes a speedy shortcut and other times a serpentine, scenic byway. Break up habits with the interspersion of less familiar places, props, and times.

Don't be bashful in your birthday suit. A gentleman's naughty creativity turns ordinary into erotic, especially with unexpected attentions and succulent asides. Don't give lip service . . . to lip service; overdo it to delight once in a while. Moreover, like the deftest topographers, use entrancing digits and a lickerish tongue to thoroughly remap your lover's clean lines, surveying for elusive valleys, firmer grades, and previously untapped natural resources.

Instead of using scholarly and poetic prose to explain preferred necking and lovemaking techniques, we offer a few bonded secrets. Always keep a full quiver, even if you only need one arrow.

PHINEAS'S PHAVOURITES

1. Like a footballer in a World Cup match, go hands-free and use the upper body. Complement pelvic tilt through sensuous arm pinning and employ a clever header with the chin and nose.

2. Practice the long vertical lick, centralized on the chakra meridian that proceeds from pelvic cleft, past the navel, through the mammary valley, over the smooth neck area, and to the waiting lips.

3. Induce gentle hot zephyrs as you hover beside an ear, followed by deliberate circling of the outer ear with the tongue, never entering the ear canal like a misused Q-Tip. Precede with a gentle parting of silky locks, exposing the tender aural flesh.

4. Upon initial penetration and for a brief time afterward, engage only the first one-third to one-half of your member.

5. Be the maestro of your own baton for a change, playfully teasing around lips and into a waiting smile before ceding control and leaving it in better hands.

6. Don't just piston-mimic; vary your speeds like a veteran left-handed pitcher, occasionally bringing the action down to a light simmer.

TESAURO'S TITILLATIONS

1. Word to your lover: Turn up the audio and let expressive exclamations telegraph what tickles your fancy. Scribble couplets with your tongue or imitate motorboat sounds with pursed lips.

2. Prolong and tease by peppering oral pleasures with plenty of hand jive. Use different utensils for different dishes, don't mix peas and carrots; and never explore the fundament too early in the count.

3. Tempo and Tantric breath control is the multiorgasmic male's Ace of Tarts. Near climax, acceleration coupled with short, fiery breaths incites release; to moderate passion, use elongated cooling breaths.

4. During heightened penetrating moments, challenge your discipline and practice teasing withdrawal or stoppage. Pause to reengage in erogenous-zone stimulation or impassioned kissing and then return to intercourse.

5. "I'm-all-thumbs." Fortified by a decade of texting, your opposable digits are dexterous tools for manual stimulation. Position your comely someone atop diddling thumbs and see if this lover gets the message.

6. The refractory period: don't make all performances a one-act play; enjoy a brief intermission, but save some spunk for an encore. If necessary, bring in the stunt double.

Incidentally, there are infinite finish lines besides orgasm and physical intimacies beyond intercourse. Do not neglect gentle nibbles at the hairline, the soft undersides of wrists, fingers, and those sexy toes. Pay attention to tucking the tongue under the waistband and sashaying across the panty line. For the real epicure, journey lips from the sensitive clavicle, through the forbidden armpit, and up the tasty elbow.

MORNING AFTER
• • • Absinthe or Pernod • Dash of anisette • I egg white • Top with club soda • • •

THE AFTERGLOW

Don't feel pressure to communicate verbally immediately after your bodies have disengaged from sticky discourse. The tenor of pillow talk varies for lovers with three hours or three years of history, yet a sincere "I feel close to you" never fails. Light candor should govern; it's no time for a "We shouldn't have" morality chat, which must wait until business hours. Avoid asking the loaded, "What are you thinking?" but if asked, respond with a quaint "You . . ." or a wry "Boy, my wife is sure gonna kill me." Recapping highlights can settle the insecurities for new lovers or for couples debuting props. Playful profanity aside, crude comments are out-of-bounds until the initial vulnerability of the act lifts.

A partner's postcoital offering of water signifies hydration loss and is a glowing compliment that punctuates continued desire. Talk of clothing's whereabouts hints at adjournment, but mention of next Thursday signals burgeoning relations. An offer of a shower from a flushed lover is a promising prelude to frolic, now or later. Though do not request one except on a harried weekday morning when a return home is impossible.

Next-morning relations are the sweetest plum, but don't linger like a house pest. Despite a frolicsome a.m., never entrap a mate for the remainder of the p.m. unless plans organically coalesce. Before departure, take a rapid inventory, lest you sacrifice a bold new Zegna tie to the connubial Goddess of Casual Sex. For unplanned stay-overs scented with regret, either tiptoe out or feign sleep. Nothing can be gained from an awkward interrogation when a bedmate (or you) is caught slinking out, singularly shod. Exits of this type indicate a poor selection of lovers in the first place.

TO THE POWER OF [3]

On the winding stretch of sexual exploration, pad your résumé with statistical analyses of the cube root. Some couples opt to troll the bars or Craigslist for willing dames like hungry cheetahs stalking lame wildebeest on the Serengeti, while others count upon alcoholic serendipity. Regardless, there's no better way to incite an adventure than through an ambassador, namely your bi-curious girlfriend. To many a strange lady, an invitation to group sex is a leering, creepy overture. Yet when your girl catalyzes the affair, the unexpected entreaty loses its seedy edge in a flirty blur of lip gloss.

Scenario: the sought-after tango occurs between a couple (A and B) and a mutual attraction (C). Troikas are not necessarily premeditated, but signs of possibility have been exchanged in prior flirtation. Participants are ideally prescreened to be open-minded, healthy (or filthy) individuals who are mature enough to separate love and lust. For this discussion, the gentleman assumes the role of A.

DRESS REHEARSAL

Warm up by stretching the twosome plus one into a shared three. Since A and B are a couple, celebrate the preexisting bond first, especially when C is present. As flirtation rises, carefully extend the affections to C. Invite C into the space A and B share by participating in playful activities that accelerate intimacy (cooking, swimming, dancing, gaming, or a late-night fashion show).

Engage the vortex with swooning conversation, enlivened with shared secrets. Talk of poetry, art, and passion raises the pulse and evokes sensual vulnerability. Like an old salt, raise a dampened index finger to read the prevailing winds. Vast inequalities or jealousies are toxic (A and C get along famously, as B stews alone). If the vibe wavers, scrap the fantasy to prevent serious damage to the underlying relationships. Better to save A and B's future than to jeopardize it for a chance to see what's behind Door Number Three.

With the group exchanging shared experiences, here is the time to get tactile. Fingers drumming on trigger points of the neck are irresistible, as are offers to massage toes. You have one hand for each neck or foot, thus it is best when B and C are closely corralled. With the growing intimacy of the trio, introduce tender behaviors and do not exclude C from a furtive kiss, open adoration, or stroke of fingers through the hair.

Note: any trois is invigorated by wine, candles, pillows, or a long, thin joint. Neck rubs blossom into bare back touching and quasi-naked backgammon. Lose when necessary; cheating for the sake of strip poker is within acceptable limits.

THE CURTAIN RISES

Act I: Exploration. Let your tongue speak a randy mind, and a night's worth of synchronicity will answer back in the form of vital signs rising, including deeper talk of sexual fantasies, laughter with smatterings of flitty kisses, and suggestions for more intrusive activities (spin the bottle, examination of body art or racy undergarments).

Act II: Threshold. Before leaping over the carnal fence, consider whether flirting and coquetry are as far as it should go. Secure final consent with a wide-open display of finger licking, lip kissing, or naughty suggestions. At this point, if B or C flashes the red card ("I don't feel comfortable"), the game is over. Retreat need not be awkward if everything has been on consent.

Act III: The Close. Open love is shared by all. Maintain a balance of attention in giving and receiving. If B or C lingers too long as the other two play, he or she must be immediately seduced to rejoin. A and B's beckoning hands are a confirmation to C that C's inclusion is vital. Strays are thus reinvigorated.

Act IV: Tidying Up. After cozy interaction, poeticize about the denser regions of sexuality. In the afterglow, reaffirm relationships by revering B as your continued favorite and acknowledging C as a welcome intimate. Always kiss last the one you loved first. In the end, A, B, and C should still know whose bed they're really sleeping in.

THE SOFT THREE

When the strip poker cards land a three-of-a-kind in your lap during a friendly or the tequila's been especially dented, let your inhibitions turn to exhibitions. It's rarely impolite to get randy with your own mate amidst an intimate circle. Would your make-out session inspire another? Feel out potential candidates by getting even randier. When party friends crash three to a bed or end up with a cozier-than-usual skinny dip, a simple invitation might qualify you for an extra roll, not unlike the upper-section thirty-five-point bonus in Yahtzee. If they're game, this is an easy invitation to accept passively (watch without participating) or bow out of gracefully ("I'm going to let you two lovebirds roost alone").

SIDE EFFECTS

A blanket policy protects against relationship stress by codifying exactly where/how far things can progress under the sheets. Likewise, third partners have their own ethic and may bring to the table modest upper limits that trump your twosome's liberated designs. Thus, hands off initially. No groping a new other without welcoming gestures—a "yes" to a threesome does not imply an "all you can eat" buffet. Treat threesome play instead as a limited, after-hours menu that doesn't include every entrée. Sometimes you'll simply be a spectator. Other episodes will find you facilitating and assisting, handling tools and fetching fresh batteries. Enjoy the vistas, but look for special cues of consent before inviting your other hand. Once you've logged some flight hours, earn clearance from the tower for more sordid sorties and let matters really take off.

Incidentally, "You've been tagged . . ." should never be followed with "in an album titled 'Last nightz screw." Cagey and clever updates, "Colombia topped Virginia in a heated match-up" or "Got so little sleep last night, you could measure it in inches" are encouraged if you're prepared to moderate responses.

MAIDEN'S BLUSH

• • • • • • • Gin • Triple Sec • Dash grenadine • Dash lemon juice • • • • • • •

Chapter Nine

TROUBLE

STICKY SITUATIONS & SOLUTIONS

Chaos seeps in. Whether transpiring across a booth or pillow, sticky situations demand deft strategy. Extraction with poise defines character. There are no prescribed responses or panaceas; rather, tactful strategies that don't incite second-guessed oafish acts and thoughtless blurts. Herewith, romantic quagmires and resolutions for skirting disaster.

HOW MANY PEOPLE HAVE YOU SLEPT WITH?

Scenario: Pillow talk moves from tittle-tattle to résumé. Minor secrets have been exchanged, but the relationship has not progressed into complete openness. As romantic and sexual histories unfold, the question is posed.

Motive

The inquirer already has an acceptable number in mind; the goal of this joust is to fall within a range. The number must be high enough to demonstrate proficiency, yet low enough to evince selectivity. This line of questioning is a vane, gauging the prevailing winds of trust. An evasive or hostile attitude corrodes developing bonds.

Amorous dalliances of old have little to do with feelings of present. Yet bedmates expect a certain amount of libidinous disclosure. Such information is ostensibly relevant to STDs, though it makes unfair fodder for stereotypes. Until the relationship is ripe for frankness, answer with gourmet delicacy. Brutal honesty about numbers may tarnish fond feelings and ultimately cheapen a budding relationship in a cloud of machismo. Why show a full house when three of a kind wins the hand?

Consider yourself a hostile witness. Open with a saucy reply and impeccable eye contact: "Including you? Two . . . give or take." If pressed further, remain cagey and state with deadpan delivery: "Once I settled my tumultuous hormones, I focused my concupiscence much more judiciously." If still on the stand, refer to the charts that follow.

Even the unchaste gentleman knows the number, within a trio. A lost count admits an unadvisable looseness of intimate affairs. To bolster believability and soften a hard total, round down to the nearest odd integer. Numbers ending in zeros sound staged—take a page from retailers who hoodwink shoppers with alluring price tags of $19.99. Why say "twenty" when "nineteen" may coax this potential lover to reach a milestone? This answer will stand for the length of your relationship.

THIRD DEGREE
· · · · · · · · · · · Gin · Sweet vermouth · Dollop Pernod · · · · · · · · · · · ·

Cues & Clues

This question rarely springs out of the blue; recognize the prequels. Start computing when conversation turns to sexual pedigree—"When did you lose your virginity?" or "When was your last serious relationship?" The carnal-tally query is close on the heels.

Be prepared to clarify and justify your answer. Follow-up questions include: "How many times have you been in love?" or "How many one-night stands?" If you are rustling your notes at the podium, focus the discourse on qualifying, not quantifying, your experiences. Talk of late bloomers, prudish upbringing, or boarding school periods of promiscuity helps triangulate your target number and conjure what range will fly.

Incidentally, play coy. You may invoke the Fifth Amendment and refuse to incriminate yourself. This cavalier attitude is reserved for flings. Or, after fessing up, profess indifference to hearing their number.

The Demure Dozen
Once asked for your tally, opportunity arises to return fire. Schooled in evasive maneuvers concerning weight or age, the snappy modern lady might retort, "I've enjoyed a demure dozen." Further prodding is unnecessary. Must you know more?

Tally Tables
Based on age, Reported Earnings helps determine an appropriate response when you don't know the questioner's tally. The Philander Forecast plots a safe tally relative to the questioner's known total. These charts are gender nonspecific and are meant to quell discomfort, not create a sexist upper hand.

REPORTED EARNINGS

Biological age	Reported Number
Teens (at this age, women will titter at whatever answer is given)	Report 100% of your earnings, but no more than your age
20–24	Report no more than 50% of your earnings
25–29	Report no more than 60% of your earnings
30–Retirement	Not more than two baker's dozen
Retirement and Beyond	Report entire earnings + 20% for poetic license

THE PHILANDER FORECAST

Theirs	Yours
1–5	≤ 11
6–10	≤ 17
11–15	≤ 23
16–25	≤ Two baker's dozen, with smirk
26–49	Full candor
50 +	Full candor + literary license

SO, YOUR FRIENDS THINK SHE'S A DUD?

Unsolicited bons mots about a long-term mate signal a quality lover, but a distinct silence portends that the masses find your bedmate an unstable wreck, a controlling wombat, a snooze, or a second-rate flibbertigibbet who should be returned before the warranty expires. A scattering of tepid reviews is normal, but when both male and female friends—gay and straight, married and single, god-fearing and hot-tubbing—offer a thumbs-down, take a sober reassessment of your relationship before trading in your hip studio for a Walden Two compound bungalow for two.

Absent a sodium pentathol drip, most chums are chary of disclosing her low Tomato rating lest such honesty sour the friendship. Even if hounded, opinions are spoken in coded half-truths. ("She's okay, a little bossy. Have you called Di recently?") Ironically, it's only after a breakup that candor reigns. Avoid needless heartache and learn to spot a dud: (1) you are your mate's spin doctor, explaining away last night's freakout; (2) double-date invitations are politely rebuffed, but solo hangouts are accepted with glee; (3) she abhors your friends, meaning that the feeling is mutual.

Perhaps the crew caught quiet Simone at a loud club that wasn't her scene, or during a crazed workweek. In the end, though, the

Chorus is rarely wrong and can save a lovestruck sap from learning the truth from monosyllabic movers asking if the living room flamingo lamp is going in the truck.

YOU'RE IN LOVE WITH YOUR MISTRESS . . .

A rocky stretch of marriage or prewedding jitters is tiddlywinks compared to the bittersweet turbulence of a hot mistress by day and cool unsettlement by night. The average affair with the buxom trystette fizzles out if attentions aren't regularly stoked by secret text messages and stolen motel room hours. When two hungry souls accidentally fall in love, however, it's an intricate affair. On the one hand, falling in love is a rare treasure, and there's nothing like a paramour to fill in what's missing at home, yet the constant, seismic breach of trust gnaws at a gent's integrity and siphons juice from the primary relationship. Keep your night moves on the QT, since the second worst moment for a wronged partner is finding out she was the last to know.

Despite the perfidious high, forestall any grand plans. Like a stress test administered to a failing bank, scrutinize the home relationship to determine if it has too many liabilities or enough outside investors and working capital to provide a prosperous future. Even if a life change seems inevitable, it's unwise to unwind a long-standing relationship because of six to eight weeks of new coitus (which is approximately the average shipping time for a novelty product to arrive in the mail). Forbidden love is a problem of scale that requires sober decision making. A stable relationship, solid or shaky, lacks the short-term rev to upstage the burst from the untarnished vibrancy of a fresh lover. Moreover, it's impossible to make an informed stay-or-go decision when you're still whispering woo to your secret lover. Hollering "I love you!" to your doxy sometimes solves the problem by forcing her to admit that it's just carnal, baby, not emotional. Hopefully, such a near miss with a mistress will galvanize a valuable home relationship and dissuade the wanderer from another agonizing affair.

Lateral moves are for serial ruffians, and a change should mean an upgrade across the board. As in a civil trial, an unmarried gent needs to prove that the new lover is a better match than his current squeeze by a preponderance of the evidence. However, a married man is held to a higher standard before jettisoning a household with a near criminal act of abandonment, namely, the mistress must be superior beyond a reasonable doubt.

CONVERSATIONAL GAFFES

Take that fully shined, patent-leather shoe and shove it in your mouth. Even the most adroit gentleman stumbles on occasion. Don't panic—show poise like an Olympic skater whose triple lutz ended ass-first on the ice.

Recognize the avoidable gaffes and look to the cures when catastrophe strikes. Whatever the remedy, don't inflate a minor boner or trivialize a flagrant oops. Whitewash foolhardiness with panache and stand tall for half gaffes. In case of serious fallout, don't play word games.

There is no magical Rescue Remedy for any particular gaffe. Deploying the proper one depends on several factors.

Severity: Forgetting a punch line might warrant a Groucho-like Slink Away or Change of Topic, while the more serious gaffe of a racial slur begs an Immediate Confession or Subsequent Redress.

Personality: A lack of comedic improvisation or quick thinking limits use of the Troubadour. Less poetic tongues might pass the Hot Potato or engineer a friendly Turnaround.

Venue: Handle muffs at raucous parties and lively bistros with a Recruitment or spirited Full-Court Press. Formal ceremonies justify the Ambassador or a conciliatory Olive Branch when the mouth misfires.

CARDINAL GAFFES

Off-Color Joke	Racial, religious, cultural, political.
The Killjoy	Legal, medical, financial, and other morbid topics that bring the curtain down.
Arcane Reference	Inside joke, obscure quotation.
Imprudent Apple Polisher	Uncomely sexual advances in the wrong direction (other's spouse, roommate, boss, altar boy).
The Cricket Chirper	After your wisecrack, silence is deafening.
Slip of the Lip	Blown cover; divulgence of secrets or past misdeeds.
Drunken Insult	Unintended malice, candor, or profanity.
The Rerun	Breaking old news and revisiting thrice-told anecdotes.
More Than I Needed to Know	Overreporting of undesirable details.
The Musical Chairman	The music stops and you're caught shouting.
The Undue Erudite	Spare the townsfolk your liberal arts vocabulary.
Jargon Junkie	Excessive use of shop-talk tech lingo and governmental acronymns: GATT, TARP.
Junkie Jargon	Exhibiting too deep a résumé of fringe enterprises, narcotic slang, and paraphernalia.

RESCUE REMEDIES

Immediate Confession	"That was a poor choice of words."
Change of Topic	Move on, no major damage.
Recruitment	Raise a quorum to defend a position: "Tell 'em, Tesauro—Bon Jovi's from Sayreville and Bruce is from Freehold."
The Troubadour	Deft save with improvisational brilliance.
Full-Court Press	Stand on convictions: "You heard me— Elvis is still alive, bloated, and kicking."
Hot Potato	After a fumble, pass the mic to a surer-footed emcee.
The Turnaround	Follow up an Immediate Confession with complimentary candor: "Pardon my flattery, but your dress is quite fetching."
Slink Away	Two-word aside followed by swift departure: "Tough crowd."
The Fill-In	Footnote a historical reference or clarify obfuscated language.
The Ambassador	Dispatch a diplomat to smooth a faux pas.
Subsequent Redress	Apology proffered slightly after the fact: "I'm sorry for last night."
Olive Branch	Peace offering of small gesture or drink.

SECRETS, LIES, & CONFIDENCES

Secrets are deviously decadent, a sort of black-market trade between friends. White lies are the President's Physical Fitness Test of impromptu lyrical dexterity; though big, fat lies are treasonous. Confidences are gifts that should never be taken for granted.

WHITE LIES

I speak the truth not so much as I would, but as much as I dare,
and I dare a little more as I grow older."
—MICHEL DE MONTAIGNE (1533–1592)

Small departures from hand-on-Bible testimonials, white lies evaporate with little risk of serious fallout. Lame excuses are the most common white lie, typically aimed at saving face. Keep them believable: one part fact with sixteen parts make-believe is a rude assault on intelligence. Excuses are useful for deflecting blame when full-blown lies are inappropriate—tell the boss traffic was heavy, not stalled by a fifteen-car pile-up. Offering falsities that would be awful if true—such as apocryphal family death—is ominously prophetic. Also, don't sling insincere compliments about dress and appearance because you think you have to. However, altruistic quasi-truths meant to spare feelings are acceptable ("Honey, of course you don't look fat").

LIES OF CONVENIENCE

When the truth is too long a story or the kernel of justification is buried in complexity, one might simplify. Lies of convenience are dashes of condensed fiction in place of truth, but they can backfire. They are best used when you're innocent of any wrongdoing, yet circumstantial evidence is stacked against you. The lie you tell: "I'm late because I ran into Gordon." The truth you don't tell: "I'm late because I ran into Gordon, who was with my old flame Rebecca." Mere mention of her name would've led to indigestion. Used sparingly, lies of convenience are a proactive thwart of spats and past wounds. Snags occur when a convenient lie isn't enough or the full story comes to light and forces you to reconcile two stories.

HYPERBOLE

Rampant among the juvenile and midlife-crisis sets are tall tales of fast cars, fat bank accounts, and phantom sexual encounters. Lying for ego gratification is laughable at best, pathological at worst. Make life a pastiche of reality and fantasy, but don't pretend to be someone you're not.

However, don't get huffish over the use of exaggeration for the sake of making a point or relating a furious tale. Aside from chats with insurance adjustors and detectives, embellishment is spice to the often bland dish of fact. Only the bore forsakes the imagination of poetic license in the interest of exactitude. In the name of fancy, add a few inches to the marlin that got away or the bustline of your first love. Watch for overkill, however, and don't jeopardize an honest nature with needless supersizing of unremarkable events.

Several excuses are always less convincing than one.
—**ALDOUS HUXLEY**

CHERRY-PICKING

Relatively harmless, half-truths are still lies. Don't be guilty of consistently excluding those tidbits of truth that paint you unfavorably. Your relationship with the listener determines when censorship is called for. For instance, omit details of excess in front of the boss. Even worse is "truthiness" or the flouting of integrity through a steely façade of half-truths until the actual truth becomes hopelessly irrelevant. Boldfaced fibs should never be trotted out to protect your ego or sell an unprovoked foreign invasion.

BIG, FAT LIES

These tumorous canards are buildups of small and midsized lies, a Gordian knot of untruth. Expect inevitable collapse and a flurry of shrapnel. The only way to avoid detection is to tell more lies and deceive more people. The aftermath includes disappointment, scorned trust, and torched friendships.

THE GREAT SECRET

• • • • • • • • • Gin • Lillet blanc • Dash bitters • Orange twist • • • • • • • • •

CONFIDING

Have at least one tight-lipped trustee to unequivocally rely upon for silence. The ideal confidant doesn't need to be sworn in before each secret—sensitive information is assumed protected. Prefacing a divulgence with "Can you keep a secret?" is practically asking for top secret material to end up on Wikileaks. Sometimes, telling one person is telling two—secrets confided to a married friend invariably reach the spouse. Before you invite someone into your sanctum of trust, consider the intent: are you seeking to gossip, gain counsel, or unload a stewing burden? For example, share a Saturday-night escapade with a racquetball buddy, but whisper moral dilemmas to a close comrade.

Incidentally, once there's enough classified material between friends to fill two manila envelopes, you've reached the MAD (Mutually Assured Destruction) phase whereby neither of you needs to worry; one call to the authorities by either party would end up sinking both.

CONSPIRACIES

Conspiracies are collective secrets with the joint responsibility of keeping things hush-hush. Following clandestine acts, coconspirators are subjected to on-the-spot debriefing about what they can or cannot discuss, what did or didn't happen, and with whom they may share this information. For example, bachelor-party adventures are sealed unless the groom himself lifts the veil of silence. Groups of friends should forge certain alliances of incognito to affirm the strength of their bond.

PERJURY REQUEST

Sometimes you are made accessory after the fact by being asked to corroborate a false alibi, ranging from the harmless ("Tell him I forgot my phone") to the precarious ("Tell her you saw me leave alone"). Perjury requests are a lose-lose situation. You are lying for someone else's benefit, and should the web of deceit unravel, your character will be impugned. Though perjuring is to be avoided, it is sometimes inevitable, an occupational hazard of socializing. Ideally, perjury requests call for a single fib or omission and not a flowchart of contingency lies to cover all angles. After this one dishonest detour, the path of truthfulness is resumed.

STATUTE OF LIMITATIONS

Secrets, like soy milk, have long shelf lives. Certain secrets come to light; others lose their efficacy. A confidence that has lost its damage potential is obsolete. For instance, a friend's wine dinner philandering is inconsequential once a divorce is finalized. When a truth is finally declassified, you are free to discuss it openly, though it's prudent to withhold the particulars of what you knew and when you knew it.

The responsibility of a confidant does not end when the friendship spoils. Prior confidences are grandfathered even after friendly and romantic relationships sour. Former friends and lovers deserve continued respect. Befouling a confidence at the first squabble or breakup marks you as an impetuous cur.

TEMPTATION

• • • • • • • • • • Whiskey • Dash Pernod • Dash Dubonnet rouge • • • • • • • • •

• • • • • • • • • • • • • Dash Cointreau • Orange twist • • • • • • • • • • • • •

OFFICE ROMANCE

You've been huddled over a stack of reports at the office for thirteen hours, and your back has developed a slight kink. After a friendly rub, a dinner break is suggested. Glasses of wine are lifted and talk strays from work.

After seeing the same pretty face every business day, familiarity may breed ill intent. Fight this urge—office romance is an avoidable minefield of corporate incest with more booby traps and legal complications than a prenup. However, due to their industry or position, certain workers are exempt from the dangers of office romance. Entry-level workers with replaceable jobs needn't fear the pink slip. In the service industry, the ethic of postshift drinks, shared smokes, and nocturnal confessions makes romantic trysts inevitable. In any case, don't prey on fresh hires, and when beginning a new job, observe a thirty-day waiting period to decipher the office culture.

Steer clear of affairs with the office magpie. If inclined, associates in other departments and part-time help are prudent prospects. Lay flirtatious rap outside working hours where shoptalk casually slips into personal life. An office romance is not a one-step close—it may require several lunches and a few group outings in weekend attire.

NONDISCLOSURE

Eventually, mutual attraction leads to candid conversation: "Do we know what we're getting ourselves into? Are we up for a little cloak and dagger?" Establish the ground rules soon after consummating romance: "Perhaps we should keep this to ourselves." Make sure there is a firm understanding of the difference between discretion and absolute secrecy. Err on the side of the latter.

TREFOILED AGAIN

Another hazard of the workplace is meddling moms and dads shaking the charity cup. There is always a troop leader lurking behind the next cubicle like the office bookie. These cookie emissaries corner you during a weak moment and threaten you with Tag-a-Longs, Thin Mints, and the abominable Do Si Dos. Read your office harassment policy and do not succumb to this type of Lemon-Drop shakedown.

To be sure, enjoy the occasional Samoa with morning coffee. But, as with quality psychotropics, always buy directly from the source and not through some patsy runner doing the Brownie's dirty work. This goes double for personalized calendars, jump-rope or lay-up sponsorships, marching-band chocolate bars, and the dubious magazine subscription whereby some eighth grader tours Paris while you endure a full year of *Popular Mechanics*.

DISCRETION

When engaging in under-the-table amour, monitor outward appearances. Googly eyes at the copier are as fatal as a sudden, cold-shouldered evasion that registers as highly unusual. Keep it off the network: affectionate jots of intraoffice email and hushed phone calls arouse suspicion. Don't risk blowing your cover with surreptitious trips to the supply closet and elevator rides shared alone; anticipation kept pent up from nine to five will be well worth discharging in the p.m.

Office romance is not for habitual cheaters or the otherwise indiscreet. Think twice before risking career and reputation on a thoughtless dalliance. In ordinary romances, poor behavior disrupts your home life but not office life. In the workplace, a rogue cheats on his spouse with a subordinate and faces double jeopardy of a divorce and a career nosedive. Leave extracurricular activities to the company softball team.

Until an office crush proves more serious than a fling, conceal your cross-dressing fetish and other provocative leanings, lest you give the other party embarrassing ammo that would sink you if broadcast. If things unravel, you are only one email away from torpedodom.

POINT OF NO RETURN

Take stock and perform a six-month review, before things become so emotionally entrenched that a bad breakup necessitates someone's resignation. Even mature adults can't work amidst snickering coworkers and lingering hostilities following an unpleasant end. If the relationship review earns an optimistic thumbs-up, consider a public declassification. Speak to your immediate superiors before open hand-holding in the break room. To avoid future litigation, some companies will request each party to sign a "Love Contract" or consensual relationship agreement.

═══ **TOP SHELF, BOTTOM DRAWER** ═══

As a young lad visiting Dad's office, you eyed high muckamucks pulling bottles from desks and pouring strange brown booze. As an adolescent, you watched the tube in awe as Larry Tate deftly produced the office deal-closer for (the old) Darrin. Now it's your turn. Brandish booze for celebratory closings and late-night bracings with weary colleagues. The liquor must be of excellent quality, and brown (bourbon, rye, or Scotch). Accompanied by at least two rocks glasses, it must be stored upright in that deep bottom desk drawer behind the hanging files. Non-compliant desks indicate that you are too low on the totem pole for this privilege: like at the rental car counter, twenty-five years or older, please.

LOSING IT

[boiling kettle]   [pent-up steam]

Don't make me angry. You wouldn't like me when I'm angry.
—**DR. BRUCE BANNER,** *The Incredible Hulk*

Temper, temper. Even after counting ten Mississippis, taking a time-out, and sipping valerian tea, a gentleman occasionally spews his bile. When a lifetime of Deepak Chopra videos and est seminars fails to cool the hot coals of emotional indigestion, losing it is the last resort.

The gloves come off, secrets are spilled, and the sphygmomanometer mercury spikes until the conflagration detonates into complete self-destruction. Plot your outbursts on the following Bile Barometer.

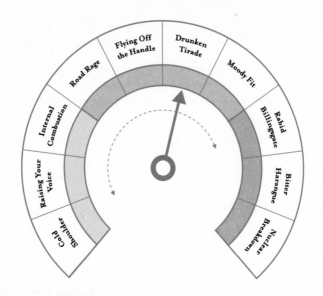

THE BILE BAROMETER

- **Cold Shoulder**: A tight-lipped and temporary uncomfortable silence; haven't had a conversation since mile-marker 57.

- **Raising Your Voice**: You can't bite your tongue any longer, so you dish out at an elevated pitch.

- **Internal Combustion**: Anger-management techniques prove ineffective; holding your breath and "going to the happy place" is not working. Shoulders are tightening—yoga class recommended.

- **Road Rage**: Knuckles white, face red, talk blue, traffic light green, and you're still stuck.

- **Flying Off the Handle**: Distinct episode of ire. This tidy tempest is typically sudden and short, a minor blemish on an otherwise pleasant day.

- **Drunken Tirade:** Now your vituperations are getting on others' nerves. Your jibes and playful breedbating have soured into an ugly stream of drunken tequila-quy.

- **Moody Fit:** Your slow-burning wick has enflamed those around you. Beyond irksome banter, this mushrooming dark spell ruins your day.

- **Rabid Billingsgate:** *You f@#%!$g so-and-so! And another thing . . . !* Eat a soft-soap sorbet for an intermezzo; your palate is feculent and foul. Crowds gather to rubberneck, take notes, and *ooh* and *aah*. Parents cover toddlers' ears, and the bouncers are summoned.

- **Bitter Harangue:** Now it's personal. Ancient history is dredged up. Your rapierlike spite not only probes soft spots, but twists the blade and seasons the wound with rancor. Sacred confidences that were once affectionate are now weapons of war.

- **Nuclear Breakdown:** A Vesuvian, Deepwater Horizon, Chernobyl-like calamity: it's all over. Book a room at Bellevue and burn your address book—no one's coming to visit.

A gentleman has a long fuse. Like a well-balanced pressure cooker, let off steam in small, frequent doses and avoid the histrionic supernova that leaves a high body count in its wake. When you start to feel the Bile Barometer rise, it's time to self-monitor. After a bad day at the office, slug the heavy bag in the gym, not a fifth of Cutty Sark. Minimize ulcerous things: unpaid bills that linger, long bouts with traffic, clinging acquaintances, a non-HD television, or the New York Mets circa 2007–2009.

A note on getting physical: putting fists through sheetrock and side-arming dishes are unhealthy channels for anger. Violence toward people and animals is wholly unsavory, excepting the deer that hop the garden fence and munch your mums.

THE APOLOGY

When excuses expire, tempers explode, and the ash settles, practice penance and apply a mild, medium, or extra-spicy apology strategy. The Culpa Continuum efficiently divides faults, foibles, flubs, muffs, mistakes, oversights, grave miscalculations, and other blunders into a PowerPoint presentation. From the lightest transgression to the darkest betrayal, the gentleman is fittingly contrite. Oops.

MILD

The land of boo-boos, boners, and goofs. For the mildest, "I'm sorry" is not necessary—instead, sprinkle the occasional "Pardon" or "Excuse me." Treat forgetful foozles at face value, and don't turn simple lateness or one forgotten trash day into a trust issue. Even if you have one, don't waste good excuses on trifles. However, habitual misdemeanors accumulate on your rap sheet—every blizzard begins with just a few flakes.

MEDIUM

The arena of lapses, transgressions, and infractions. For medium-low derelictions, impromptu-yet-meaningful apologies are a start. In addition to remorseful words, furnish a modest act of good karma, such as flowers, lunch, or the more practical offer of dry-cleaning reimbursement. Close friends should shrug off these botches as long as your slate remains clean for the following week.

Medium-mediums call for premeditated words or a contrite letter. Lob an excuse to help explain your thoughtlessness. Further, you must furnish greater retribution, such as a homemade meal, a night on the town, or a tasteful fruit basket.

The most serious mediums also require a revisit, as an insurance adjustor would do, to assess the damage and confirm relationship integrity. Hopefully, the passage of time renders your fault historically curious. The phrase "I owe you one" was never more meaningful. Often, emotional scars are less the result of severity of offense and more the consequence of untimely neglect. Despite conciliatory emails, don't assume everything is jake until forgiveness is sealed by a handshake.

EXTRA-SPICY

The pit of iniquity. One may spout profuse regret until morning, but this is merely the first peace offering of the healing process. The victim needs time and space to process the upset before renewed contact. Extra-spicy sins require third-party moderation to shuttle messages and broker a deal. This is the time to come clean and surrender. Lay yourself at the mercy of the wronged. Excuses are despicable and represent a shallow understanding of the devastation. Apologies shouldn't focus on the reviled act, but the wake of battered emotions.

Often you will be required to endure a difficult interrogation, with repetitive questions, uncomfortable details, and incriminating evidence. Bypass pride and answer with humble sincerity. You are lucky to be talking at all.

DEVIL'S COCKTAIL

· · · · · · · · · Port · Sweet vermouth · 2 dashes lemon juice · · · · · · · · ·

CULPA CONTINUUM

MILD: FORGETTABLE WITHIN MINUTES TO ONE DAY.
DEGREE OF FAULT: 0.0–2.5

0.5	Sneeze, cough, mild brushing in public, wearing a black belt with brown shoes, failing to return a friend's disposable pen.
1	Mild lateness, failing to hold the door, undercutting a fellow hailer by fifty feet to snatch a cab, filching office supplies.
2	White-wine spill, household chore defalcation, encrusted frying pan still in sink after five days of "soaking," forgetting to feed roommate's goldfish or turtle, ignoring Wet Paint sign.

MEDIUM: TIME WILL HEAL, RELATIONSHIP WILL EVOLVE.
DEGREE OF FAULT: 3.0–6.5

3	Gross lateness, blowing a mild favor, belching at a dinner party, minor fender-bender in friend's car, premature ejaculation, souring of an evening with your grumpiness, borrowed clothes imbroglio.
3.5	Red-wine spill, arriving home extra late and waking housemates with ruckus, failure to take dog out resulting in unseemly mess, being an irksome overnight guest, online posting of bloated photo of pal, failing to repay debt, mixing lights and darks.
4	Standing up friend without calling, blown favor leaving friend in lurch, sharing secrets with nonrelated party, borrowing without asking, blowing off a family affair, drinking a friend's top-shelf booze and replacing it with rotgut.
5	Breaching trust, forgetting intimate's birthday or other significant date, getting visibly aroused with a lover's best friend on dance floor, distressing host with extended guesting, fistless skirmish.

| 6 | No note, major letdown, ignoring an intimate's crisis, accusing others without confronting them, major drunken spectacle, heated dish hurling, sticking others with large bar tab. |
| 6.5 | Slip of the lip that sinks friend, thoughtless racial or homosexual slur in wrong company, saying "I love you" to get sex, butting into a breakup before the smoke has cleared. |

EXTRA-SPICY: THERAPY AND SOUL-SEARCHING;
RELOCATION TO NEW CITY AN OPTION.
DEGREE OF FAULT: 7.0–10.0

7	Caught in big, fat lie with fiduciary; car accident with cover-up; sharing secrets of inner circle; intentionally writing bad checks to friends.
7.5	Negligent pet care resulting in death of prized small mammal; unexplained, last-minute absenteeism at close friend's wedding.
8	Conspiratorial affairs; infidelities; getting caught with explicit, nonconsensual video; breaking up after coaxing a lover to pay your credit card debt; black-eye assault.
8.5	Accidental killing of a family cat or dog, abandoning pregnant lover and other perfidy, cheating in the marital bed.
9	Grand larceny, fraud, abuse, and other basic unimaginables that warrant police involvement; losing your wedding band in a hooker's lair.
10	Dreadful, irreversible consequences that affect multiple parties and, indirectly, the cosmic balance; evening news–worthy betrayal. Congratulations! You just reserved that hard-to-get corner booth in Circle VII, Ring 3, of Nether Hell alongside heathens who did violence against God, Art, and Nature.

BETRAYALS OF LOVE

If your felonies have affected a lover, mind your distance in the heated aftermath. After betrayal, expect recoil from even the most tender caresses and hugs. Don't be cold, but offer to sleep elsewhere.

After extensive Q&A, it's time to gauge whether the relationship is worth salvaging. It falls upon the offender to attempt casual recontact without pressure. Wait until the recipient responds before proceeding further. You are on eggshell probation until further notice.

Final points:

- Reduce your sentence by turning yourself in before grapevine discovery makes your infraction public knowledge.

- Pie-in-the-sky promises won't get you off on a lesser charge. Even if you think you should say it, don't utter "I'll never do it again" or "I'll never look at another woman."

- For medium bungles, offer (or accept) sincere apologies from good friends and keep going.

- "I was drunk" is a valid excuse for offenses 3.5 or lower; "The Devil made me do it" works for those grade 2 or lower.

Incidentally, no "to be continued . . ." Upper-medium transgressions left unsalved by an apology quickly fester into extra-spicy wounds. Clear the air before leaving town, driving away, or hanging up.

part four

The

WAYFARING GENTLEMAN

[A] racing car is very much like a woman. . . . You must treat it with smoothness and caution. . . . Let's take one corner, for instance. You're approaching at maximum speed, maybe 200 miles per hour, and you've got to decelerate sharply to go round. You don't wait until the last second and then stamp the brakes. . . . And as you're gearing down, you're not banging through the gears; you're taking them smoothly. . . . She doesn't want to be rushed. . . . Now you have to take the apex . . . which can be measured in inches, and this precise spot is the climax. . . . Maybe you're going to apply a little bit of power because she's coming but you haven't really reached it yet; and that last bit of extra power does it. She's done it beautifully, and you've done it with her. . . . The fact that every car is like a woman, of course, means that you can do all the right things with her and she still may not respond.

—JACKIE STEWART (Scotsman and former World Champion
Grand Prix driver), Interview, *Playboy*, June 1972

TRAVEL

MOTORING

[authority vehicle] [dreaded siren]

In Italy, where machismo and horsepower merge on winding highways, the law of *il sorpasso* (to pass with an automobile) dictates Andretti speed and blind passing. In America, preserve riders' sanity by not stopping hearts with near misses, hair-raising banked turns, or shoulder passing. Unless on the run with a blonde moll, do not drive the way you drive alone. Running red lights, slamming on brakes, and doing donuts in snowy parking lots are reserved for easily impressed sophomores. The most overlooked aspect of a seamless ride lies in the driver's artful ability to start and stop smoothly. With a full manifest on board, consciously manage brakes to prevent rocking quease and miniwhiplash at every stoplight.

Incidentally, the Modern Gentleman always uses his signal, not necessarily to ask permission, but to indicate intent.

SPEEDING

For novices, a posted speed of 65 mph does indeed suggest a limit. Interpret speed postings as a gauge of terrain. Typically, 75 mph signs aren't found on winding trails. Of course, there is the law. One weighs the benefits of speed with the inconvenience of moving violations and night court. In general, reserve the lead foot for open stretches, familiar territory, and summertime trips with the top down.

No need to break into triple digits except to test new wheels at full throttle. Speeding is utilitarian for the perpetually tardy, but recklessness is reprehensible, especially in a shimmying, prebankruptcy GM jalopy.

Sharpen eyes for fellow Sunday drivers flashing headlights and return the favor next time you see the sheriff poised in a shaded gully. Ease off the accelerator at intersections, bridges, on-ramps, and swaths cut across woodsy highway medians where cruisers make U-turns. Drop to reasonable speeds when approaching the crest of a hill or a stopped vehicle. Ludicrous speed is unnecessary; enjoy the countryside.

Incidentally, play "follow the leader" and draft slyly behind a blazing sports car with its radar/laser detector LED lights beaconing from the dashboard (and hopefully a good speed trap smartphone app). Don't fret; like Lee Majors, the 'vette will be the fall guy when Smokey emerges from the median.

SCOFFLAW

· · · · · · · Rye or bourbon · Sweet vermouth · Dollop lemon juice · · · · · · ·
· · · · · · · · · · · · · Dollop grenadine · Dash bitters · · · · · · · · · · · · · ·

CLOCKED

If stopped for speeding, pull over slowly, turn off the engine, unroll the window, and place your hands on the steering wheel. Before a word is spoken, you must appear unarmed and compliant. Always address the officer with a clear, curt "Good day, officer," and nothing more. Wait and allow the deputy to explain your defalcation before volunteering any excuses. Never answer the question, "Know how fast you were going?" with an actual integer. If pressed further, state valid excuses with contriteness, not drama. The most effective requests for leniency are truthful (medical or family emergencies, relationship heartache) or a simple petition ("Could you kindly issue me a warning this time?"), though best of luck in those municipalities in debt where ticket quotas are needed to fund the sheriff's pension. Alas, the waterworks and flirtatious smile reside solely in the ladies' quiver.

DULLARD ON BOARD

A gentleman does not parade cutesy back-window stuffings, windshield-obstructing rearview-mirror danglings, or side-window suction-cup signage. Eschew the stupidity of fake limbs dragging from the trunk and raccoon tails in the gas tank. Window placards announcing mothers-in-law or toddlers on board are the marquee of blockheaded drivers and guarantee curbed courtesy from other motorists. A single strand of Mardi Gras beads is permissible, but graduation tassels, cheap garters, or rotating CDs are unwelcome dashboard trinkets. Festooned fuzzy dice are encouraged for vintage hot rods.

PASSENGER ETIQUETTE

Take control when the driver's radio and climate choices have nullified the joy of being chauffeured. Before usurping the host with a discourteous stretch across the console, preface with a statement. When engaging heat: "Mind if I throw a log on the fire?" Never touch the FM radio dial that is in the Indie Zone (that is, to the left of the 90MHz or to the right of 107) unless you're older, cooler, or have a backup ride home. And after a palpation-inducing drift into another lane, drivers' mobile devices may be confiscated.

Shotgunners should earn their keep by helping navigate. Know that north and south are different from up and down, watch exit signs, and make sure the driver isn't suffering from highway hypnosis or Moon-Pie deprivation. Take the wheel when the driver needs to shed a sweatshirt. Keep the car straight and compensate for bad alignment. Decline requests when traveling at excessive speeds or if the car is careening down a mountain pass with more curves than late-night Cinemax.

ROAD TRIPPING

Motoring for the sake of rolling scenery and the joy of crossing state lines is worth more than discount airfare. Peanut baggies at thirty-five thousand feet have nothing on craggy coastlines and the salty wind smacking at your T-top along the cruise north on U.S. 1 from Los Angeles to San Francisco. At the rental car counter, always inquire about convertible upgrades, except for January visits to Fargo for the Eastern North Dakota State Curling Finals.

Don't leave home without: a pack of tissues or wet-naps, coolered drinks, crunchy snacks, beach towel for dips and spills, travel journal, night-driving stimulants, and music collection all-stars covering moods from daytime rock and operatic exuberance to mellow acoustic. Designate a rest-stop brown bag for litter to prevent thoughtless defenestration of empties.

With or without a map, solitary road trips are therapeutic and clarifying. Forget a bad breakup, decide on a grad school, or merely feel space beyond the city block. Stop at a scenic overlook and get high on the mountain air. Skip the broadest routes and interstates. Hop off the exit and get lost on a back-road whim. With an empty passenger seat, periodic cell phone shout-outs satisfy cravings to share. Learn the madness and unexpected joys of the car radio functions Seek and Scan when in unfamiliar air space. Slip out of shoes and into pyjamas, or after a dash to the sea, sit on a sandy towel in swimming trunks.

HONKING

Horn blowing, on the decline, has been unduly criminalized in some areas. Gone are the halcyon days of Saturday afternoons filled with intermittent beeps commemorating victory by the varsity football team.

Sound off vuvuzela-style in the following situations:

- The light turns green and you are immobilized behind a luxury sedan, driven by a reptilian matron buried in her Chanel compact. Lay it on, hopefully causing creative beauty lines.

- When lively conversation in the cabin boils over in delight, give a medium burst to alert the heavens to such joy.

- Give a bunt to persistent lane-drifters, a soft staccato to alert cyclists.

- While respect for the elderly is a proper pillar of society, sharing your lane is another matter. Let her ring.

Incidentally, an honest mechanic who resists the temptation to invent fictitious transmission problems deserves a small sum along with your continued patronage. Off-the-main-drag repairmen who fix minor problems on the spot deserve a Jackson or two. Find yourself filling up on an extremely chilly night? Slip the station attendant a few extra bucks just for working.

ASKING DIRECTIONS

Except for Prince Henry and a GPS satellite, no navigator is infallible and everyone should employ a certain amount of navi-guessing. For those caught without GPS, ask for directions before a passenger suggests it—this nip in the bud will save your gentlemanly reputation. Local yokels may be queried about venues in the general area; otherwise, it is acceptable to stop at a gas station to quietly peruse a map.

Steer clear of sinking, ominous auto vibes that pall the cabin after the discovery of an unplanned twenty-mile detour. Everyone dreads the realization that precious life energy was drearily squandered on a barren country road or interstate. After such a mood blow, regain bearings. Like a Saint Lawrence breaker, smash the conversational ice, lest you have a boatful of sulking, Caine-Mutinous passengers ready to pounce on a single four-way-stop hesitation. Should morale plummet, give up the keys and fall upon the mercy of clamoring backbenchers.

WHICH WAY

• • • • • • • • • • • • • • Brandy • Pernod • Anisette • • • • • • • • • • • • •

BUMPER STICKERS

These auto op-ed pieces incite tailgaters to honk in good humor, recognize fellow alums, or dream of later keying your fine hatchback. Bumper space is valuable: the gentleman limits himself to two items on the fender, if any. Sticker creep is not tolerated; peel away refugees that have migrated to the lower trunk. Err on the side of none.

Choices are legion; taste is limited. Express affiliations, music tastes, and philosophical leanings, not corporate pap or travel logging ("This car [and 40 million others] climbed Mt. Washington"). A single university decal is modest, but expired seasonal decals denoting access to exclusive beach communities scream showboating. Election-time stickers, like holiday lights, should be taken down in timely fashion—after defeat in the primaries. Before applying a sticky witticism, suppress your giggle and ask: will it be witty to an irascible motorcade during a ten-mile summertime backup?

Like a tattoo, the bumper sticker is personal, if less permanent. Avoid giving too much away. Be proud of proclivities for skiing or bathhouses without the rear-window advert. For the botanist who fancies hydroponics, posted cannabis leaves are probable cause for police stops in suburban enclaves.

Be a sticker stickler. Select clever over choleric, zippy over zealous. For instance, "My other car is a Ferrari" might work best pasted on the muffler of a moped. "Keep Honking, I'm Reloading" is common, but the lesser-known "I brake for hallucinations" is more expressive. "My karma ran over your dogma" is well regarded by these gentlemen, though the baffling "I ♥ Quisp" is more singular.

Incidentally, pithy old saws or ironic idiocies printed on T-shirts are the sidewalk equivalent of vapid fender signage. "Don't bother me now . . . my brain's out of order" and other dreck displayed on your chest places in serious doubt your respective share of the planet's oxygen supply—a mere 21 percent of the total atmospheric gas content.

SLEEPER TRAINS

Sleeper trains connect the gentleman to century-old luxuries across the bucolic tracks of Americana. Read some Ambrose Bierce, order a whisky in the club car, and enjoy the caboose, as sleeper cars are typically found at the rear. There's something particularly hypnotic about gazing down the tracks as endless rail converges in the distance.

Today's sleeper trains are tops in rail travel, well worth a coachfare upgrade. Designed by calculus-wielding space maximizers, sleepers waste no square footage. Pack light so luggage neither cramps the area nor blocks the air-conditioning vents. Most sleepers feature top and bottom single bunks with little extra room, though a spooning twosome can squeeze onto one and toss baggage onto the other. The toilet is similar to an airplane lavatory, with a fold-down sink that harkens back to days of bedside washbasins. Travelmates not accustomed to an open bathroom-door policy might splurge for a first-class sleeper with a separate three-quarter bath.

For maximum privacy, close the door and draw the drapes to avoid peeping passersby. Conversely, leave the sliding door open to catch the corridor breeze. Bed linens are provided, and there's a set of straps either for securing yourself in sleep or restraining a lover. Either way, they are best deployed during bouts of turbulence.

BLUE TRAIN

• • • • • • • • • Gin • Cointreau • Lemon juice • Dash blue curaçao • • • • • • • •

Nice touch: When booking a compartment, select the sunrise side; leave the shades open and awaken to the percussion of a chugging locomotive at first light.

THEOREM DE VALISE

The classic overpacker chokes his bag with a different ensemble for every moment and mood. Conserve. Mix, match, and plan to depart and return in the same outfit and bulky coat. Tote workout attire for unexpected fitness opportunities. A full wardrobe isn't at your disposal when traveling; no one will fret if black pants get a second-night reprise. Learn from prior packing mistakes. Notice what was left unworn from the last trip and pack lighter next time.

Our Theorem de Valise replaces guesswork with mathematical certainty. Dust off your abacus and read on for practical packing ratios that measure shirts, pants, and shoes against nights away.

BAGGAGE CLAIM

Prepare to snake your way through the clutter of golf clubs, snow skis, and caged pets to lay claim to your effects. Get a ringside spot but avoid standing mesmerized in front of an empty carousel before the bags are spit out. Once ready, get in the paint, box out, and crash the boards; it's all about positioning and the occasional off-the-Samsonite rebound. Since you're not the only one with a black duffel bag, adorn your valise with a marker, ribbon, or travel tag. Be nice: rescue a wayward bag that has turned the corner out of someone's reach, assist a neighbor with lumbering trunks, and clear the mouth of lodged impediments to maintain flow.

Beyond efficiency, traveling affords the chance to pack your closet's greatest hits. Instead of taking two months' worth of hot-date ensembles, tote a bagful of favorites for four days and three nights of nonstop style and mood changes. It's okay if everyone thinks you dress this way all the time. Know the mercury and itinerary ahead of time. City avenues and mountain hikes call for different clothes and shoes. For long weekends, pack daytime kicks and a snazzy pair for the evening. Shoe color, black or brown, determines pants and belts. Fill a valise with interchangeable clothes that match these shoes. Shirts and pullovers are the wild cards that stretch two pairs of slacks into four different outfits. Special shoes that go with one outfit are forgivable for extended stays when extra footwear isn't frivolous.

Five steamer trunks is overkill for a simple getaway, but stowing a little comfort is essential. Before stuffing a suitcase with practical items like toothbrushes and airline tickets, gather personal bits of home. Turn any motor inn into an inviting abode without paying $8.95 for the edited late-night feature. Stow a pet photograph, pyjamas, choice tunes, and a strong dose of vitamins to counter local bacteria.

Nice touch: Don't forget the fun stuff—water pistols for a picnic, handcuffs for the fetish club, flannel for a hayride, or a ski mask if short of cash.

TOILETRY KIT

Something small, black, and durable, containing at least two compartments, is adequate for all affairs. Skip the haphazard pile of beauty products strewn about the bottom of one's luggage. A toiletry kit should reflect simple preparedness without medicinal overabundance. Travel-sized products or holders ease congestion and mass. With purchase of this book, you hereby promise to destroy forthwith your old, periwinkle-blue or vomit-beige, wide-stitched, canvas-like American Tourister toiletry bag won at the church raffle ten years ago.

In addition to reloadable basics like deodorant and toothpaste, have an inventory of in-a-pinch essentials like a diminutive bottle of aspirin and multivitamins, decongestant, extra contact lenses, bowel remedies and antacids, disposable razor, condoms, small bar of facial soap, safety pins, nail clippers, Band-Aids, and styptic pencil.

CHECKLIST

Pack carefully before embarking for a wedding or formal gala that requires a bevy of accoutrements often left behind. Perform a thorough sartorial rundown before zipping the bag. A simple recitation averts a last-minute trip to a sporting-goods store for black tube socks to wear under tuxedo pants.

A garment bag oral checklist (literally meant to be spoken aloud):

❑ Shoes	❑ Socks	❑ Pants	❑ Reversible Belt
❑ Undershirts	❑ Boxers	❑ Shirts	❑ Jackets
❑ Ties	❑ Cufflinks	❑ Handcuffs	❑ Glasses/Contacts

ADVANCED TROUBLESHOOTING

Don't forget the extras that are bag mainstays: business and playing cards, pens, phone chargers, extra earbuds, loose change, and matchbooks from prior trips for nostalgia. To lower stress, pack a spare pair of dress socks in case of an inadvertent step into a hotel bathroom puddle. Moods change between packing day and the big event. Bring various dress shirts and ties and decide at the last moment. When going to a black-tie event, be the warm-bosomed schoolmarm: stow a cheap spare bow tie and set of cufflinks in your tuxedo pocket for a forgetful chum. To prevent a mishandled-luggage catastrophe and an immoderate dry-cleaning bill, store shampoo, cologne, hair gel, and other powder kegs in a sealed zip-locking bag.

THE THEOREM ITSELF

Algebra serves a gentlemanly purpose: whether your triangle is isosceles or scalene, you are bound to find value in this easy, plug-and-pack Theorem de Valise—a mathematical construct as riveting and complex as Fermat's own. Punch in your data to calculate how many glad rags should be packed for the holiday and minimize those airline baggage fees.

This is not your father's quadratic equation.

$$\text{SHIRTS} = \sqrt{(\text{PANTS}^3 + \text{SHOES})} + \text{NIGHTS/DAYS}$$

Note: nights/days refers to the respective number of days and nights away.

Equivalents: shorts = 0.5 pants, sandals = 0.5 shoes,

short sleeves/pyjamas = 0.5 shirts, sportcoats/sweaters = 1.5 shirts

A WORD PROBLEM

Phineas is taking a beach weekend in the Hamptons. He is leaving Thursday after work and shall return late Sunday afternoon. He will bring a pair of dress shoes, a pair of casual shoes, and sandals. He will also pack one pair of jeans, evening trousers, and swimming trunks. After work, he will board the 5:51 p.m. eastbound train from New York; however, a westbound train leaves Montauk at 6:10 p.m. Both are traveling at the same speed. How many shirts should Phineas pack?

Hint: the gentleman departs and returns in the same ensemble, thus his travel shirt, pants, and shoes are not packed (or counted). Also, do not forget the lounge-about T-shirt (pyjamas may be substituted) for lazy mornings. You will not receive credit for the answer if you don't show your work. Let's compute:

$$\text{SHIRTS} = \sqrt{\{(2.5)^3 + (1.5)\}} + 3/3$$
$$\text{SHIRTS} = \sqrt{(15.63) + (1.5)} + 1$$
$$\text{SHIRTS} = \sqrt{(17.13)} + 1$$
$$\text{SHIRTS} = 4.14 + 1$$
$$\text{SHIRTS} = 5.14 = 5.0$$

Incidentally, a wifebeater is not 0.14 shirts. Stick to the nearest half integer. To avoid overpacking, always round down.

Phineas should pack two stylish shirts for Friday and Saturday nights, one casual short-sleeve shirt for the days, a sweater for protection against an evening chill, and one polyester pyjama set.

Other formulae solve for different variables:

$$\text{SHOES} = (\text{SHIRTS} - \text{NIGHTS}/\text{DAYS})^2 - \text{PANTS}^3$$

$$\text{PANTS} = \sqrt[3]{(\text{SHIRTS} - \text{NIGHTS}/\text{DAYS})^2 - \text{SHOES}}$$

GUEST DECORUM

Be a welcome guest, not a trying inconvenience. Common sense, privacy, and humility go a long way—even long-standing college intimates deserve a tad of respect. Be nice: offer to walk the dog, wash the dishes, or make the mortgage payment. In addition to consolidating your bags and wiping excess toothpaste spittle from the mirror, learn a few other considerations.

"Make yourself at home" doesn't mean dialing 1-900 numbers or ordering pay-per-view UFC specials, drinking out of the milk carton (even the buttermilk carton), belching like a rabbinical shofar blower, drawing an uninvited bath, recharging anything larger than a laptop, annexing the living room like a conquistador (clothes strewn, sofa bed out, coffee table littered, multiple pizza boxes holding court), making your presence known as an early riser, parking it anywhere not designed for sitting, bringing home an unsolicited nightcap to your aunt's house (if you have broken this guideline, do not invite your guest to breakfast), ball-playing or nakedness around the house, leaving adult magazines by the bed, exhibiting

New Age or ethnic idiosyncrasies (lighting incense, frying curry, or curing soprasetta from the rafters), hanging undergarments (especially black bikini briefs) to dry from the shower rod, packing a load of laundry (except when visiting Mom), blanketing the bedroom with a multitude of empties, smoking dope indoors (blowing smoke out the window is still considered inside), guitar strumming after 10 p.m., using the living room as a putting green, hosting an all-night poker game.

Incidentally, if you need an extended place to stay, say so up front instead of fudging intentions. If your "brief" stopover begins to affect the host's electric bill or your guest towel sours, you have overstayed your welcome.

DON'T TOUCH

By reaching for the wrong drinking glass or sitting in "that" chair, every guest irks the host with a thousand silent indignities. It's best to touch as few things as possible and avoid raising a fuss about anything when everyone is famished and short-tempered. The sooner a guest learns to live with fewer amenities, the smoother the stay for all. The easiest way to be a noodge is to indulge these trouble spots: lengthy showers that tax the hot water heater, constant foraging in the cupboards, and slamming of doors and cabinets or otherwise roughhousing the fixtures. That being said, the guest room is fairly free from regulation and a guest can leave a maelstrom of blankets on an unmade bed (except on the last day) and a deluge of spent clothing around an open suitcase that spans at least half the room's square footage.

Incidentally, couples in guest rooms who are stewing or screwing should learn to disagree or climax in muffled tones, lest they wish to be switched to the no-invite list, alongside nosy cousins, creepy introverts who scribble in their journals, and portly stoners who sleep prone and bare-assed on the living room pull-out sofa.

As a wrap-up, keep away from: prescription bottles, the dining room or any room designated for "hunting"; the "master study" (unless accompanied by a snifter of brandy); the humidor or stash; the wine cellar; anything autographed; any piece of furniture with a historical or explanatory placard; the whisky decanter; the family car, even with a note; hope chests; glass curios or anything in an étagère; other people's razors; any family member (in that way) including great aunts, cousins, babysitters, and farmer's daughters.

BRING A GIFT

A doniferous guest bestows upon the hosts a small token, larger if the visit is significant. Something personal should suffice, such as a bottle of infused olive oil, bounty from your garden, or an obscure Xavier Cugat vinyl LP. For others, vices are appropriate. A bottle of vino or liquor is proper if nothing more original comes to mind. However, wrap the bottle in something other than a recycled brown paper bag, and don't forget the bow. Regional comestibles are winning ideas. For example, outsiders will appreciate Vermont maple syrup, New York City bagels (however, the Sunday *New York Times* is not a gift, but a gesture), Kansas City BBQ sauce, or local fresh flowers or plants. When in doubt, browse a museum shop or patisserie, or mail a gift ahead via the Internet. The savvy gent stows a few small colorful bags in the closet for gifting. Nothing speaks to a slight lack of class more than presenting a gift in a plastic supermarket sack (aka "cat shit" bag).

Want to make a bigger impression? Think small, overlooked pleasures: thousand-piece puzzles, stationery, or an array of jams, fine teas, or coffees. Indulge the host's hobbies: a twin-boxed set of playing cards for a big whist player or quirky lemon reamers for the gourmand. Follow up with a onesie for the infant, cool toy for the toddler, or irreverent T-shirt for the schoolboy and you'll garner the softest towel in the joint.

Something tucked into the valise for a "meet-the-parents weekend" arrests querulous sizing up and might upgrade you from the basement couch. Gifting forges a favorable impression, earning clemency for those festooned with body art or lacking viable careers. Bestow shortly after arrival or the next morning following breakfast.

E-FRIENDS

The provision of WiFi and limited computer privileges is standard, on par with offering guests a fresh, nonstained towel. To avoid hassling the host for a blank CD, guests wishing to copy MP3s and photos should pack their own flash drive. A host's computer is like the bathroom cabinets—no peeking in the file folders or other private corners of the space. Internet usage should be limited to email checking, news sites, and social media updates, not surfing and downloading malware-laden apps. If you wish to endanger the host's property, bring home a felonious tramp or chain smoke in bed after helping yourself to a fistful of Valium.

LIFE RESET

Big change can be a personal choice or be thrust upon you; either way, a crisis is a terrible thing to waste. Whether loveless, jobless, clueless, or just suffering from a chronic case of ramblin' on your mind, maybe it's time to reformat the hard drive of your life to avoid early obsolescence (the first symptoms being a reversion to canned beer and the leasing of a new Kia, usually in that order). Reassess your assets, rediscover self-reliance, and iron out some psychic and waistline flabbiness. By definition, young punks still years from their first gray chest hair aren't eligible for a life reset, since they haven't yet had a life journey that needs rejiggering. For artists or burnt-out professionals, however, these decisions are investments in the complexity of one's character.

Older souls whose life isn't so easily packaged in the rear of a hatchback need more of a bankroll to start over, but everyone else merely needs a passport and a determined look. Whether you land in a new place or just leave Wall Street for the pickle biz, expect a period of hard work, minor frustrations, Salvation Army drop-offs, boozing, and reconnecting with old friends who've stayed with you through many erased address book entries. There's an element of escapism, but a life reset is not an extended spring break—the latter ends with debt and a racy Macbook slideshow, the former with new friends, fresh digs, and an updated skill set. While a life reset doesn't require a master plan, there should be an overriding, if vague, goal beyond exorcising demons or attaining enlightenment, otherwise the big change is like hitting the Hyperspace button in Asteroids—yes, you've sidestepped trouble, but your wayward ship could reappear tragically inches from a hurtling space boulder (and life, unlike Atari, does not grant extra lives every 25,000 points).

CRASHING AND BURNING

An open-ended crash extended to foreclosure victims or banished infidels requires an agreement on the material terms, including length of stay, closed door policies, visitation rules, and the list of no-nos that will invite immediate expulsion. The crasher may plead the Fifth with his estranged wife, but in exchange for free accommodations, the host is entitled to one unexpurgated retelling of the guest's ejectment. When relations fray and sickly cats expire due to the crasher's negligence, goodbyes can be awkward, so agree on the propriety of eviction by text message. Crashers should start off favorably with a grand gesture—beer and pizza for everyone. A closing gift is another winning method to obtain a positive seller rating, since even if it ended on a sour note, you'll still garner a "Hey, at least Hollander left behind a nice bottle of rye."

With the vacancy sign illuminated, don't then ask for the car or other favors that trample a saintly pal's patience. For some hosts, an extended crash is overdue time with a ne'er seen friend; other hosts are unenthralled after the third day. If the latter, be scarce, but if the former, engage in camaraderie lest you hear the clarion, "What are we, your free hotel room?" Either way, the "green" crasher leaves little impact on the host's environment. The shit, shower, and shave troika is indeed performed during off-peak hours, lest the host encounter an ingracious ninny smoking a butt in the tub behind a locked bathroom door.

The
CEREMONIAL
GENTLEMAN

*I cherish little notes from some of my old lady friends
in their eighties, because they know how to turn
a sprightly phrase in even the briefest notes
while some of my contemporaries freeze up
at the sight of note paper. . . .*
—*Amy Vanderbilt's Complete Book of Etiquette,* 1958

Chapter Eleven

PUBLIC

RELATIONS

POLITICS OF FRIENDS

Old friends, tarnished and patinaed, remind you where you came from and act as a governor on ego and the usual whitewash that comes with promotions and accolades. New friends are the spice of life and the source of extra continuing education. However, they require several rounds of regard before they can exist without monthly momentum, so don't blow "We should really get together" aspirations early on or a new association will fizzle like a July sparkler. When strolling or driving, use the magic telephone time slots (Mon–Wed, 7:30 p.m.–10 p.m.; Sat–Sun, 11 a.m.–3:30 p.m.) to connect for happy birthdays or bigger fond hello downloads. When the procreation bug hits, store spouse's name and kids' names and ages in your contacts info to flawlessly exhibit your bonhomie.

Nice touch: Arrive on time to a close friend's soirée to help with candles and last-minute ice runs and act as an early seat filler when the first guests buzz.

PICKING UP THE CHECK

The true joy of having an ample bank balance is the ability to bestow largesse to close friends. "This one's on me" means just that, with no explicit future expectation. Options include the tableside big flourish, without any hint of irony about the frequent flier points, or the sly gobbling of the check during a bathroom break. Notably, if someone else is picking up the check, do not actually *pick up* the check, as those who've been bluffed out of the pot may not view the winning hand. Dole out the Bohemian Subsidy to ensure that thin-walleted, nonconformist pals don't plop down grocery money for Thai food and exorbitant cover charges at after-hours clip joints.

FRIENDLY FIRE

Sometimes even the funnest members of your platoon slump from lady of the hour to persona non grata. Bite your frown, though. Since Jacqueline is big in publishing and Amy Lee can get you a table at the hot café with but a finger snap, best to just ride out this temporary wave of annoyance.

Serial Proposer/Canceller Chancellor: The smiley quick-draw who is forever declaring, "We should . . ." but rarely follows through, or sends the "Something came up" text with but little notice.

Judge & Jury: Finger-wagging acquaintance who disapproves of your lifestyle.

Moocher: Erstwhile friend who comes calling only when it involves your pool, your beach house, and your booze.

Flashpointer: High-maintenance pal always in crisis. "Can we talk now?" "Can I crash at your place tonight?" "Are you a notary?"

The 7-10 Split: When you love one half of the couple but despise the other. As on the PBA tour, even top pros can rarely make this spare.

COLLECTIVES

Postcollege or grad school crews are valuable lifers, the ones who come to visit in twenty years with but a sprig of hair and an enlarged prostate, yet still tote a one-hitter and a taste for cheeseburgers with a side of yellow rice. Note the sociological ebb and flow as the perpetual ne'er-do-well is the first to settle down (though the second to divorce), while other professional-grade alums catch the gambling bug. If you lose a few Franklins to a pal in transition, at least you'll be repaid when saucy pics of his new trophy mistress grace your inbox.

For the first decade after tassel time, the group might stuff into a rented beach house once a year to relive their formative years, this time with bottled beer and New York strip. However, as once-hardened bachelors enter the taedium vitae of middle age, tight cohabitation becomes untenable and summer reunions fall away. The group's majority whip will forcibly attempt to garner support for a weekend blowout, yet it's fortunate if the gang can muster its regional forces for a Sunday get-together at David's new McMansion. It's copacetic; in a group of a dozen stalwarts plus mates there are bound to be lines of discord, in-dating gone bad, and silent feuds, such that most of the clan is unaware that Eli is in *broyges* with Peggy. Since the group organism won't perish, the individual cells learn to play nice and minimize contact with begrudged others. The result is comical and a lesson in Office Politics 101: email lists pruned for certain messages, splinter groups that meet without the offenders, and the delicate interplay of asking permissions to invite so-and-so if what's-her-name will be present.

IOUs

With a handshake as collateral and favorable no-interest terms, the friendly lender happily forks over a wad of cash and expects certain integrity in repayment. While a loan to an out-of-work chap to keep the lights on is implicitly a long-term debt, a payday loan to a pal with a surefire filly in the fifth race at Pimlico requires prompt repayment within the calendar month. To prod a defaulting lendee, send an email reminder explaining why you need the money: "Taking Tamar out and she's more foie gras than drive-thru. . . ." With no PayPal transfer in sight, double dates will dry up to avoid pubic airing of the "debt." Although small-time stakes under $250 are usually waivable by a solvent lender, a deadbeat with a string of unpaid dinner check advances and shared car rentals will eventually be cut off with a stony "Sorry, bank's closed."

Good friends don't disappear when a floater comes due. A pal shouldn't feel like a loan shark fiend for asking for his own money back. A good faith payment or a simple "I'm working on it" eases the bankroller's agita. If lacking the funds, offer to barter favors. Certainly a $500 debt doesn't brand a borrower an indentured serf, but a smart lender will not write it off before receiving pennies on the dollar. Debtors may not flinch when requested for demolition work or brush duty on house-painting chores under 700 sq. ft.

Incidentally, many a friendship has been splintered by a business deal or IOU gone bad. Don't offer up amounts that represent a real percentage of your net worth; that way, when you get Madoffed by an old pal you can still pay the rent and move on, with or without him.

SOCIAL SYSTEM: THE FIVE RINGS OF FRAMILY & FRIENDSHIPS

Astronomically speaking, syzygy is the positioning of three or more celestial bodies in a straight line. On this side of the ionosphere, it's vital to understand the concentric orbits of friends, framily, acquaintances, and other heavenly bodies. Among your closest contacts, there's less of a premium on social engagements and more significance placed on personal responsibility. Both of you are on call for white collar labor, kind-ear listening, and crisis management. With mere acquaintances, one missed soirée may doom a tenuous relationship, yet intimate friendships can survive broken dinner plans as long as you're there to offer jumper cables at I a.m. or an impromptu place to crash after a friend's blonde live-in finds an incriminating red curly on his boxer shorts. Whereas new friendships take energy to start, fully developed friendships take energy to stop. And though there's always wiggle room for gaffes among intimates, everything is amplified in the start-up phases of friendship, with each party on probation as peccadilloes come to light.

Venus and Mars aren't changing their respective paths, and neither are lifelong friends that maintain a strong gravitational pull over your life. You can, however, capture cohorts stuck in outer orbits with frequent appearances and small sacrifices. Make plans that stick, offer professional advice gratis, and help with the move so that friendship grows; on the other side, it's easy to relegate what's-his-face and what's-her-name to the nether regions of regard by being generally unavailable or refusing to drive crosstown in the rain. For artist friends, entry-level benefaction is required and encouraged. No, you don't need to commission a major piece, but attend her latest trunk show and pony up some clams for a modest work.

Incidentally, do new pals pass the Excedrin test? If you've got a headache *this big* and it's got New Pal written all over it, calculate whether he offers more hang-ups than cool reasons to hang out. High-maintenance friends are like wines that take twenty years to mellow and mature: long-term investment or vinegar? Hopefully the former.

* * *

The following are the five tiers of amity in your Gentrocentric Universe, with would-be grenade-fallers in a synchronous orbit and that favorite newspaper kiosk guy, hawking smut rags under plastic, light-years away.

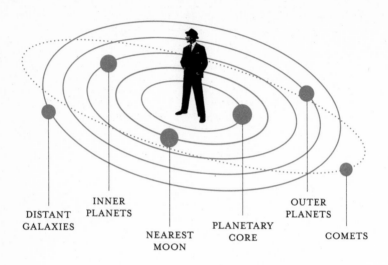

DISTANT GALAXIES • INNER PLANETS • NEAREST MOON • PLANETARY CORE • OUTER PLANETS • COMETS

PLANETARY CORE:	Pallbearers Best friend/faithful Achates Inner circle/confidants/emergency contacts Groomsman/officiant Lived, trekked together Close siblings/brother by another mother Known each other >15 years Childhood friends/framily Weathered crisis/litigation
NEAREST MOON:	Close-Knit Crew Four/five digit loan repaid Exes (the ones you still talk to) Worked together (3+ yrs) Grad school/college alums/fraternity buds Did time/rehab/tour of duty together Known each other 10–15 years/distant siblings Studied abroad together Studied a broad together Carnal knowledge

INNER PLANETS:	Cheek Kissers Best friend's close friend or relative Hallucinated together Worked together (<3 years) Long-time neighbor House-sat/dog-walked/held their stash Accomplices/teammates/professional contacts Man's best friend Volunteering/civil disobedience cohorts Survived kerfuffle/fender bender
OUTER PLANETS:	On the Radar Family friend/Christmas card list Helped them move/seen them naked Bartender who knows your drink Beloved houseplant Three digit loan . . . never repaid Intramural softball right fielder Her monthly friend Foreign pen pals Celebrity friend "Token" friend Association members and industry hacks
DISTANT GALAXIES/ SPACE JUNK:	Chum (the fish, not the friend) Pygmalionistic objects Drunken rescue; shared toothbrush (by accident) Fellow barflies/nameless "Hey" recipients Neighborhood denizens and townies Familiar service personnel Your sweetie's exes Your exes' sweeties Distant Facebook friends whose status you check Reluctant Facebook friends whose status you hide Business card pile miscellany
COMETS:	Once-in-a-Lifetime Encounters Soul-quaking one-night stand Mardi Gras/Burning Man/summer camp mate Influential teachers Disaster cosurvivor Hostel hottie who stole your heart and Eurail pass

CORRESPONDENCE

If all your post arrives in windowed business envelopes, it's time to dust off thy wax seal, clean thy nibs, and write a letter. Despite the deluge of email and texted everything, there is nothing more intimate than a smudged pen-and-ink shot of love.

LONGHAND

Personal correspondence is ideally in longhand, written with a favorite pen (not the Eraser Mate 2) or clacked out on a manual typewriter with quirky, crooked characters. The best letters are intimate, humorous, and insightful, if slightly illegible. Pour a glass of port, light a candle, and click off the wireless router. Crack epistlers suffuse a note with at least three non sequiturs and one self-fashioned abuse of the official lexicon. If keyed on a computer, do not justify the margins or otherwise gussy up a note with fancy fonts and fallacious French phrases. Seal it with wax and an embossed stamp, then kindly ask the post office clerk to hand-cancel the envelope to avoid marring the presentation. Keep a stash of illustrative postage for adorning personal mail. Try to match philatelic themes to receiver or subject matter. For example, Enrico Fermi for the scientist, carnivorous plants for the vegetarian. Beyond the prosaic, consider assembling a care package for homesick and overseas chums sans access to local goodies and contraband.

PENMANSHIP

Outside of midterm-examination blue books, hen scratch should morph into fluid cursive or cogent Courier. Befuddle the graphologist with a ransom note but delight an interstate pen pal with crackling imagination and fine handwriting. Revel in loopy letters with soft strokes or slanted etches with sharp, inky jerks; but be it print or script, wield a mostly legible font. For garnish, trademark a few oddities: crossed zeds, typewriter-style a's, double-scooped 8's, and flamboyant serifs.

Invest in a fine stylus that transmits a prominent line. Black or blue ink is recommended for most correspondence, but colored pencils are appropriate for birthday cards and construction-paper projects. Practice your autograph on the take-out menu while waiting for a pizza and master the perfect expression of your name in ink. A gentleman has a few signatures to work with:

- **The Half-Second Scrawl**: For unimportant documents like package delivery receipts, put your mark by the X but omit the last few letters of a long surname.

- **Simple Script**: For job applications and personal checks, nothing fancy, but apply unique characters that are forgery proof.

- **The Ornamental Hand**: For stationery, cards, and documents of consequence, apply a distinctive John Hancock.

P.S. YOU ARE AN IDIOT

A P.S. is acceptable for small oversights, randy asides, or last-minute news flashes. P.P.S. dangles you over the precipice, and anything more "post" than this likens you to a fifth-grade note passer. XOXO may be used only for doting mothers, matronly kin, and long-distance tic-tac-toe games. "Sincerely" and "Very Truly Yours" are staples for business letters. For cozy communiqués, use more creative and endearing forms, ranging from "Fondly" to "Love and Other Words Between Lick and Lycanthropy in the Dictionary."

GREETING CARDS & SOCIAL PAPER

We prefer a slice of stringy notebook paper with actual sentiment over a store-bought greeting card scribbled with a meager "Dear ___" and a signature. Artistic blank cards serve all-purpose use; a box of smaller thank-you cards and classic bond stationery are versatile. Whatever you'd use for a first-class résumé makes handsome social paper. Don't rule out craft-class scissor work or deft use of graphics software to create a distinctive letterhead.

THANK YOU

Most guests inform a host or hostess they have enjoyed themselves. Few will affirm it the following week; rarer still, the guest who mails a note of gratitude. Thank you, get well, and congratulations are common sentiments commonly overlooked. Discipline yourself (and your lover at times) to deliver essential thoughts in a timely fashion.

═══ LETTER OPENERS ═══

Long the favored murder weapon of Ellery Queen serials, the letter opener outclasses the paperweight as an ancillary desk accessory. We prefer a stand-alone hand-me-down to an opener poorly paired with matching pens and a tape dispenser. A stiff index finger swipe is the default opener, but why ruin a good manicure mangling 24.9% APR credit card offers? For the everyday pile of utility bills, have a standard sabre, preferably lifted from the conference room or won at the company-picnic egg toss. When the mail escort delivers personal post and airmailed curios, unsheathe a top-shelf opener bequeathed by Grandpa. Savor plunging the blade into the folded nape of an envelope.

FLORA

A gentleman stops to smell the *Rosa borboniana*. A thorny crush on Gregor Mendel's snap peas is not a gentlemanly prerequisite, but the core curriculum mandates basic floral proficiency. Ever been to an arboretum? A cultured man's recognition of a dozen plants on sight, Latin names excluded, adds to the joy of selecting a winning nosegay.

- Visit a botanical garden yearly. It is a glorious scientific and visual feast, not to mention an ideal early date or "me time" venue.

- Frequently (at least fortnightly), brighten up a white-walled apartment or bare kitchen table with a modest arrangement.

- Banquet affairs feature flowers and centerpieces. Take the blossoms to go and bestow pick-me-up forget-me-nots upon down-and-out souls on your stroll through the cityscape.

Flowers are best bought from nurseries, florists, roadside stands, or groceries, not filling stations and bus-station kiosks. Stow a tasteful glass vase in the kitchen to accommodate floral surprises. Before displaying, trim any wilting foliage and snip the stems diagonally, at varying lengths. Change the water to avoid the noisome vapors of biomass decay.

PASS THE PISTILS

Flowers are a gift that needn't be reciprocated—every lady enjoys the receipt of flowers. With the panoply of choices, bland purchases belie creative verve. Tulips, daisies, phalaenopsis, or hydrangea strike a more redolent presentation. The surprise single flower, even a vacant-lot dandelion, plucked on a whim, is never misguided. Despite the fine gesture, seventy-five-cent à la carte carnations and baby's breath (which is a weed) should not be exchanged with even a pestiferous foe.

═══ BOUTONNIERE ═══

The boutonniere blossomed in the late nineteenth century and has all but disappeared from men's fashion. Yet a lonely sport coat lapel seems unpollinated. If you're not sporting a lapel pin de cause célèbre, a simple blossom from the backyard garden is far better than an elaborate topiary, and a modest triple bloom is less formal than a single flower. Try a small ivy berry or a pinned silver vial of flowers to complement an evening jacket. For added panache, wear the local flower when traveling: Virginia Beach, dogwood; Scottsdale, a saguaro cactus flower (prickly danger while hugging); Tennessee, a small TV satellite dish.

Nice touch: After hours, encourage a lover to play "He loves me, he loves me not." Count the petals beforehand to ensure the desired outcome.

TULIP
· · · · · · Calvados · Dry vermouth · Apricot brandy · Lemon juice · · · · · ·

GIFTING

[carefully wrapped present] [bow] [ribbon]

A gentleman's gifting skills should transcend the holiday fruit-cake or elk-embossed wool sweater. Do friends and family bellow, "Whoa! Where did you get this?" or force a tight, polite grin and trail, "Ohh . . . that's nice. Thanks"? The most expressive gifts wow not with expense, but with the unmistakable stamp of "I knew you would like this."

Gifts to best friends, a fraternal sibling, or house pets should be so individually tailored that in anyone else's stocking they would make little sense. Garner insight into tastes and listen for unconscious clues dropped as you and a future giftee pass shop windows. Thoughtful gifts are sourced from need (a new raincoat or hi-fi equipment), personality (playoff tickets), hobbies (wine, workout gear, or binoculars), and guilty pleasures (caviar). A good test: does the gift mean something to you? If tempted to keep it for yourself, the only thing better is bestowing it upon an intimate.

Don't be a December 24th rote wrapper. The best gifts are those you serendipitously stumble upon months before the occasion. Though it's only May and a friend's birthday isn't until October, better to snatch up that combination backscratcher/shoehorn you know she'll love than be caught scrounging at the last minute. A wish list recited months before is forgotten by the time a ribbon-wrapped box is in hand; the recipient will be doubly delighted by such premeditated gifting.

Be attuned to occasions when gifting is an obligation of relationship maintenance. Such gifts of duty to the in-laws, a cubicle mate, or the doting probation officer are efficiently bought and delivered without the usual mires of cost and selectivity—like a vacation souvenir.

Incidentally, wrapping is rarely optional. The surprise is enhanced with thick paper, colorful trappings, and a small card. Even if it's your favorite Snoopy pattern, don't eye the paper for reuse.

FOR THE LOVER

Never give a gift that would make the recipient uncomfortable. Thus diamond-studded earrings after the third date are inappropriate, while a small book of poetry or objet d'art is fun. Always be cognizant of subtle hints or casual asides. Does she repeatedly linger over something in the same shop window? Or perhaps she used a more direct approach ("Umm, I really want that catamaran").

The most memorable gifts are often uninitiated notions handed over without occasion or bestowed on nontraditional holidays (such as half-birthdays, Arbor Day, or First Carnal Anniversary). Do you want to be another afterthought at the dusty bottom of her overstuffed jewelry box, or the first to escort her to a ball game? Fine alternatives: sniff out sumptuous foodstuffs, frame a picture of the two of you, take your thoughts to paper (a poem or sweet letter) or canvas (can you watercolor?), or hit the wood shop for a handcrafted creation.

Nice touch: Present four courses instead of a one-dish meal. A bevy of books, framed photographs, and bathtub pamperings are ne'er amiss.

GIFTING PITFALLS

A gift bespeaks your relationship with the recipient. Beware these common gifting blunders when exchanging affections:

- **The Stale Hint:** The lady offers a clue, but failing to act on it quickly proves fatal. In a whimsical mood three months ago, she may have wanted that Belgian teakettle, but now . . .

- **The Projection:** The six-DVD Sean Connery James Bond set is a great gift . . . for you.

- **The Candy Dish:** "Look, honey, another toaster." The wedding gift table is sagging with Crock-Pots and food processors. Think harder.

- **The Useless Gift:** Oops . . . that fantastic imported lamp has an Albanian-issue European five-prong plug and would short out a city block if used.

- **The Obvious Overpay:** Don't show up with a velvet box when she's bringing a paper bag. A velvet-boxed necklace is an expensive commemoration of a two-year, not two-week, relationship.

- **The Wild Pitch:** A gift so off the mark that it raises serious talk of a trade. Expect a mound conference with the manager.

- **The QVC:** Don't pawn off shopping-channel schlock hawked by Rachael Ray as something special.

- **The Agenda Gift:** "I got you this LSAT review book, just in case you ever tire of life in the theatre." Don't push your hidden agenda through gifting.

WEDDING GIFTS

Brace yourself for the four-year, nonstop, summer-wedding binge, beginning at age twenty-six and petering at age thirty. A wedding gift is a dual gift for the bride and groom. No golf clubs or monogrammed bowling balls.

Writing a check or choosing from the registry is always suitable, though family members and closest friends deserve singular attention. Don't give your lifelong chum a seven-piece saucepan set; let others make the domestic purchases of bone china and candlesticks. Creativity aside, a cash gift of $200+ for struggling newlyweds is on the money. Anything less barely covers your chair-rental cost at the ceremony. If the pockets are light, pool resources among friends for a colossal bequeath of a 3-D television or first-class hotel accommodations on the honeymoon. Lastly, do not impose your avant-garde tastes upon the conservative. Margaret and Donald might not like the geometric mobile sculpture or minimalist armchair.

Belated gifts are acceptable only when tardiness is superceded by the overwhelming thoughtfulness. Thus, a paltry check mailed eleven months and twenty-nine days after the wedding smacks of a miser's crazy scheme to earn interest for an additional fiscal year.

HANDY GIFTING GUIDE

The following is a red-hot poker to stoke the fires of creativity.

PRACTICAL

Soft leather wallet; change purse; high-thread-count linens; silk boxers/dress socks; fine white dress undershirts; oxblood dress belt; hardy houseplant; homemade jam; MP3 player or e-book reader;

travel clock; wine fridge; scarf, wrap, or cloak; silver brooch or lapel pin; framed print; dress watch for the sophisticate, training watch for the athlete; loose teas and accessories; acoustic guitar; peppermill; BBQ tools; plush towels; digital camera; comfy wool socks; wall clock; silk pyjamas or lingerie; film noir DVD collection; deluxe ear buds; hobby-oriented magazine subscription; uncommon glassware and cordials; distinctive kitchen accessory (pizza stone, thick bamboo cutting board, juicer, tortilla press, popcorn popper); artisanal olive oil; colorful cups and saucers; external hard drive; loaded toolbox; whistling teakettle; cylindrical sex toys; top end vacuum cleaner; pocket umbrella; French press or espresso machine; local restaurant guide; cordless power drill and new toolbox; air purifier; dried flower arrangement; leather satchel or briefcase; sushi bowls and chopsticks; wine or spirits reference book; unabridged dictionary; board game; slippers; subprime mortgage—backed securities.

Nice touch: Identify a well-used cream or elixir on the bathroom counter. Replace this sundry with a fresh one. Tie it with a bow and slip it onto the shelf as your sweetheart bathes.

CLASSIC

Fine cigars and smoking accessories; fountain or glass pen set with inkwells; liqueurs or cordials; a flight of wines with rack; pearl earrings; desk lamp; first-edition classics; monogrammed handkerchiefs; orchids; flask; caviar spoon; stocked picnic basket; cuckoo clock; antique corkscrew; cufflinks; shaving equipment (brush, mug, mirror); stationery and wax correspondence sealer; fragrance; soft-covered address/phone book; puppy or kitten; napkin rings and serviettes; vinyl LP (first pressing); antique picture frame with photo; decanter; portable bar set; manual typewriter; personalized cocktail napkins; soda siphon; vintage toiletry kit; worn copy of a favorite children's book; specialized obsolete item (slide rule for engineer, old Singer sewing machine for clothier); shoe-shine kit; wine and cheese basket; telescope; talc; homebrew kit; baseball mitt or football (especially for a lady); world globe; cocktail shaker set; chess, backgammon, or cribbage set; autographed picture or book with dedication; anything created by you (poem, painting, drawing, elementary-school diorama); pocket journal; flowers delivered to the office; original work of art; set of pilsner glasses.

MORE INDULGENT

Gift certificates for spa/massage/salon visit; scented bath salts and lotions; paraffin or aromatherapy lamp; feather bed; caviar; stocked exotic aquarium; imported chocolates or candies; wall sconces and decorative vases; vintage arcade console or pinball game; luxurious shower head; microbrew of the month club; Armagnac from recipient's birth year; cashmere anything; ornate Persian rug, vintage champagne; flight of wine from split to double magnum; hot-air balloon ride; mistress slush fund; hard-to-get theatre or sports tickets; surprise party; hobby lessons (such as music, language, cooking, craft, pole dancing, trapeze); express-mailed smoked meats, cheeses, exotic fruits, and dessert specialties; museum membership; paying off a credit card balance; the entire *Modern Gentleman* recommended reading list or classical/jazz recordings.

Incidentally, don't go empty-handed to a friend's home affair or to the office on Secretary's Day. Stock the pantry with small notions for unexpected exchanges or last-minute offerings for hostesses. A cupboard full of candles, teas, and tins of sweets that are wrapped and ready saves the day for the thoughtful . . . and absent-minded.

Chapter Twelve

BEYOND BACHELORHOOD

THE FOURTH DECADE

The twenties had breakups, student transfers, landlord kerfuffles, and agendaless love, so after hitting the big Three-O, welcome a salmagundi of Capital M responsibilities—money, mortgage, marriage, medical, ministerial, moisturizer—and with it a newfound perspective about your parents' travails in raising your misbehaving ass.

The "My life is half over" crying jag isn't ripe until forty candles, so revel in the hard-won maturity granted by the gods of chronology. If college was Shangri-la on the cheap and your twenties were an amusement park ride with a permanent in/out hand stamp, then your thirties is the hardcover life: quality hooch, direct flights, and a willingness to pay extra for personal space. With another decade of vibrant experiences, you're instantly 28 percent more magnetic (even if 30 percent less hirsute), a social chameleon who can chat indie rock with the youngsters and Otis Redding with the silver hairs. Simple getaways are supplanted by international jaunts (biking in the Basque instead of hooking up at Hedonism). Picking up the check doesn't require a mental bank balance check, and twenties and fifties are dropped harmlessly for café lunches and charity auctions. The musical chairs for turn-ons and turn-offs are over; no one starts smoking Luckies at age thirty-five.

Sexual exploration might have peaked at age twenty-seven, but the fourth decade offers delicious play plus access to seasoned belles seeking considerate chaps. While one's sexual frequency formerly had spikes and droughts, the fourth decade boasts linear progressions, since you are either married or committed, steady with a side Betty, or comfortably single and rarely without a sweetie on call.

Nice touch: Revel in the art of "screwfinding." Mature lads not trawling the streets for birds should still keep an up-to-date hot-to-trot list for visiting dignitaries, new-to-towns, and the recently split. It's not a pimp-out, since the dynamic guest still has to close his own deal; think of it as introducing two free radicals with available covalent bonds.

Check in with long-term goals, fight your slowing metabolism, and say goodbye to the ragamuffin relics of the past. Lackluster friendships fall away and newer, varied intimates arrive, not necessarily sourced from school chums or flatmates but rather from soirées and the occasional petite orgy at a friend's beach house. Watch for signs of "getting too old for not growing up," such as a bank balance in the three digits and dingy threads. Break out of these predictable ruts:

- **Social:** The same haunts . . . you're now the oldest patron.

- **Leisure:** While other people are learning new languages and carpentry skills, you . . . discovered that eggplant and veal parm can be combined into one super sub.

- **Financial:** Raided 401(k)s and flimsy IRAs. "I might have to eat Alpo in a group home, but have you seen my new laptop with the killer graphics card?"

- **Betterment:** The same old anecdotes and empty lines that rouse no one—"I think I'll start taking classes again."

Eventually, it's time to trade the "shot of Jack and a beer back" lifestyle for a stable romantic commitment. It feels right when the mature id finally releases its iron hold and the hungry belly stuffed with scrumptious youthful excess feels full for the first time, allowing the heart to push toward the higher stakes of human equity. Without such a smooth transition of psychosexual/analytical power, you're bound to make bad choices. Indeed, a marriage conceived, spurred, nurtured, consecrated, and maintained solely by one's johnson will inevitably result in finances examined, drained, garnished, and expropriated by a shrewd divorce attorney.

THE ROCK

[hers] · [stone] · [his]

Never mind the two-months' salary dictate—it was disseminated by insidious gemstone cartels like Communist dogma. For the man of means, his booming wallet buys a shiny boulder with change left over for airfare to the South African diamond pit from which it was mined. For a young couple with postgraduate degrees and staggering loan debt, wouldn't $5,000 be better spent on a down payment? No bring-home-to-Mom girl wants a husband in serious hock for a rock, anyway.

In any case, don't sell your lover's unique qualities short with a dime-a-dozen design. Search for rings worthy of bequeathing to grandchildren. Visit a sophisticated dealer, find something vintage, or commission a signature piece from a local artisan. You can't get a gourmet meal at the Arby's drive-thru (despite the delicious Horsey sauce), so do not expect to wow a lover with strip-mall trinkets.

Selecting a ring is the ultimate romantic surprise and a demonstration of taste and confidence. Yet, bring along a female pal to prevent the purchase of a four-pronged nightmare. Moreover, there's nothing unromantic about a long-term couple on the inevitable marital path shopping for a ring together with its price and "delivery date" remaining a mystery.

In contemporary relationships, the diamond rule is no rule at all. Respect the customs and indulge her ring-finger fantasies, but don't constrain creativity. Emeralds, rubies, sapphires, and other beguiling precious stones have bejeweled countless crowns and digits with timeless beauty. Rediscover these gems (though when you enter the next tax bracket, expect a smart lady to promptly request at least diamond earrings). Phineas, nevertheless, warns against a lazy skimp who substitutes for imagination with a chintzy, champagne-colored pebble. The eclectic option is reserved for like-minded modern couples for whom tradition is merely a point of departure for their own customs.

Do your homework regarding the Kimberley Process and the four Cs (color, clarity, carat, and cut) lest you end up with second-rate conflict diamonds. Browse through the Tiffany's showroom for facts and classic ideas. Don't be prejudiced on weight alone, as bright, brilliant jewels are more eye-catching than massive, dull duds. As for flaws, if a suitor has forgivable imperfections only seen under a lover's loupe, can't a B+ engagement ring commemorate A+ thoughtfulness?

Final note: For those with frozen garlic toast on their grocery list, by all means, put a day's pay toward a cubic zirconia. If even the tiniest speck of a real gemstone is prohibitively expensive for you, offer another token of betrothal. Ask Grandma for an heirloom to proffer as symbolic collateral toward your commitment. Paint a picture, write a poem, or hang one of your rings about her neck. At the very least, slip a candy Ring Pop onto her finger and promise to deliver actual minerals before it is licked to a nub.

PROPOSALS

You will remember the time, place, and details of this day until both of you are gumming food in the Florida sunshine. Be creative. A lover should be swept away by torrents of affection. Besides, magnificent tales of surprise and romance are more fun for her to brag about later. Do not divulge the big news to any friends or coworkers until after popping the question.

Creative presentation suggests mystery and astonishment, along with hidden accoutrements (champagne, glasses) for afterward. It's too intimate for a crowded restaurant (possibly a sexy bistro) or the football stadium Jumbotron scoreboard, where a hesitant "yes" may simply be polite aversion to embarrassment. Instead, select a secluded spot that promotes unchecked emotions and passionate, bare celebration.

ASKING PERMISSION

Before taking the lady aside for a heart-to-heart, make a pilgrimage to her papa. Asking for a love's hand is less about permission and more about declaration. Certainly, an unsupportive relative may throw a spanner in the works with a flat "Over my dead body, Tesauro." Still, in-law rapport was likely cemented during courtship. When a face-to-face is impractical, a letter in longhand is a better alternative than email, postcard, or balloon-o-gram. Follow up with a phone call.

DECLARATION

Prepare a few cogent phrases beforehand, but skip crib notes scribbled on sweaty palms; for those in broadcasting, a teleprompter is permitted. By now, you've visualized the scene. Be assertive and engaging, and break from the working script when appropriate. If you have prepared a snazzy sonnet, recite with fervor. Kneeling is optional—those with thinning hair may want to strike a more flattering pose.

Verbal options abound. Whether it's a premeditated love monologue or courageous blurt of sincerity, there is one essential closer: "Will you marry me." Note that the statement ends with a period; you're already attuned to the answer. Lastly, do not ruin the moment with disclaimers or a follow-up: "I'll get a job" or "Did you hear me?" Permit the words to sink in, and remain quiet until the answer is given.

Surprise is preferred, but measure an unsuspecting mate's mood and choose a time befitting the moment. Know the calendar date and its significance (is it a full moon, *her* moon, Yom Kippur, or a somber family anniversary?). Once you're prepared, consider the upshot. Is there time and a place to kiss, cry, and embrace afterward? Are you running late for a flight? Make sure appointment books can be tossed aside in deference to engaged merrymaking. Plan to spend the rest of the date together and brace for awesomely tender and powerful lovemaking that affirms the proposal and delivers the relationship unto new heights. Once the news is ready for publicity, relish making the round of calls to close friends informing them of the big announcement.

VOWS

Do not completely neglect the classic template—the exchange is not an avant-garde production, performance-art piece, or three-hankie affair. Honor, respect, and loyalty share the stage with spirit, pleasure, cherish, and fetish. Write realistic vows, uncluttered with minutiae, lest broken promises be hurled against you in a domestic scuffle. For example, "I promise to fulfill each and every one of your dreams, however small," inevitably spawns a needling spouse two years later: "Honey, it's my dream that you take out the trash, clean up your whiskers, and just forget about that pipe dream you mentioned over dinner." Skip the archaic "obey," as this term needlessly and rightfully angers even nonmilitant women. Besides, an overly pliant mate is dull—isn't someone who requires cajoling and sensual favoring more interesting? This goes both ways, as a man shouldn't be an uxorious, shackled simp.

═══ **BRIDAL TOURNAMENT SELECTION** ═══

Just like the NCAA hoops tournament, there are automatic and at-large bids. Upstanding family members and long-time compatriots are easy picks; other groomsmen are culled from the larger lot of prospects. Choose persons relevant to the relationship who share a smooth rapport with your fiancée. Create a sacred inner circle that is the fount of integrity and energy for the ceremony. If you have to count upon a rented wedding band playing that tired Righteous Brothers song to effuse sentiment, perhaps elopement is a better idea. An older I Do'er may discover that he has more friends whom he stood with on the altar than available groomsmen spots at his own affair. Instead of fielding a cricket team of be-tuxed nitwits, shrink it to two or three—best man, plus siblings or lifelong confederates, designating the remaining intimates for readings during the ceremony or speeches at the rehearsal dinner.

At the altar, answer with an unblinking "I do," not the corny "I will" (which suggests compliance in the indeterminate future, not necessarily anytime soon). To seal the blessing, plant a soulful-but-tasteful kiss, namely, a slight open-mouthed smooch that appears presentable from the third row. Marriages consecrated with a prudish, cold peck are doomed from the start.

Nice touch: During that spare moment between the groomsmen's processional and opening bars of "Here Comes the Bride," steal a nip with the best man during a feigned shoe-tying conference. Nerve-quelling benefits aside, surreptitious altar flasking is a fond farewell to the unhitched you, but don't mouth "I Do" with whisky breath.

HONEYMOON

· · · · · Calvados · Bénédictine · Dash curaçao · Lemon or orange juice · · · · ·

THE GOOD HUSBAND

You are hard work.
—DANIEL ROOP, *Love Poem #39*

Divulged ATM PIN numbers, commingled laundry, and a ring exchange equal marriage. That was the easy part. Be the kind of husband who makes her friends want to find a man like you. And cultivate in-law rapport, even if you don't call them Mom and Dad (or call them).

She's still the same person, especially if cohabitation preceded the nuptials. Marriage is a confirmation, not a poker bluff to exact behavioral changes concerning fidelity, maturity, passion, or finances. The real change should have occurred after the engagement, when practical concerns and latent insecurities were aired and resolved. For instance, check-balancing acumen demonstrated responsibility and wading through sexual turbulence proved thick-or-thin commitment. Now that you're hitched, maintain the parallel paths that got you here. Branching off into excessive solitary pursuits (vice, religion, crochet) leads to alienation and, eventually, divorce.

═══ TRY A LITTLE TENDERNESS ═══

The good husband knows expressions of love more potent than screwing, and his acuity alerts him when tenderness trumps physicality. When a couple hasn't spent enough time together, tenderness is their carnal chicken soup. Sometimes, heavy emotions (upset, making up, erectile dysfunction) call for more than high-impact p.m. tumbles. Tenderness and explicit acts are not incongruous; however, it behooves the good husband to recognize when the sport of ass-smacking cardio sex diminishes the sacred union. Ease off the lust. The path to exciting, kinky sex is not always through the toy chest. Sacred sex establishes trust and opens the door to experimentation. Sex within the context of tenderness is less goal-oriented to your orgasm and more focused on caressing, talking, or just lying naked. Such heartfelt lovemaking ends with sighs of contentment.

RENEW THE WOO

Newlyweds are pegged by their glowing demeanor and a distinct lack of seasoned scowls, but courting should not stop when the honeymoon is over. Anyone with a long-playing Sade record can sustain three to five weeks of unbridled humpery, but continued courtship rituals and flirtation make you feel lionhearted and her feel alluring. Set aside "alone" time, compliment her daily, and surprise her with the kind of passion you exuded way back on the third date.

JEALOUSY

You are not the only man who will recognize the goddess in your woman. Her tall black boots and sexy clothes are not just for you. Interfering with her night on the dance floor with single friends is an insecure sign of ball-and-chain mistrust. After outings without you, sit her down for an adventure recap and not a strap-down on the polygraph.

MONOGAMY

A wedding ring is a badge of respect, if a tattoo of restraint. Don't quash longings; discipline is about boundaries, not numbness. Nightclub distractions that cloud judgement and evoke swinging days of singledom are to be brought home as kindling for the eternal fire of your marital bed. Fantasized sex with today's stranger is best expressed during tonight's lovemaking.

Run temptations through the filter of fidelity. It's about channeling, not romanticizing about what single life was really like. In marriage, you relinquish the infrequent serendipities of mind-blowing casual sex—those beachheads of pure lust, connection, and unexpurgated ecstasy that defined bachelorhood. What you're getting in return are rainy-night security and a baseline of sensuality that define your life the other 364 days of the year.

Consummation of fantasies is not the first, but the final, step of an infidel. Should you entertain extracurricular affairs, measure the risk. Will a rendezvous leave you satisfied or burdened with constraints of lies, treachery, and compensation? Are you just horny or has the home bed gone all the way cold? A spouse's dearth of sexual passion is but a symptom of more fundamental turmoil. Sex is a barometer of relationship wellness, and the closed heart of a philanderer is a poisoned apple among the fruits of monogamy.

Incidentally, a long, leering look is worth a thousand thrusts. Just knowing that you could have it is enough; reaffirm sexy esteem and cash in on the fantasy value. Avoid the heartache and karma-crunching logistics of bad decisions that set in thirty nanoseconds after climax.

AFTERWORD

A gentleman is a gentleman is a gentleman. Being married, involved, single, gay, or naked doesn't dictate one's character or charm. Similarly, the venue or medium of interaction should heighten, not hamper, exchanges. Engaging and keenly naughty behavior is possible in nearly all situations. Wherever you are, be the dashing demiurge and don't just take up space. Cultivate an energy that makes people smile and then watch your stock rise.

The Modern Gentleman offers a slide rule of respect for solving the deepest conundrums of love and vice. Respect decency, life, and the dignity of men—their rituals and foibles. Respect women and the virtues of their grace and intuition. Respect quality over greed, meaning over appetite. Respect action and fitness, health and spirituality, learning and enrichment. Seek a diversity of experience, and respect the liberating and instructive fruits of fun and frivolity. Keep your eyes open and respect the potent allure and sometimes grotesque beauty of vice and its peripheral curiosities. Join us in intellectual fellowship as you rejoice, read Joyce, and "forge in the smithy of your soul" the man of your own desire.

Applying *The Modern Gentleman's* lessons is a contagious process that evolves into effortless gestures. It begins by bringing relaxed charm to a first date, trying a new cocktail, perusing new aisles in the bookstore, or peeking into the leather store. Then, like any discipline, it will infuse other aspects of livelihood, from timely thank-you cards and delicious text messages to the joys of flasking when the theatre lights are low. Others will take notice and inquire about the steady inner improvements.

Put simply, your refurbished character is like last year's wardrobe: updated, enhanced, and pruned, with the outmoded remnants boxed and donated to charity. The idea is continual growth, not personality replacement or complete makeovers. On occasion, a gentleman should take stock of past achievements and miscues. Be proud of inspired revelry and review limitations, the mishandling of last year's love affair, or flagging friendships in need of a handwritten letter.

Best of luck to you, noble Cavalier of Life. Go forward with strength, grace, mindfulness, and an occasional glass of Chartreuse. The world will follow behind you.

In the life design he navigates
A gent strives to be these 9 traits

Genuine
mann Ered
dari Ng
cul Tured
articu Late
laudabl E
Mindful
s Avvy
se Nsuous

BIBLIOGRAPHY

Ames, Elinor. *Elinor Ames' Book of Modern Etiquette.* New York: Walter J. Black, Inc., 1935. The book Grandma lived by. Terrific for niceties of classic social affairs: gifting, correspondence; features a what-to-wear chart.

Aywyós. *Hints on Etiquette and the Usages of Society with a Glance at Bad Habits,* third edition. London: Turnstile Press Ltd., 1836. Compact bedside primer. Quick essays with terrific color illustrations. A little stuffy at times and loose with the term "vulgar."

Black, Kathleen. *Manners for Moderns.* New York: Allyn & Bacon, 1938.Very practical regarding group dynamics, proper courting, and introductions. Eye-catching 1940s caricatures and sound, accessible advice from an American perspective.

Censor. *Don't: A Manual of Mistakes and Improprieties More or Less Prevalent in Conduct and Speech.* Whitstable, UK: Pryor Publications, 1982 (originally published circa 1880). Headmaster finger-shaking etiquette. Hilariously outdated, yet useful. Get a sense of how far "nice" society has come (or how far we've degraded it).

Diescher, Victor H. *The Book of Good Manners: A Guide to Polite Usage for All Social Functions.* New York: Social Culture Publications, 1923. The book of true gentility, not pretense. Whereas the *MG* touches on Prophyletiquette, Diescher touches on finger bowls.

Dornenburg, Andrew, and Page, Karen. *What to Drink with What You Eat.* New York: Bulfinch, 2006. They've stolen back drink pairings from fusty gourmands and brought it to all the fun foodies who've ever risked carpal tunnel while stirring risotto only to wonder what wine to pair.

Duffy, Patrick Gavin. *The Official Mixers Manual.* New York: Halcyon House, 1940. A mixological masterpiece. Classic and complex: more cocktails listed under absinthe and Calvados than under vodka. Infallible recipes and essays on wine and beer.

Editors of *Esquire* magazine and Ron Butler. *Esquire's Guide to Modern Etiquette.* New York: J. B. Lippincott Co., 1969. More loose in its rules than any of the preceding titles. How to look the part. Slanted toward the male perspective, hitting modern topics like sporting etiquette and sex in the office.

Eichler, Lillian. *The New Book of Etiquette.* New York: Garden City Publishing Co., 1940. Wonderful prose and commentary about the self-improvement and sincerity of manners, not just table dressing.

Flusser, Alan. *Clothes and the Man.* New York: Villard Books, 1989. Worth tracking down this gem just for the fold-by-fold pocket-square and cravat-knotting tutorials.

Gasnier, Vincent. *Drinks.* New York: DK Publishing, 2008. A marvelous reference book that, ahem, distills the world of booze into five hundred beautifully organized pages for both the tyro and the learned lush.

Green, Jonathon. *The Big Book of Filth.* London: Cassell, 1999. F!*$@%# indispensable phrase book for honing the well-balanced, profane tongue.

Herbst, Sharon Tyler, and Herbst, Ron. *The Ultimate A-to-Z Bar Guide.* New York: Broadway Books, 1998. Keep it next to the jigger; it's okay if you spill on it. Handy reference for everyday concocting.

Hix, Charles. *Dressing Right.* New York: St. Martin's Press, 1979. Casual and fanciful splashes of clothing; dressing for "now," not necessarily for all time. Great explanation of fashion terms and collar styles.

Kingwell, Mark. *Classic Cocktails: A Modern Shake.* New York: St. Martin's Press, 2007. Finally, someone else is writing snappy prose about booze packed with literary references, dynamic vocabulary, and frothy personality, not to mention a professed love for *The Savoy Cocktail Book* and an enlightened "Ehh" attitude toward vodka.

"M." *The Sensuous Man.* New York: Lyle Stuart, Inc., 1971. Worth the purchase for "Party Sex Etiquette" and the list of ten exercises not involving dumbbells that will make you a better lover. By age seventeen, you should've already perused a stolen copy from your great-uncle's study.

Mario, Thomas. *Playboy's Host & Bar Book.* Chicago: Playboy Press, 1971. So much more than a recipe book. Barmanship, embellishments, party planning, and a Code of Conviviality that everyone should subscribe to.

Martine, Arthur. *Martine's Hand-Book of Etiquette and Guide to True Politeness.* Bedford, MA: Applewood Books (originally published in 1866). A man ahead of his time. A concise guide, written before the era of etiquette tomes. Relish the art of carving, taking wine at the table, and etiquette on the street.

Meade, Marianne. *Charm and Personality.* New York: The World Syndicate Publishing Co., 1938. This book gets into the charm and grace of things. The author stresses that before one can excel in social manners, one must tend to inner care and hygiene.

Mrs. Humphrey ("Madge" of "Truth"). *Manners for Men*. Whitstable, UK: Pryor Publications, 1993 (originally published 1897). A small book with sidebars for easy reference on classical etiquette on and off the omnibus. Especially helpful refresher on the formal calm and order at dinner parties.

Post, Emily. *Etiquette (The Blue Book of Social Usage)*. New York: Funk & Wagnalls Co., 1945. Classic treatise, perfect for gleaning the fundamental principles. Written in friendly language—the early, preagitated Miss Manners.

Potter, Stephen. *The Theory and Practice of Gamesmanship: Or the Art of Winning Games Without Actually Cheating*. New York: Henry Holt & Co., 1947. A humorous guide to the subtle art of gentlemanly jousting on the golf course or billiard table. Every gent should master a few psychological ploys to unnerve a pesky opponent.

Random House Hostess Library. *The Random House Book of Etiquette*. New York: Random House, Inc., 1967. Great source for practical etiquette such as gifting, tipping, and party manners. Classic cover art on an early 1970s Italian restaurant banquette—red hardback.

Reid, Lillian N. *Personality and Etiquette*. Boston: Little, Brown & Co., 1940. Finishing-school textbook with manners exercises. A family book, perhaps read to young children before the "Birds and the Bees" lecture.

Sherwood, M.E.W. *The Art of Entertaining*. New York: Dodd, Mead & Co., 1892. A revisit to the classic age of parlor games and cocktail hours around the piano. Breaks down entertaining into popular venues—in the city, on a picnic, clambakes.

Shopsin, Kenny. *Eat Me: The Food and Philosophy of Kenny Shopsin*. New York: Alfred A. Knopf, 2008. A wonderfully simple cookbook from an eccentric New York restauranteur. The joy is reading the musings and singular wisdom about food and life that make the recipes seem almost an afterthought.

Steele, Valerie. *Fetish: Fashion, Sex, and Power*. New York: Oxford University Press, 1996. Less a how-to book than a visual dictionary, with a slight bit of history. Good for your fetish vocabulary and for corroborating your mischievous fantasies.

The Savoy Cocktail Book. New York: Arno Press, 1976 (originally published 1930). A glorious reference and recipe manual for atmospheric drinks. Best illustrative art of any cocktail book. Though recently rereleased, track down a worn copy if you can.

Vanderbilt, Amy. *Amy Vanderbilt's Complete Book of Etiquette*. Garden City, NY: Doubleday & Co., 1958. One day you'll be stuck setting a tea tray . . . The comprehensive, authoritative text from the etiquette maven, with line drawings by a young Andrew Warhol.

ABOUT THE AUTHORS

Besides the times a-changin', they've evolved as well: Phineas Mollod's Baddha Utthita Parsvakonasana (bound sideangle pose) is more balanced and pretzely, and Jason Tesauro's last 10 K race time was a youthful 40:30 (rumors of Chartreuse-tinged PEDs proved inconclusive). As a writing duo, they've grossed three children (one, you might say, for each mistress, divorce, and narrowly averted short sale on their rap sheet), and just enough grays around the temples to earn the term "Distinguished" in front of "Gentleman." Phineas received his law degree from Vanderbilt University and lives in downtown New York. He is a staff writer for a national firm and esquires just enough to keep his attaché out of hock. He's a proud co-op apartment owner, whereas Tesauro remains above the poverty line but below the Mason-Dixon Line and "just might be the most popular man in Richmond, Virginia," or so says *Details* magazine. He pulls corks for Barboursville Vineyards and flits about various metropoli hosting MG soirées and seminars.

Phineas and Tesauro coauthored *The Modern Lover: A Playbook for Suitors, Spouses, & Ringless Carousers* (Ten Speed Press, 2004) and between them have contributed to *Men's Health*, *Maxim*, Match.com, Luxist.com, *Sommelier Journal*, *Washingtonian*, the *Sunday Paper* (Atlanta), and *Richmond*, among others.

Stay connected via TheModernGentleman.com.

INDEX